Taming the Presumption of Innocence

Recent Titles in

Studies in Penal Theory and Philosophy
R. A. Duff and Michael Tonry, General Editors

Popular Punishment
On the Normative Significance of Public Opinion
Jesper Ryberg and Julian V. Roberts

Just Sentencing
Principles and Procedures for a Workable System
Richard S. Frase

Punishment, Participatory Democracy, and the Jury
Albert W. Dzur

Retributivism Has a Past
Has It a Future?
Edited by Michael Tonry

Taming the Presumption of Innocence

RICHARD L. LIPPKE

OXFORD
UNIVERSITY PRESS

OXFORD
UNIVERSITY PRESS

Oxford University Press is a department of the University of Oxford. It furthers the University's objective of excellence in research, scholarship, and education by publishing worldwide. Oxford is a registered trade mark of Oxford University Press in the UK and certain other countries.

Published in the United States of America by Oxford University Press
198 Madison Avenue, New York, NY 10016, United States of America.

First Edition published in 2016

Library of Congress Cataloging-in-Publication Data
Lippke, Richard L., 1954– author.
Taming the presumption of innocence / Richard L. Lippke.
pages cm. — (Studies in penal theory and philosophy)
Includes bibliographical references and index.
ISBN 978–0–19–046919–1 (hardcover : alk. paper) 1. Presumptions (Law)
2. Presumption of innocence. I. Title.
K5469.P7L57 2016
345'.06—dc23
2015032005

9 8 7 6 5 4 3 2 1
Printed by Sheridan, USA

CONTENTS

Acknowledgments vii

Introduction 1

CHAPTER 1 The Presumption of Innocence: Sorting the Claims 11

CHAPTER 2 The Human Right to Be Presumed Innocent 33

CHAPTER 3 Nonproceduralism and the Presumption of Innocence 57

CHAPTER 4 The Presumption of Innocence in the Trial Setting 81

CHAPTER 5 Justifying the Proof Structure of Criminal Trials 105

CHAPTER 6 Do We Need a Pretrial Presumption of Innocence? 129

CHAPTER 7 Pretrial Detention and the Presumption of Innocence 155

CHAPTER 8 Incomplete Prosecutions and the Presumption of Innocence 177

CHAPTER 9 The Presumption of Innocence Postpunishment 213

Epilogue 233

Notes 237

Bibliography 265

Index 273

ACKNOWLEDGMENTS

My interest in the presumption of innocence began with an invitation from Antony Duff to present a paper at the University of Minnesota Law School's Robina Institute for Criminal Law and Criminal Justice in April 2012. I had just finished a book on plea bargaining and was spending some time researching and thinking about the role of prosecutors in the US criminal justice system. When I received Antony's invitation, I decided to write a paper about prosecutors and the presumption of innocence. I was intrigued by the question of whether, if at all, they were bound by it. I had, at the time, a fairly amorphous understanding of the presumption, one that, I am sorry to say, persisted as I worked on the paper. At the conference, someone (I think it was Zach Hoskins, in his commentary on my paper) asked about the difference between a presumption of innocence and a nonpresumption of guilt. Since I had not really thought about the question, I said so and indicated that I would have to think further about it. When I got back from the conference, I did just that. In many ways, this book is the result. As will become apparent to readers of the following chapters, I became convinced that much of the burgeoning scholarly literature on the presumption of innocence failed to take seriously the distinction between it and a nonpresumption of guilt. The latter often makes sense in contexts in which the former does not. Or so I argue.

In addition to Zach, Chad Flanders (my other commentator) and others at the Robina Institute conference had numerous important comments and suggestions about my paper. I thus learned just how complicated the scholarly debate about the presumption of innocence had become. My early attempts to grapple with the questions that debate raised produced several articles that are incorporated, in revised forms, in this book. Chapter 4 previously appeared as "The Presumption of Innocence in the Trial Setting" in *Ratio Juris* 28 (2015): 159–79. Chapter 5 previously appeared as "Justifying the Proof Structure of Criminal Trials" in the *International Journal of Evidence and Proof* 17 (2013): 323–46. Chapter 7 previously appeared as "Preventive Pre-trial Detention without Punishment" in *Res Publica* 20 (2014): 111–27. I thank these journals for their kind permission to reuse some of this material in the present manuscript. I should add that anonymous reviewers for the journals offered many criticisms of the earlier papers that enabled me to substantially improve them. Two reviewers for Oxford University Press also offered numerous helpful comments on the manuscript.

I owe special thanks to Antony Duff, not only for his sagacious and consistently challenging work on the presumption of innocence, but also for encouraging me to submit my book to the OUP series that he coedits with Michael Tonry. Also, many thanks to James Cook, the Sociology and Criminology editor at OUP, for believing in the book and pushing it forward through the review process.

Finally, as always, I am enormously grateful to my wife, Andrea Wiley, and my children, Aidan and Emil, for their love and support.

Taming the Presumption of Innocence

Introduction

IN RECENT YEARS, CONCERNS about expansion of the criminal law, the harshness of penal sanctions, and the lingering effects on persons of entanglement with the criminal justice system, have led some scholars to cast the presumption of innocence as a panacea, of sorts, for many of the perceived ills of our contemporary approach to crime and punishment. Instead of conceiving of the presumption of innocence as confined to the criminal trial, where its function is clearly defined, if not always well-understood, scholars have posited other roles for it. Some seek modest extensions of the presumption—to the pretrial phase, invoking it to ward off the erosion of due process protections, limit the damage done to the reputations of the accused, or discourage the use of pretrial detention.[1] Others have sought to extend its protections further back into the criminal justice process. Some see it as a normative constraint on the kinds of conduct that can be legitimately criminalized.[2] Others go further, extolling a substantive human right to be presumed innocent, one that persons are alleged to have independently of whether they have fallen under any official suspicion of criminal misconduct.[3] Such a right has implications for the social interactions of persons outside the ambit of the criminal law. Finally, some scholars envision roles for the presumption posttrial, especially when individuals have been acquitted of all or some charges against them, or have fully served whatever sanctions have been assigned to them by the courts pursuant to convictions.[4] Here, the idea is that there comes a point at which persons who have been caught up in or punished by the criminal justice system ought to have their status as citizens in good standing fully restored.

One of the principal themes of this book will be the difficult questions with which we must grapple if we extend the presumption of innocence (hereafter, I will usually employ the abbreviation PI) outside of the trial context. In that context, there is some consensus about the rules governing the presumption. Persons accused of crimes are to receive the PI at the outset of their trials; it is jurors, or judges in bench trials, who are charged with presuming their innocence. The burden of bringing forward evidence that establishes the guilt of the accused is squarely on the government. The standard of proof that the government must meet in order to obtain convictions—beyond a reasonable doubt—is exacting. If the government satisfies that standard, then the court ought to convict the accused. The outcome of conviction is the assignment of some form of legal punishment, with its characteristic censure and hard treatment. In short, in the context of criminal trials, who is to presume the innocence of whom, for what purpose, what rebuts it, and what happens when it is rebutted, are all readily identifiable.[5] This is not to say that there are no uncertainties concerning how to understand the operation of the PI during the trial process. There most assuredly are, as we will see in chapter 4.

However, the perplexities surrounding the PI in that context pale in comparison with those that will have to be faced if we take up the invitation to cast the PI in roles outside of the trial. To gain some sense of these perplexities, consider the notion that we should extend the PI to the pretrial phase of the criminal justice process. The pretrial phase begins with official suspicion or accusation and ends with the advent of a trial, or, more likely, a guilty plea by the accused. Since the PI is a presumption, and thus seemingly a deliberately adopted perspective on suspects or formally accused persons, we must first ask who is to presume their innocence in the pretrial context. The police or prosecutors directly involved in arresting, investigating, and processing charges against the accused? These are officials who might have seen substantial evidence of the guilt of the accused, or worse, heard full and free confessions of guilt from them. As a result, it is unclear whether instructing such officials to presume the innocence of the accused makes much sense.[6] More importantly, we might worry that, if they really attempted to do so, it would interfere with their assigned tasks, which involve detecting crimes, investigating them thoroughly, and pursuing charges against those whom they conclude have committed them. When the crimes in question are grave, it would seem that we want police and prosecutors to be proactive about preventing or interfering with them and dogged about bringing suspected perpetrators to justice.

Next, consider the victims of crimes, if there are any. Should they be instructed to presume the innocence of those who victimized them? This seems a dubious proposition as well, especially for those individuals who are certain that it is the accused who stole from, assaulted, or threatened them. Perhaps it is members of the public more generally who should presume the innocence of suspects and formally accused persons. Such an admonition seems more promising, except that most of the time the public will be unaware of which individuals have been charged with what crimes.[7] Only in cases of serious or notorious crimes does the public become cognizant of them and the persons alleged to have committed them. If the public is to actively presume the innocence of suspects and accused persons, then it seems that it will have to be considerably more engaged in the workings of the criminal justice system than it currently is.

Further, what evidence or other considerations should be understood as rebutting the PI in the pretrial context? Proof beyond a reasonable doubt? That seems an unlikely candidate, since evidence of that kind (including evidence that has withstood contestation by the defense) will usually be unavailable until a trial has progressed almost to its completion. Other evidence standards exist, but which of them to select—"probable cause," "the preponderance of the evidence," "clear and convincing evidence,"—seems a somewhat arbitrary decision, at least until we have some better idea of what follows if the standard is satisfied in any given case. What presumably does not follow is that persons suspected or accused can be subjected, without further ado, to legal punishment; for that, they have to be tried and convicted, or convinced to plead guilty. Is it that once the standard is met, whatever that standard is, it is all right for some or all of us to think less of the accused, to regard the accused as something other than law-abiding? And can we then withhold more than our good opinion of them, perhaps denying them some of the myriad benefits of social cooperation, ones that we extend to persons whose good citizenship is not in doubt? Now the problem is that it is hard to see how such responses on our part are not premature. They would seem to be, especially for those scholars who insist that, until they are convicted of one or more criminal offenses, we ought to treat persons *as if* they are innocent.[8] How do we treat accused persons as if they are innocent if we withhold things from them that we would ordinarily offer our fellow citizens?

As will be shown, puzzles and problems such as these are not unique to a pretrial PI. In fact, they exist in more baffling forms once we consider proposals to extend the PI outside of the criminal justice process altogether—to lawmaking or to our treatment of our fellow citizens quite independently of any official suspicion of them. This brings me to a second principal theme of the book. Much of the work that some legal scholars would have the PI perform outside the trial context can be, I argue, performed as well, if not better, by utilizing other moral constructs or by reminding legal officials of the harms that their actions risk if they do not adhere strictly to due process. For instance, police or prosecutors should be circumspect in their public comments about accused persons, not because the accused are presumed innocent, but because such comments might irreparably harm the reputations of persons who are never actually convicted of crimes. This, in turn, will make it more difficult for the formerly accused to resume the full exercise and enjoyment of their basic rights as citizens. In particular, public statements by police or prosecutors that impugn acquittals seem to be illicit efforts to impose some of the social costs of criminal conviction on persons who have not been found guilty by the courts.

Instead of trying to make the PI do more work than it is capable of or suited for, I argue that we ought to tame it: We should confine it to the trial context, where what it means, how it functions, and what are the consequences of its rebuttal can be tolerably well-defined and defended. Before attempting to tame it, I first examine proposals by scholars to expand its role in the criminal justice system. In chapter 1, I provide an overview of the full range of claims that have been, or might be made, about the PI, sorting these claims into various categories and offering some initial clarifying remarks about them. The aim of the chapter is to provide readers with some sense of the lay of the land in recent scholarship on the PI.

In chapters 2 and 3, proposals to extend the PI outside of the context of official suspicion or accusation within the criminal justice system are examined in close detail. Chapter 2 focuses on the boldest of these proposals—the claim that there is substantive human right to be presumed innocent. Initially, I raise doubts about whether the right to be presumed innocent can be substantive, rather than procedural. I then scrutinize the rationales supplied by the leading proponents of a substantive right to be presumed innocent and find them unconvincing. In place of such a right, I develop an account of the ways in which the investigation and prosecution of alleged offenses should be restrained due to concerns about how they impact more familiar substantive rights—to liberty, privacy, and autonomy. I contend that it is respect for and concern about such rights that should lead criminal justice officials to proceed cautiously in investigating crimes and charging individuals with them. Those officials should also be required to have and provide justifications for infringing the rights of individuals as they proceed with criminal investigations and charges.

Chapter 3 takes up two distinct kinds of claims made by scholars who see the PI as more than narrowly procedural but who do not explicitly identify it as a substantive human right. First, there are claims that the PI should function as a constraint on the content of the criminal law. Various criminal law provisions have been seen as contravening the PI, and, indeed, many of the provisions scholars have expressed concerns about are troubling. However, I maintain that their problematic character is not helpfully explained by invoking the PI. Instead, the provisions tend to be overbroad or unduly harsh in their penal consequences, or they make individuals liable to punishment who have not engaged in serious, culpable wrongdoing. Second, some scholars would have the PI regulate our everyday interactions with our fellow citizens. These scholars claim that we should not regard or treat our fellow citizens as inclined to prey upon or assault us, or else we act contrary to the spirit of the PI. However, I contend that not treating or regarding our fellow citizens as active threats to us must be distinguished from presuming them innocent of legal wrongdoing. Also, we can be civil to people about whose law-abidingness we are far from certain. Finally, many people live in circumstances in which they rightly fear some of their fellow citizens, and some occupy those circumstances more or less continuously. A blanket prescription to the effect that they should "think the best" or "not think the worst" of their fellow citizens is neither wise nor defensible.

One strand of argument that emerges in chapter 3 is worth highlighting. It might be plausibly claimed that there is a societal presumption against legal punishment of the innocent. Such a presumption can be seen as the basis for objecting to overinclusive legal prohibitions or strict liability provisions that expose the innocent, qua undeserving, to legal punishment. I do not deny that there is something like a societal presumption against punishment of the innocent. But I do not believe that it is equivalent to a presumption *of* innocence. Instead, it is a principle, one that carries enormous weight. Indeed, it is hard to imagine what "evidence" would rebut it if it is a presumption *of* innocence. What we can imagine is something different, namely, that there might be competing principles to which we subscribe that outweigh it in special kinds of circumstances. Yet principles are not presumptions, at least not presumptions of the sort that the PI is usually thought to be, and little is gained by conflating the two.

Having cleared the ground of false starts in our thinking about the PI, chapters 4 and 5 constitute the theoretical heart of the book. In them, I develop and defend an account of the PI in the context in which I believe that it makes the most sense—namely, the criminal trial. I cast the PI as a vital aspect of the "proof structure" of criminal trials, wherein the accused get the presumption of innocence, the burden of proving guilt is on the government, and the standard of proof, beyond a reasonable doubt, is exacting. In chapter 4, I characterize the PI as a deliberately adopted perspective on accused persons, one that is designed to motivate jurors (or judges in bench trials) to subject the government's evidence to close and exacting scrutiny. I also contrast it with competing perspectives that they might adopt and attempt to show its superiority in shielding accused persons from unjust conviction.

In chapter 5, I detail how the proof structure of criminal trials makes them the appropriate kinds of stern tests of the government's evidence against the individuals who have been charged with crimes. Trials are characterized as elaborate "moral assurance procedures." Accused persons should be able to demand them and we should accommodate this demand in order to assure ourselves that we act justifiably when we inflict legal punishment, with its potentially life-altering effects, on them. I also contrast my account with more familiar error-distribution accounts of the proof structure of criminal trials.

The narrow account of the PI developed and defended in chapters 4 and 5 is challenged in chapter 6. For many scholars, it will seem obvious that the PI has implications beyond the trial, most particularly in the pretrial context. Individuals suspected of or formally accused of crimes are to be presumed innocent, or so we are often told. By whom, for what purpose, and what rebuts that presumption, are questions that are less often answered. I suggest an alternative to the PI in the pretrial context, one that I believe is sometimes confused with it in the literature on the subject. This brings me to a third principal theme of the book: The PI must be distinguished from a nonpresumption of guilt. The nonpresumption of guilt is consistent with having substantial doubts about the law-abidingness of persons. Yet it counsels criminal justice officials, and others in society, to avoid presuming that the individuals suspected of or accused of crimes are guilty or will be found guilty—the former because the criminal justice process is fallible and we know this, or ought to by now; the latter because it is unpredictable. Caution in jumping to conclusions about suspects, a willingness to keep the door open to doubts or confounding evidence in cases, and a firm commitment to full and fair due process are all things that we can sensibly urge, particularly on the legal officials involved in the prosecution of crimes. More than this, we should continually remind police and prosecutors to avoid practices that are known to produce mistaken convictions.[9] These include pressuring suspects to admit their guilt, relying on jailhouse snitches, prompting reluctant or uncertain witnesses to decisively identify suspects, coaching witnesses, and concealing or destroying exculpatory evidence. My contention is that providing periodic and clear reminders to the police and prosecutors concerning the dangers of tactics such as these will do much more to prevent errors than hectoring them about the presumed innocence of those whom they suspect of crimes and often have amassed considerable evidence against.

In chapter 7, I continue my examination of the PI in the pretrial context by focusing specifically on the controversial practice of pretrial detention. Such detention, especially when it is premised upon the belief that accused persons are apt to commit further crimes before the current charges against them have been resolved, has been portrayed by numerous legal scholars as contravening the PI. Not surprisingly, since I reject a pretrial PI, I am unpersuaded that the abundant grounds we have for limiting pretrial detention have much to do with it. In its place, I urge reforms in the conditions of pretrial detention, so that it is much less like legal punishment than is currently the norm. I also support drastically less use of such detention, on the grounds that relatively few accused persons can be shown to present dangers to the public. However, some do pose substantial risks and their pretrial detention can be justified.

In chapter 8, I take up the topic of "incomplete prosecutions." I employ this catchall phrase to refer to persons who become entangled in one way or another in the criminal justice system but who are not convicted of any crimes. They are arrested but never charged, charged but the charges are dropped, or charged but acquitted after trials. All subjects of incomplete prosecutions are apt to suffer adverse social consequences because of their involvement with the criminal justice system. Employers who find out about their arrests or charges will be leery of hiring them. Credit agencies might refuse to extend them loans and licensing boards might decline to offer them credentials. Various remedies aimed at limiting the damage done by incomplete prosecutions have been proposed: the expungement of official records not leading to convictions; required explanations from legal officials concerning why prosecutions were discontinued or never pursued; forms of acquittal disambiguation; prohibitions on publication of the names of suspects; and antidiscrimination provisions designed to protect individuals who have not been convicted of crimes. Some scholars will see the PI as providing support for these remedies. However, I contend that the PI might not support such remedies or might lead to the adoption of unwise versions of them. I propose an alternative framework for analyzing such remedies, one centered on the nonpresumption of guilt.

Such a framework permits us to weigh the value of the information that the various kinds of incomplete prosecutions provide us about our fellow citizens against the costs of letting their histories of entanglement with the criminal justice system continue to hinder them.

It might seem that once persons are convicted of crimes, then there is little remaining role for the PI to play in relation to them. Yet most of the individuals convicted of crimes and sentenced for them will eventually complete their sentences. Once they do so, are they to be presumed innocent again, and for what purposes? These questions are made more pressing by the common practice of imposing myriad "collateral consequences" on convicted offenders, including ones who have fully served their sentences.[10] Ex-offenders encounter all manner of restrictions on their liberty, privacy, civil, and welfare rights. Often, these collateral consequences are defended on the grounds that ex-offenders pose risks to the public. Chapter 9 focuses on our treatment of ex-offenders. The discussion is split into two parts. In the first, I examine whether such collateral consequences should be viewed as they often are by both the courts and legal scholars—as mere adjuncts to legal punishment, not inherent parts of it. I propose a novel account, according to which the restrictions and legal disabilities imposed on ex-offenders should be counted as integral aspects of their official sanctions. As such, they should be assigned prospectively by sentencing judges, not added on after offenders have served their sentences. They should also be subject to proportionality analysis; doing so would require sentencing judges to evaluate the entire package of censuring losses imposed on individuals convicted of crimes. In the second part of the chapter, I examine collateral consequences through the lens of the PI. Instead of casting the imposition of such consequences as contrary to the presumed innocence of individuals who have fully served their sentences, I argue that they are better understood as unjustified infringements of the rights of full and equal citizenship, to which those who have completed their sentences are, once again, entitled.

As will become apparent, I take literally the notion that the PI is a *presumption.* As such, it is a deliberatively adopted perspective on persons suspected of or formally charged with crimes. It is tempting to deny this, to cast the PI as consisting of no more than certain rules of conduct for criminal justice officials. On such a conduct-centered approach, it matters little what such officials, or others in society, believe about the accused, or what perspective they take on them. The PI is honored if criminal justice officials refrain from statements suggesting the guilt of suspects and see to it that they get full and fair due process. I regard such a conduct-centered account of the PI as implausible. It is hard to square with much of the rhetoric surrounding the PI, rhetoric which suggests that it matters not only how criminal justice officials, and all of us, for that matter, treat the accused but also how we view them. More importantly, it seems undeniable that how criminal justice officials view suspects and formally charged persons will pervasively affect how they treat them. In particular, the perspective such officials take on the accused will determine how carefully and thoroughly they investigate the actions of the accused, whether they heed doubts about the evidence they have gathered, search for or give proper weight to exculpatory evidence, and whether they go to extraordinary lengths to prove the guilt of the accused, including the employment of measures well-known to produce mistaken convictions. Of course, I have already indicated that I do not believe that the appropriate perspective on the accused in the pretrial context is one involving a presumption of their innocence. Instead, the nonpresumption of their guilt is, I will argue, a viable alternative perspective, one which criminal justice officials, and indeed all of us, ought to adopt. Only in the trial context does a full-on presumption of innocence, on the part of those tasked with rendering verdicts, have a defensible role to play.

Most of the claims that I make throughout the coming chapters should be acceptable to theorists who subscribe to a range of competing views about the aims and scope of the criminal law, as well as the purposes of legal punishment. This is a book primarily about the procedures that the criminal justice system should employ in the detection, investigation, and prosecution of criminal offenses, as well as the responsibilities that criminal justice officials have toward the accused. The book also discusses the attitudes and conduct toward offenders, or suspected offenders, that members of the public ought to exhibit. What ought to qualify as a criminal offense, and for what purposes we punish, are relatively distinct questions that are mostly beyond the scope of my discussion.

Nonetheless, I would not want my efforts to tame the PI to be interpreted as signaling complacency about the operations of many current criminal justice systems. We criminalize too much conduct and punish it too harshly. I would confine criminal prohibitions to serious wrongs that culpably harm, or threaten to harm, other persons.[11] Though I believe that the reduction of crime is a legitimate justifying aim of legal punishment, it is one that should be subject to retributive constraints. Legal sanctions for offending should be kept strictly proportional with both the comparative and absolute severity of crimes, and we should assiduously avoid the use of inhumane and degrading criminal sanctions.[12] More to the point, although we grant police and prosecutors enormous discretion, we know that they do not always exercise it responsibly.[13] Yet we do much less than we should to monitor, guide, or restrain their actions. The result is mistaken convictions and blatant inconsistencies in the treatment of offenders, not to mention brusque treatment of those suspected of crimes. We should also undertake reforms to ensure that nontrial forms of charge adjudication, which are far and away the ones on which most contemporary legal systems rely, are fairer to accused persons and operate in accordance with the justified aims of legal punishment.[14] Yet the good reasons we have for being concerned about all of these things, and many others as well, have little to do with the PI and are not helpfully illuminated by invoking it.

CHAPTER 1 | The Presumption of Innocence

Sorting the Claims

A BEWILDERING VARIETY OF claims have been made about the meaning and implications of the presumption of innocence in the criminal law. Given its apparent elasticity, it is natural to wonder whether the presumption is an honorific concept, one that is mostly empty and therefore adaptable to the needs and interests of legal theorists of diverse kinds.[1] Far from confining it to the criminal trial, which seems its native habitat, legal theorists have proposed that it applies not only to the pre- and posttrial contexts, but to humans generally, whether or not they have fallen under suspicion of any criminal conduct. Other theorists claim that the presumption ought to act as a constraint on the content of the criminal law.

Anthony Duff has written that inquiry into the meaning of the presumption of innocence involves asking "what must be presumed by whom, about whom, to what effect; what can defeat that presumption; and when (if ever) the presumption need not be made."[2] Duff's succinct statement of the complexities raised by the presumption of innocence anticipates many of the distinctions I draw in this chapter. In it, my aim is the limited one of bringing some initial order to the claims made about the presumption of innocence, though I also foreshadow some of the issues discussed in subsequent chapters. We must first gain some clear sense of the diversity of the claims made about the presumption; later we will see which of them can be utilized in a defensible account of it.

I divide the claims made about the presumption into seven categories: the meaning of "innocence"; the context in which the presumption is held to apply; whether the presumption is a substantive right or a procedural one; the strength of the presumption, meaning what kinds of considerations are taken to rebut it; whether the presumption requires only certain kinds of conduct by public officials or citizens more generally or whether it also requires them to take up or maintain certain attitudes toward their fellow citizens; and the relationship between the presumption and other aspects of criminal procedure. Before turning to the categories, I offer some clarifying remarks about the nature of presumptions.

Presumptions: Legal and Otherwise

Numerous legal scholars have noted that the PI is not one of the kinds of presumptions that is familiar in the law, a so-called presumption of law.[3] Presumptions of law authorize the courts to draw inferences from certain established facts to other facts: If the prosecution has proven P, then the jury should presume Q, even if, in extralegal contexts, Q might not follow of necessity from P. For instance, in public corruption trials, there might be a presumption of law according to which if the government can prove that a private contractor gave a gift to a public official who had the authority to allocate government contracts, jurors should presume that the gift was a bribe. The public official will then have the burden of proving otherwise. As Antony Duff notes, the PI is different. It is "foundational" in the sense that it obtains (or is supposed to) independently of any proof adduced by the government.[4] Persons charged with crimes are entitled to the PI; neither they nor the government has to prove anything to activate the presumption.

Nicholas Rescher has suggested that presumptions are "tentative claims to truth," ones that allow individuals "to navigate the vast domain of uncertainty."[5] As such, presumptions are provisional, standing until undermined by conflicting evidence or, in some cases, by other provisional claims to truth. Applying this to the legal context, and specifically to the context of a criminal trial, it is plausible to believe that jurors come to the task of rendering verdicts in criminal cases not knowing quite what to believe about the individuals accused of crimes standing before them in the courtroom. Jurors might suspect that most of them are guilty, that the accused would not be where they are unless the authorities had strong evidence implicating them.[6] But the task of jurors is to reach a verdict based on the evidence presented during the trial, not based on things that they have heard outside of the courtroom or believe about accused persons more generally. To anchor them initially, we might therefore instruct them to presume the innocence of the accused—that is, to take it as a provisional truth that the accused has not committed the crimes with which she is charged. Why we might do this and whether it makes sense to do so are questions to which we will return in chapter 4. For now, what matters is the stipulated and provisional nature of the presumption, along with its limited duration. No proof is offered of the innocence of the accused, and it endures for no longer than the trial. Jurors are told to view the accused as innocent and to evaluate the government's proffers of evidence in that light. They are also told that the burden of proving otherwise is on the government and the standard of proof, the quality of the evidence that the government must adduce to rebut the presumption, is high.

However, it would be an error, it seems, to hold that the PI instruction involves telling jurors to *believe* that they accused is innocent. Beliefs are not the kinds of things that can be willed or intentionally taken on.[7] Also, accused persons are not like friends, relatives, or coworkers, individuals with whom one might have had numerous encounters over time and so some basis for forming beliefs about whether they are persons of good character or not. Accused persons in criminal trials are strangers, or should be. But if we are not telling jurors at the outset of criminal trials to believe that the accused is innocent, then what are we telling them to do? The answer, I believe, is that we are telling them to deliberately and provisionally take up a perspective on the accused—to view them in a certain way. Much as we might tell a person who is harshly critical of the behavior of a group of raucous schoolchildren to view them as she would her own children, we instruct jurors (or remind judges) to view the accused as they would a person in whose law-abiding character they are confident. They are then to evaluate the government's evidence of the accused's guilt through the lens provided by that perspective. The perspective can and should be abandoned if the evidence brought forward is strongly persuasive.

Notice that in the trial context, the answers to Duff's questions—who is to presume the innocence of whom, to what effect, and what rebuts the presumption—are fairly clear. It is the jury, or the judge in bench trials, who is to presume the innocence of the accused in relation to the criminal acts alleged by the government. The focus of the jury is on one or more specific past acts and the evidence for them. The government is tasked with persuading jurors to abandon the perspective on the accused according to which he or she has abided by the relevant legal provision or provisions. If it can do so, and indeed persuade them beyond a reasonable doubt that the accused is guilty, then the jury must convict. The outcome of conviction is a criminal sentence, imposed by the court.

All of this is familiar. It bears mentioning because the answers to Duff's questions when the PI is taken out of the trial context are, as we shall see, anything but clear. In fact, I contend that the answers will often turn out to be either indecipherable or nonsensical. But I am getting ahead of myself.

The Meaning of "Innocence"

With what sort of "innocence" is the presumption of innocence concerned? It seems clear that its purview is not "moral" innocence, if by this we refer to whether or to what extent the conduct of individuals is above any kind of moral reproach. Whatever the presumption of innocence means or entails in a properly constituted legal system, it does not concern whether individuals are innocent of all wrongdoing, especially wrongdoing that is not appropriately within the remit of the criminal law.[8] Such extralegal misconduct might be the concern of divine beings, if they exist, or of coworkers, friends, spouses, or family members, in certain contexts or on certain occasions. But the criminal law's focus is narrower than moral innocence.

It is legal innocence with which the presumption of innocence is concerned. However, "legal innocence" is ambiguous as between what have been termed "material" and "probatory" innocence.[9] The former refers to innocence in what is perhaps its most intuitive sense: Individuals are materially innocent of crimes just in case that they did not, in fact, and perhaps contrary to the suspicions of legal authorities, commit them. Yet this account is too simple, since individuals can satisfy *actus reus* requirements of the criminal law, and so have in one clear sense "committed" criminal acts, but fail to satisfy mens rea requirements. Or, accused persons can have legitimate justifications or excuses for having violated the law if they satisfy both kinds of requirements.[10] Hence, "material" innocence must be understood to encompass both individuals who did not act as the authorities allege they did and individuals who did so act but who should not be held liable to criminal conviction and punishment. Or to put it a bit differently, to presume the material innocence of persons is to presume them to be "without reproach" by the criminal law, or as "citizens in good standing" with respect to the criminal law.[11] In subsequent chapters, I use the abbreviation PI_m to refer to the presumption of material innocence. PI_m is, I believe, the most plausible interpretation of the PI, though many legal scholars seem hesitant to say so.

Instead of interpreting material innocence as all or nothing, some have suggested that we interpret the PI probabilistically. For instance, the PI could require members of the public, or judges or jurors during criminal trials, to adopt a perspective on the accused according to which they are regarded as equally likely to be materially innocent as guilty.[12] Alternatively, the PI could urge the adoption of a perspective on the accused according to which they are regarded as more likely than not materially innocent, or perhaps much more likely than not materially innocent. A third approach would peg the probability of material innocence to the frequency with which the offenses of which persons have been accused occur in the general population. The less frequent the offense in the general population, the higher the probability of material innocence the PI would require us to assign to the accused. All three of these approaches might lead us to resist our natural suspicions about the accused and would, therefore, if adopted, provide some degree of insulation to the accused from too quick or facile judgments of guilt. However, none of them provides the degree of insulation from suspicion or doubt that a full-on presumption of material innocence provides.

If it is not material innocence with which the PI is concerned, then the alternative would seem to be "probative" innocence. The most straightforward way to then characterize the PI would then be as follows: Individuals suspected of or formally accused of crimes are to be presumed probatively innocent, meaning that they should be regarded and treated as if their legal guilt has not been established by a duly constituted authority, which is presumably a court of law. It should be apparent that the absence of proven guilt is fully consistent with the material guilt of individuals. Guilt might not have been established beyond a reasonable doubt, yet exists (materially) just in case the individuals in question did, in fact, commit the crimes of which they are suspected or formally accused. However, so characterized, the PI does not really embody a presumption of *innocence*; instead, its implications are more negative, to the effect that the guilt of persons suspected of or accused of crimes has not been authoritatively established. Worse than this, such a formulation threatens to turn the PI into little more than a statement of the obvious, for of course individuals only suspected of or formally charged with crimes have not yet been *proven* to be guilty. Much more needs to be done before we can justifiably regard and treat them as other than law-abiding. Perhaps the formulation can be rescued from this implication by interpreting it as a much-needed reminder to criminal justice officials and members of the public that mere suspicions or accusations are far from convincing demonstrations of guilt. True enough, but this does not convert the PI into a presumption of *innocence,* as opposed to a nonpresumption of probative guilt.

It will not help matters to suggest that the PI should be interpreted as a presumption that the probative *innocence* of persons suspected of or accused of crimes is authoritatively established or is likely to be. The legal system does not concern itself with proving the innocence of persons, except, perhaps, in rare cases in which the courts attempt to determine whether an individual has been falsely convicted of one or more crimes.[13] Even then, the focus is apt to be on whether the evidence relied upon by the courts in convicting individuals was somehow tainted or short of the reasonable doubt standard. Interpreting the PI as a presumption of the probative innocence of persons would turn it into what Larry Laudan terms an "idle wheel."[14]

Another way in which "innocence" might be interpreted besides material and probatory innocence involves what can be termed the "clean slate" approach. It has been suggested that jurors, at the outset of trials, should be told to ignore everything they have heard about the accused, or which they believe about accused persons in general, and thus to let the evidence presented at trial be the sole determinant of their verdicts.[15] It is debatable whether the "clean slate" approach amounts to a PI proper; it does not enjoin jurors to regard the accused as materially innocent, that much seems clear. But it does require jurors to adopt a perspective on the accused that is not wholly intuitive and might give the accused fighting chances at acquittals. Viewing the accused as having clean slates seems more advantageous to them than viewing them as probably guilty, for instance. The "clean slate" perspective on accused persons could also be urged more generally, to members of the general public, as well as to government officials not directly involved in the investigation of crimes. To urge a PI would thus involve encouraging all of these individuals to suspend judgment about the accused until there is an authoritative finding about their guilt, or lack thereof, by a court. But to be clear, doing so does not encourage government officials or members of the public to regard or treat the accused as either materially or probatively innocent.

Context

The US Supreme Court has held that the presumption of innocence properly applies only in the context of a criminal trial.[16] In that context it is said to require that the burden of proof must be borne by the government and the government must establish the guilt of defendants beyond a reasonable doubt. The Court has rejected the contention that the presumption applies to the pretrial context, though its claims to that effect seem little more than bare assertions.

Everyone agrees that the presumption applies in the trial context, although there is disagreement about what it means in that context. There is also disagreement about whether, or how far, the PI is consistent with requiring accused persons to shoulder the initial (or any) burden of proof when they assert various affirmative defenses.[17] These are matters to which we return in later chapters.

Many scholars contend that the PI applies outside the trial context and quite a few of them take it to be obvious that it does. For instance, many believe that the presumption applies in the preadjudication context, by which I refer to the context that commences once an individual falls under suspicion of having committed a crime by the authorities and ends when the authorities decide not to file charges, do so but drop them, or the charges are adjudicated via plea bargaining or criminal trials.[18] A typical formulation of the presumption in the preadjudication context holds that the authorities, and sometimes members of the general public, ought to regard and treat those under suspicion, or formally charged with crimes, *as if* they are innocent, so far as possible.[19] What "innocent" means in this formulation is not always specified, although it seems fair to say that it is material innocence that most of its proponents have in mind. On this interpretation, the "so far as possible" qualifying phrase is crucial, since persons arrested, detained, investigated, charged, and perhaps held on remand are most decidedly not treated, or perhaps regarded, *as if* they are materially innocent. Indeed, even with the qualifying phrase, it is unclear what the admonition requires and of whom it requires it. Perhaps it necessitates only that government officials not seek to impose punishment on suspects or accused individuals, or portray them publicly as, in fact, guilty. It seems doubtful that it requires those same officials to regard suspects and defendants as if they are materially innocent. But it might require members of the public to believe this or act like they do. These are issues to which we will return.

Interpreting the PI in the preadjudication context to mean that suspects and formally accused individuals are to be treated *as if* they are probatively innocent raises many of the same difficulties noted in the previous section. The criminal justice system is not concerned with proving individuals innocent; neither does it seem to make much sense to admonish government officials or members of the public to regard suspects or the accused as proven innocent, whatever that might mean. However, it might make sense to insist upon a nonpresumption of probative guilt in the preadjudicative context. This would amount to saying no more than that suspects and formally accused persons should be treated, and perhaps regarded, *as if* their guilt has not yet been authoritatively established. On this interpretation, the PI instructs the authorities, and perhaps members of the public, to keep open minds about the guilt of suspects or formally accused individuals until due process has taken its full course. The PI is thus a reminder, of sorts, that even though government officials might believe they have damning evidence against individuals, the evidence has not yet gone through the crucible of a criminal trial or been acceded to by the accused during negotiated plea settlements. Given the unpredictability of the criminal justice process in its early stages, presuming that the guilt of suspects will be proven is premature. Again, however, this interpretation of the PI seems less a presumption of innocence than a nonpresumption of guilt.

Some scholars go further, suggesting that the presumption applies to the prearrest or, perhaps, presuspicion context. Thus, Hamish Stewart claims that all persons have an innate moral right to be presumed innocent.[20] Simply insofar as they are persons, as opposed to individuals who distinguish themselves by and through their conduct, individuals are to be presumed innocent. Notice that questions about who is to presume the innocence of persons as citizens, to what purpose, and what considerations are capable of rebutting it and to what effect, have less obvious answers when the PI is taken out of the trial context, or even the context of official suspicion or accusation. Are all citizens supposed to "take up" a presumption of innocence toward their fellow citizens, one that endures until they have reason (and how much so?) to suspect otherwise? Or must only criminal justice officials do so? What kind of evidence is to be deemed capable of rebutting such a nontrial and nonprocedural PI? And to what effect?

Similar kinds of questions must be answered by scholars who hold that the PI serves as a substantive constraint on the content of the criminal law. Lawmakers, it is alleged, violate the PI if they adopt criminal provisions that, when enforced, sweep in the materially innocent as well as the guilty, or if they prohibit conduct that has not been proven, beyond a reasonable doubt, to be appropriately criminalizable.[21] On these accounts, the PI would appear to have some role to play even if no one ever violated the criminal law or fell under suspicion of having done so. Yet what exactly would it mean for lawmakers to "presume innocence" as they craft criminal provisions? Further, what kinds of considerations would rebut that presumption, and what follows from its rebuttal? These are questions the answers to which seem elusive.

The presumption has also been held to apply to the postadjudication setting, meaning after the point at which charges against individuals have been formally resolved by trial, plea bargaining, or other means. For instance, though courts in the United States permit it, many scholars contend that allowing sentencing judges to determine convicted persons' sentences based, in part, on charges of which persons were acquitted by a jury, runs counter to the PI.[22] Similarly, it has been held that permitting probation officers to rescind an individual's probation, subsequent to an arrest but before any charges related to that arrest are filed against the individual or adjudicated by the courts, is difficult to square with the PI.[23] Perhaps so, but in these kinds of cases, once again, the answers to the questions Duff poses about the PI need clearer answers than have often been given to them.

The same is true for claims made by some scholars that the behavior of officials subsequent to trial acquittals can contravene the PI. If prosecutors or police publicly impugn a jury acquittal, declaring the acquitted defendant to be guilty, such conduct has been deemed to run afoul of the presumption.[24] Likewise, aggressive police monitoring of the posttrial conduct of individuals acquitted of crimes, or worse, harassment of such individuals, might be held to violate the presumption of innocence. Once a court has acquitted individuals of the crimes with which they have been charged, the claim appears to be that the authorities ought to regard and treat them *as if* they are innocent.

Finally, it could be argued that the presumption has, or ought to have, some bite in the postpunishment context, that is, after individuals have served whatever sentences have been assigned to them by the courts. As noted in the Introduction, it is not uncommon in many jurisdictions for the law to impose various civil penalties or disabilities on individuals who have been convicted of crimes and fully served their sentences.[25] Ex-offenders routinely encounter officially imposed restrictions on where they can live, whether they can possess firearms, whether they can vote, and whether they can participate in various social welfare or educational programs sponsored by the government. It seems clear that the aim of some of these penalties and restrictions is preventive, meaning that they have been enacted with a view to making it harder for ex-offenders to commit further crimes. If that is correct, then it might seem that such restrictions run counter to the PI. Instead of viewing those who have fully served their sentences for previous crimes as, once again, citizens in good standing in the community, such provisions implicitly cast them as unreliable and therefore suspect.

Substantive or Procedural?

There is also debate about whether the PI is procedural in character, a vital aspect of the process by which we investigate and adjudicate criminal charges, or more than this, a substantive moral requirement that ought to constrain us in ways that go beyond concerns about having fair and accurate investigative or adjudicative procedures. The proof structure of criminal trials, consisting of the presumption of innocence, the burden of proof on the government, and the reasonable doubt standard, is viewed by many legal scholars as an error distribution device.[26] We know that trials can produce adjudication errors. As between errors of mistaken conviction and those of mistaken acquittal, we prefer (and perhaps quite strongly) to avoid the former more than the latter. Thus, we set up trials to be ordeals for the government officials who seek to convict and punish the individuals whom they suspect of crimes in order to achieve the desired distribution of errors. The PI is a vital part of the proof structure of criminal trials, which are conceived as normative models of fair and accurate adjudicative procedures. In a similar vein, it might be claimed that other rules or provisions governing criminal trials that some have seen as required by fidelity to the presumption of innocence are little more than procedural requirements designed to prevent fact-finders from rushing too quickly to guilty verdicts based on considerations other than the probative evidence furnished by the government. These rules include ones imposing strict limits on the introduction of evidence of the accused's past crimes, prohibiting adverse inferences regarding the accused's guilt based on his declining to testify, and prohibiting the accused from appearing in court in jail garb or shackles. Even prohibitions on pretrial declarations by police or prosecutors concerning the "obvious guilt" of the accused, or on detailed disclosure of the evidence against the accused, might be construed as merely procedural in character. These kinds of conduct by public officials might be thought to confound efforts to assemble jury pools that can weigh the evidence against the accused in an unbiased fashion.

Other scholars cast the presumption in more substantive terms. Stewart's innate right to be presumed innocent is exemplary in this regard. He argues that the presumption requires criminal justice officials to successively justify their actions as they stop, arrest, detain, and investigate individuals whom they suspect of offending.[27] The burdens of justification such officials must meet at the earliest stages of a criminal investigation might not be all that demanding, but Stewart sees them as entailed by the right to be presumed above reproach. Independently of whether they aid or interfere with fair procedures, infringements of the right to be presumed innocent should have to be justified. Also, on more substantive accounts of the presumption, inflammatory pretrial statements about defendants by criminal justice officials should be prohibited, not simply to avoid poisoning the potential jury pool, but to protect what Stefan Trechsel terms the "reputation-related aspect" of suspects and defendants.[28] It matters to all of us what our fellow citizens think about us. How they regard us will determine the treatment we receive at their hands both pre- and postadjudication, and thus the opportunities available or foreclosed to us. What police or prosecutors say pretrial might irreparably harm such reputational interests, especially if the accused are ultimately acquitted. Inflammatory posttrial statements aimed at undermining a jury's verdict of acquittal can likewise set back an individual's reputational interests. Prohibitions on such statements, it might be argued, cannot be plausibly cast as procedural requirements needed to optimize the distribution of adjudication errors. Instead, they are needed in order to protect substantive interests that individuals have in their good names and reputations.

Strength of the Presumption

Whatever else it is, the PI is only a presumption, which means that it can be rebutted or overridden. Yet it would seem that the strength of the reasons for overcoming it must vary somewhat, depending on the context in which it is thought to hold.[29] As we have already seen, if the presumption holds, as some claim, in the preadjudication context, it will have to be interpreted as rebuttable by fairly weak considerations. The police must be able to investigate suspicious conduct on the part of individuals, and this means that they must be able to request that individuals cease whatever else they are doing and answer questions. The police must also be able to prevent those who are behaving suspiciously from fleeing instead of answering questions, briefly detain them until they answer questions or refuse to do so, and arrest them if the answers they give, or other evidence readily discernible, warrants it. Even if we believe, as we surely should, that the authorities ought to have some "reasonable grounds" for such initial investigative actions, it seems unwise to set the burdens of justifying their actions very high. Granted, as investigations proceed, and official intrusions into the privacy or onto the property of citizens become more significant, or restrictions on their liberty become more extensive or enduring, the authorities, perhaps in deference to the PI, ought to have to satisfy progressively stronger burdens of justification. At the preadjudication limit, when the issue is the justifiability of pretrial detention, it might be argued that the burden of proof on the government ought to be exacting, especially since such detention is, in many jurisdictions, virtually the same as imprisonment and therefore legal punishment. Some argue that pretrial detention violates or at least sits uneasily with the PI.[30] Yet even if we do not go that far, it seems clear that the authorities should have to furnish powerful reasons for thinking that no approach other than pretrial detention will suffice to ensure that accused persons will appear for trial, refrain from interfering with the course of justice, or be prevented from committing further preadjudication crimes.

In the trial context, the strength of the presumption is formidable. If the government is to rebut it, it is widely agreed that it must bear the burden of proof and meet the stringent, reasonable doubt standard.[31] Such a hefty burden of justification makes sense given the profound ways in which legal punishment, especially when it takes the form of imprisonment, impacts the lives of individuals convicted of crimes. Legal punishment stigmatizes and hobbles offenders in ways that persist beyond the formal periods of their sentences.[32] If the government succeeds in convincing an impartial tribunal of the guilt of defendants beyond a reasonable doubt, then it seems that the presumption of innocence is not only rebutted but replaced by, or converted to, a presumption of guilt. After all appeals are exhausted, it would seem that the presumption of guilt becomes final. However, in many legal systems, once a conviction has occurred, there is a profound shift in the procedural and evidentiary rules in favor of the government, one that makes successful appeals unlikely.[33] Also, when individuals plead guilty, typically in exchange for charge or sentencing concessions by prosecutors or the courts, the presumption of guilt is quite strong. Most jurisdictions grant limited appeals to defendants who admit their guilt.[34]

What about the strength of the presumption in the sentencing context? Few scholars seem willing to defend the practice of permitting judges to sentence convicted offenders based, in part, on beliefs that the individuals standing before them committed crimes for which a court did not convict them.[35] It would seem to be sentencing judges who are to presume the innocence of the individuals whom they are sentencing, at least in relation to any charges of which those individuals have not been convicted. But this would then seem to mean that if the PI is doing the work of explaining why judges should not be permitted to consider unproven charges in determining sentences, the presumption is, in this context, nonrebuttable. For it is not clear what kinds of considerations could overcome it. Yet this seems to convert the PI into something else—a firm rule against having sentences influenced in any way by unproven charges.

Next, consider what I have termed the "postpunishment" context and the claims made by some scholars that civil penalties and restrictions contravene the PI. On the one hand, it might be unwise to dismiss all such penalties and restrictions on the grounds that they are contrary to the presumption, no matter what the quality of evidence the government has that imposing them will prevent some crimes. On the other hand, we might be wary of permitting the government to impose such penalties and restrictions, for preventive purposes, in the absence of compelling evidence of their crime-preventive potential and without proof that no other measures—ones less in conflict with the PI—exist to prevent such crimes. In short, it might seem that the burden of proof for adopting such measures should be on the government and it should be a fairly demanding one, given their likely stigmatizing, liberty-restricting, and welfare-diminishing impact.[36] That being said, it seems doubtful that the government should have to demonstrate, beyond a reasonable doubt, that some ex-offenders pose risks to the public. And we would have to specify more clearly who ought to be presuming the innocence of ex-offenders and what procedures, if any, are required if it is to be appropriately rebutted.

Conduct versus Attitudinal Requirements

As already noted, another broad division in the claims made about the PI is that between its requiring certain kinds of conduct from government officials, or members of the public, and its requiring the intentional adoption of a perspective on those who have fallen under suspicion of offending or been formally charged with it. Everyone agrees that the police and crime investigators must be given the authority and resources to detect crimes, apprehend suspects, and obtain evidence against them. There is also widespread agreement that, in doing so, they ought to have to follow certain rules or procedures, ones designed to restrain and control the use of their formidable powers, especially with a view to protecting the innocent, but also in order to respect the dignitary interests of persons. Similarly, in the event of trial adjudication, there is broad consensus that, as a procedural matter, the government should have to bear the burden of proof and meet a high standard of proof to gain convictions. There is also considerable agreement that, pretrial and postacquittal, government officials ought to be circumspect in their comments about defendants and the evidence against them, even if there is disagreement about the grounds for such circumspection. Notice that these conduct requirements, whatever they are or how they are seen as grounded, tell us little about how government officials, or the general public, ought to regard or view the individuals who have fallen under suspicion of offending, been charged with it, or had those charges formally adjudicated.

Some scholars draw a sharp distinction between the legal rules or procedures concerning conduct that they believe criminal justice officials must adhere to and the beliefs or attitudes of those officials toward the individuals being processed by the criminal justice system. The police, crime investigators, prosecutors, and even judges might believe that most of the individuals who have fallen under their purview are likely guilty. That does not matter, it will be claimed, so long as they abide by the relevant rules and procedures designed to optimally distribute adjudication errors.[37] It also might not matter what the public thinks about those who have been arrested, charged with, and either convicted or acquitted of crimes.[38] The view of some scholars is that we cannot control, or even hope to influence, what members of the public think about those who have become entangled with the criminal justice system We can only insist that the officials in charge of the system behave in accordance with certain rules and procedures, and that members of the general public refrain from vigilante action or other illicit conduct toward the accused and toward individuals who have been acquitted or against whom charges have been dropped by prosecutors or dismissed by judges.

However, one also finds support for the notion that the PI imposes attitudinal requirements on public officials and members of the general public. It is not uncommon for the press, in covering criminal investigations or announcing criminal charges, to remind the public that the suspected or formally accused are "innocent until proven guilty." Though this might amount to little more than an admonition to not act toward such individuals as if their guilt has already been authoritatively determined, it does not seem strained to interpret it as more than this, as an encouragement to regard or view such individuals in a certain way. Granted, such a reminder's import seems ambiguous: Are members of the public being encouraged to regard the accused as materially innocent or not yet proven guilty (or perhaps both)? The former might be a stretch, given the highly stigmatizing effects of arrest, investigation, and charges. Yet even if the reminder is one only to the effect that members of the public ought to refrain from concluding, too quickly or easily, that those charged with crimes are guilty, it seems one that goes beyond the prescription of conduct toward or in relation to the accused.

The notion that the presumption of innocence requires the officials involved in the investigation and prosecution of crimes to adopt certain attitudes toward suspects and defendants might seem a dubious one, given the evidence about crimes committed by individuals that those officials will have seen. But again, the distinction between material innocence and the absence of probative guilt complicates matters. It might indeed be too much to ask police and prosecutors to regard those in their grips as materially innocent, however diligent those officials might otherwise be in adhering to the rules of due process. But it does not seem quite so much to ask that they bear in mind the fallibility of the investigative and charging process, and therefore adopt attitudes reflective of that awareness and supportive of proceeding carefully, rigorously, and fairly as they do their work. This means, among other things, that they must respect the rules of due process, acknowledge their own susceptibilities to error or bias, and restrain themselves from jumping too quickly to conclusions about suspects and the evidence against them. One might attempt to cast all of these as solely conduct requirements. Yet to do so obscures the ways in which the attitudes we have influence our conduct. Simply put, conduct unsupported by attitudes of certain kinds seems unlikely to persist or be exhibited consistently.

In the trial context, there is debate about whether granting defendants the presumption of innocence is a conduct requirement or also an attitudinal one. The US Supreme Court appears to construe it as the former, indeed, as little more than a reminder that the government bears the burden of proof and the standard of proof it must meet is high.[39] Still, it could be argued that implicit in this understanding of the presumption is the prescription of certain attitudes, or at least expectations, on the part of judges or jurors. It is to the government that they should look first to make the case that defendants are guilty. Moreover, those charged with rendering verdicts should be disposed to not be satisfied, or even moved, by weak proofs of guilt.

Some scholars contend that jurors should be given explicit instructions, pursuant to the PI, about how to regard defendants at the outset of their trials. For instance, William Laufer, argues that jurors in criminal trials should be instructed to start from the presumption that defendants are materially innocent.[40] He sees this as a way of insulating them from too quickly drawn verdicts of guilt. Laufer's is an account much like the one I develop in chapter 4. Larry Laudan, who is more skeptical about how much we can affect jurors' beliefs about defendants, nonetheless holds that they should be instructed to place no probative weight whatsoever on the fact that the defendant sits in the dock before them. Jurors are to focus squarely on the evidence presented by the government.[41] This seems less an attempt to encourage an optimistic attitude toward the defendant's innocence than an attempt to discourage or combat unsympathetic ones.[42] As we have already seen, alternative perspectives on the accused, especially at the outset of their trials, might also be prescribed.

Though less often discussed, the questions of whether there is an attitudinal component to the presumption of innocence, and what it consists in, seem especially pertinent in two postadjudication contexts—when the accused are acquitted of the charges against them (or the charges are simply dropped by prosecutors or dismissed by the courts) and after individuals convicted of crimes have served their sentences. Why might it matter how the authorities or the general public regard the individuals against whom prosecutions have either failed or been discontinued? Because even if legal officials and members of the public refrain from seeking to illicitly punish the formerly accused, as they surely should, how they regard and therefore treat such individuals will matter. Continued suspicions about the formerly accused might lead the police to more actively monitor or harass them. Likewise, doubts about the citizenship in good standing of the formerly accused might lead members of the general public to shun them or treat them with open scorn or hostility. There are clear costs to individuals in being regarded by legal officials or their fellow citizens as untrustworthy or irresponsible, costs that attitudinal requirements grounded in the presumption of innocence might be invoked to combat.

Similarly, once individuals have fully served their sentences for past crimes, does the presumption of innocence get restored, such that ex-convicts ought to be regarded, once again, as citizens in good standing? As we have seen, current social and legal practices belie such a notion. Even a weaker prescriptive attitude toward ex-offenders, one that Antony Duff at one point characterized in terms of a "right to be presumed harmless," seems in conflict with existing practices.[43] Once a convicted offender, always a convicted offender, seems to better capture the official and unofficial attitude toward at least certain kinds of lawbreakers. Yet such an attitude toward ex-offenders is deeply at odds with practices and attitudes to which many of us subscribe—redemption, forgiveness, and equal treatment foremost among them. It therefore might seem plausible to believe that once individuals have served their sentences for their past crimes, we ought to revise our attitudes about them. Some regard the PI as the basis for such a needed shift.

Who Must Adopt the Presumption of Innocence?

The discussion so far has implicitly exposed a further dimension along which claims about the presumption of innocence might be sorted: Of whom does the presumption of innocence require conduct, or attitudes, or both? To see the potential complexities here, consider the interpretation of the presumption according to which suspects and the formally accused ought to be regarded, preadjudication, as if they are materially innocent. Suppose this is interpreted as stating an attitudinal requirement. It seems one thing to urge such a perspective on the accused to the general public, or to jurors at the outset of trials. None of these parties will have seen much of the evidence against individuals accused of crimes, though they might have been exposed to some of it through press coverage or disclosures by prosecutors or police. Hence, up to a point, it might make sense to insist that all of these parties should take perspectives on the accused according to which they are materially innocent.

However, as we have seen, it arguably makes less sense to insist that the police or prosecutors involved directly in the processing of cases must regard suspects and defendants as if they are materially innocent. Granted, conduct requirements of various kinds are clearly applicable to such legal officials, ones that, incidentally, have little application to others in society. Police and prosecutors can be required to meet a variety of burdens of proof as they move suspects and charged defendants through the legal process, at least some of which might be grounded in the PI. Likewise, such officials should be prohibited from making public statements about the accused prior to the charges against them being adjudicated, especially ones prejudicial to the accused being able to obtain fair charge adjudication. There should also be prohibitions against making the accused appear in the courtroom in jail garb or shackles. But to go further, and require police and prosecutors directly involved in a case to view the accused as materially innocent (as opposed to not yet proven guilty), despite the evidence to the contrary they have seen, seems a more doubtful proposition.

More dubious still would be the suggestion that those who are crime victims, and who are certain it was the accused who victimized them, ought to view the accused, preadjudication, as if he or she is materially innocent. If charges against the accused are subsequently dropped for lack of evidence, or the accused is acquitted, it still would make little sense to insist that victims ought to regard the formerly accused as if they are materially innocent. By contrast, it arguably does make sense to insist that victims regard and treat the accused, preadjudication, as not yet proven guilty. Even victims who are confident about who wronged them and how they did so might be usefully encouraged to let the criminal justice process take its full course. In the event of acquittals or dropped or dismissed charges, victims should be strongly discouraged from undertaking vigilante actions against the accused.[44] It also seems appropriate to tell victims that they should adopt attitudes of acceptance toward the adjudicative outcomes of the criminal justice system, even when those who victimized them are, for some reason, not convicted and punished.

What about the judges who must rule on pretrial motions by the prosecution or defense, oversee trials or plea colloquies, or act as fact-finders in bench trials? Does the presumption of innocence have implications for their conduct and attitudes, and does what they consist in depend on the specific tasks in which they are engaged? With respect to pretrial hearings of various kinds, it might seem sufficient for judges to focus on ensuring that suspects and formally charged individuals receive due process. How they regard or view suspects and defendants—in particular whether they should strive to view them as materially innocent or not, might not seem to matter much. In this context, judges should focus on maintaining fair adjudication procedures. During jury trials, it might also seem that whatever fidelity to the presumption of innocence requires of judges is exhausted by actions on their part undertaken to ensure that defendants receive fair trials during which the state bears the burden of proving guilt.

However, judges are also tasked with making rulings that bear directly on determining the validity of the charges against individuals. This is most obviously true in bench trials, in which it is judges who render verdicts. It could be claimed that, at the outset of bench trials, judges, like jurors in jury trials, should consciously adopt a perspective on the accused according to which they are presumed citizens in good standing. Only by doing so will they give the government's case the appropriate degree of scrutiny and not let their own beliefs about most accused persons unduly influence their ultimate verdicts. Also, in jury trials, defense attorneys might ask for the summary dismissal of charges at the conclusion of the state's case against defendants on the grounds that the government has failed to shoulder the burden of proving guilt. Rulings on such motions appear to require judges to go beyond ensuring fair trial procedures. They depend on some assessment, by judges, of the sufficiency of the government's case.

But that raises the question from what starting point judges ought to begin trials with respect to defendants' presumed innocence or guilt. Further, decisions about whether to grant accused individuals bail or to remand them are not purely procedural ones. Judges might be called upon to offer some preliminary evaluation of the evidence against individuals, either to determine whether they are likely guilty of the charges against them, or pose a threat to the trial process or to others in the community. Such judgments might also be affected by the attitudinal stance toward accused individuals that judges bring to the table. A judge committed to viewing defendants as materially innocent, as far as possible, might make very different decisions about the preadjudication detention of individuals than one who cynically regards most persons arrested and charged with crimes as guilty, or as very likely so.

In short, there is a diverse group of actors to whom the presumption of innocence might be held to apply in some form or other—police, prosecutors, judges, jurors, victims, and the public generally. An adequate account of the PI will have to accommodate this variety of actors. As we will see, some accounts struggle to do so more than others.

Relationship to Other Aspects of Criminal Procedure

Last but not least, we turn to vexed questions concerning the relationship between the PI and other critical elements of criminal procedure. In particular, there are various claims made about its relation to the right to fair trial, the burden and standard of proof in criminal trials, and the right against self-incrimination.

Some scholars see the PI as the ground for the entire panoply of fair trial rights. The presumed innocence of citizens is the normative status quo ante that must be overcome or defeated, in a court of law, by the government's production of evidence convincing to a very high standard.[45] Moreover, the accused must be afforded the right to challenge the evidence and charges, with the aid of competent legal counsel, and to call witnesses on their behalf (who must be made to appear). Only verdicts produced by such fair and rigorous procedures are deemed capable of defeating the PI.

Though they do not question the value of such procedures, other scholars doubt that all of them are entailed by the PI. It might make sense to so view the burden of proof. If those accused of crimes are to be presumed materially innocent at the outset of their trials, then it would seem to follow that the burden of establishing that they are guilty of one or more offenses ought to be on the authorities. But it is less clear whether the standard of proof that the authorities must meet is entailed by the PI. The standard of proof concerns the degree of persuasiveness that the government must meet to defeat the PI.[46] Setting it high makes it harder for the government to defeat the PI; that much is clear. But why we should make it harder rather than easier for the government to obtain convictions is a question that does not seem answered by the PI itself. Instead, scholars have suggested that we make it harder rather than easier because we strongly prefer to avoid convicting the innocent to convicting the guilty, or because we seek moral assurance that we act justifiably before we inflict legal sanctions on persons, with their stigmatizing and potentially life-altering effects.[47] In either case, our reasons for insisting on a high standard of proof seem external to the PI.[48]

With respect to the right against self-incrimination, it has been claimed that the PI is the foundation for it, the idea being that those provisionally deemed innocent should not be expected or required to prove their innocence, including with their own testimony.[49] The burden of proving guilt is entirely on the government; the accused can testify at their trials if they wish but should not be compelled to do so. Neither should judges or juries be permitted to draw adverse inferences from their refusal to testify, or else the PI is violated. One question such an account must address is whether the PI is really needed to normatively shield accused persons from harsh police interrogation, or will reasons drawn from the dignity of persons suffice.[50] More to the point is the question whether the PI should be conceived as persisting throughout trials, no matter how persuasive the government's case that the accused have committed one or more offenses. Even if accused persons ought to be granted a robust PI at the outset of their trials, it is rebuttable. The key issue might turn out to be when it is appropriate for jurors to regard the PI as rebutted—only after a verdict is reached or once the government's case seems persuasive enough to jurors to meet or exceed the reasonable doubt standard. In the latter case, accused persons who decline to testify might be reasonably thought to have to live with adverse inferences concerning their guilt. Whether such inferences contravene the PI is, therefore, not readily apparent.[51]

Concluding Remarks

The breadth and complexity of the issues surveyed in this chapter might lead readers to wonder whether they can be addressed in a single book, or even in several of them. I shall be content with modest aims: Many of the issues raised in this chapter will be confronted directly in the chapters that follow; others will receive more cursory treatment. My intention, as outlined in the Introduction, is to develop and defend a systematic account of the PI, one that assigns it an important and intelligible role in the criminal justice system. But it is a limited role, far more so than many legal scholars would assign it.

In the next two chapters, I explore proposals to give the PI a robust role in the criminal justice system and in society more generally. Though many of the concerns that animate these proposals are ones with which I have considerable sympathy, I am not convinced that hauling in the PI to clarify or address them is helpful.

CHAPTER 2 | The Human Right to Be Presumed Innocent

THE RIGHT TO BE presumed innocent has been endorsed by human rights documents as fundamental. Consider three representative documents:

> Everyone charged with a criminal offence shall have the right to be presumed innocent until proven guilty according to law. (International Covenant on Civil and Political Rights, Article 14 §2)
>
> Everyone charged with a criminal offence shall be presumed innocent until proven guilty according to law. (European Convention on Human Rights, Article 6 §2)
>
> Every person accused of a criminal offence has the right to be presumed innocent so long as his guilt has not been proven according to law. (American Convention on Human Rights, Article 8 §2)

There are some differences in the wording among these documents, though these differences appear to be minor. One possibly significant difference concerns the ECHR wording, which elides the claim that the presumption is a right. However, this hardly seems significant, given the nature of the document. Also, as Stefan Trechsel has noted, the relevant European institutions always recognized the presumption as a right.[1]

Given their wordings, these documents imply that the right to be presumed innocent comes into existence once persons have been formally accused of criminal offenses. So understood, it is natural to then interpret the right as a procedural one, entitling individuals to a variety of protections designed to shield them from the stigma and hard treatment of legal punishment until they have been formally convicted, as well as to ensure that convictions are produced by appropriate means. Even if we interpret it in this way, how we should understand such a right and what it implies about criminal procedure is subject to considerable controversy. Though important, controversies such as these will not be my focus in this chapter.

Instead, I am interested in the claim, made recently by several scholars, that, despite the wording of the human rights documents themselves, the right to be presumed innocent is a substantive human right, attaching to all persons whether or not they have been formally accused of criminal offending.[2] Such a substantive human right is seen as grounding a variety of rules and procedures to which individuals are entitled. On Hamish Stewart's account, the innate right to be presumed innocent requires the authorities, and perhaps all of us, to view and treat persons as "above reproach" simply insofar as they are persons.[3] More significantly, such a right also requires the authorities to progressively justify infringements of or intrusions upon citizens' basic rights to liberty, autonomy, or privacy as they investigate crimes and undertake formal actions against those suspected of having committed them.[4] According to Stefan Trechsel and Liz Campbell, the human right to be presumed innocent requires more than fair trial (or more broadly, in light of the ubiquity of plea bargaining, fair adjudication) rights. In Trechsel's view, it also requires the authorities to protect, or at least not injure, the "reputation-related" interests of individuals.[5] Hence, police and prosecutors must refrain from statements and actions suggesting that individuals are "guilty" when have not yet been convicted or when they have been acquitted by the courts. Campbell has similar concerns about statements made by public officials attributing criminal conduct to citizens who have not been convicted of any crimes. She would hold officials to higher evidentiary standards before they can besmirch the good names and reputations of individuals. She grounds these strictures in an account of the proper relationship between citizens and the government in liberal societies.[6]

Most ambitiously, Hock Lai Ho argues that the substantive right to be presumed innocent consists of all of the rights constitutive of fair trials.[7] Trials serve as vital checks on the use and abuse of the power to prosecute. Because individuals have a substantive moral right to be presumed innocent, they can legitimately demand that such a check be employed. Only if the government can decisively prove the guilt of the accused is the presumption of innocence fully and properly rebutted.

Many of these authors' claims contain important insights. However, I believe that they fall short of demonstrating that individuals have a *substantive* human right to be presumed innocent. I therefore endeavor to show that, insofar as their claims are defensible, they can be accommodated without such a right. Further, I argue that such a right would have unsettling implications for criminal justice practice, supporting criminal justice policies that would make it more difficult to prevent crimes, as well as to apprehend, prosecute, and punish offenders. More than this, a substantive human right to be presumed innocent does not seem like other substantive human rights. It does not directly secure liberty or basic welfare interests. Many of those accused of crimes seem willing, if not eager, to waive the right to be presumed innocent in order to reduce their punishment and thus preserve interests that they deem more important. In short, the PI seems more like a second-order, or procedural right, one that individuals accused of crimes invoke in order to see to it that their basic liberties and welfare are not unjustifiably diminished by the state's imposition of legal punishment.

The discussion in this chapter proceeds as follows: In the first section, I show how a right to be presumed innocent does not seem a good fit with other paradigmatic substantive human rights. In the next four sections, I take up the claims made about the presumption of innocence by Stewart, Trechsel, Campbell, and Ho, respectively, and show why they fall short of establishing its status as a substantive human right. Along the way, I develop an alternative account of the presumption as a fundamental procedural right. In the sixth and final section, I summarize that alternative account.

Human Rights and the Presumption of Innocence

There is considerable debate about the existence of human rights and their grounding. I shall ignore the outright skeptics and focus on those who attempt to defend human rights as vital normative constructs. Though unanimity among the believers does not exist, a consensus, of sorts, has emerged that basic human rights are grounded in the necessity of securing liberty and welfare interests that, collectively so to speak, undergird the complex capacity for human agency.[8] Rights to life, physical and psychological integrity, freedom of movement, privacy, freedom of conscience and expression, minima of subsistence, education, and healthcare, all are plausibly cast as designed to secure the conditions under which individuals can have and lead decent lives of their own choosing. Such rights are universal, that is, possessed by all humans, and equal.[9] They also seem focused on securing fairly rudimentary prerequisites of human agency.[10] Morality might require considerably more of us in our treatment of our fellow human beings than does respect for their human rights. Indeed, by exercising our agency we establish relationships with other people, and these relationships generate a host of further obligations, as well as opportunities to assist or care for other people. Which of these opportunities we take up and how we do so both develops and reflects our moral characters. It does not follow from the fact that what respect for basic rights requires of us is minimal that it is unimportant; far from it.

If something like the preceding sketch of basic and substantive human rights makes sense, then it is not apparent how a substantive right to be presumed innocent can be made to square with it. Such a right does not seem in any direct way linked to securing one or more aspects of the complex capacity for human agency. It is not like the right to physical or psychological integrity, which obviously does so by shielding us from attacks on our persons that would injure or impede our abilities to reflect, make choices, and act. Nor is it like freedom of expression, which serves to increase the conceptual and affective resources upon which we can draw in determining how our lives will go, or provides us with opportunities to act on our creative impulses and contribute to important debates about culture, politics, religion, art, or science.

Granted, if we are suspected of or accused of criminal misconduct, the presumption of innocence might serve as a vital check on the authority and ability of government officials to infringe or curtail our substantive moral (and presumably legal) rights through criminal sanctions. But this suggests that the right to be presumed innocent is a second-order right—one needed to ensure that our basic substantive rights are not unjustifiably curtailed—and a procedural one, in the sense that it entitles us to the state's employment of fair and rigorous methods for testing and evaluating the accusations made against us by the authorities.[11] Given the well-known and continuing dangers of state power, such a procedural right is plausibly interpreted as fundamental, one worthy of inclusion on any list of human rights. Though some legal scholars would try to convince us otherwise, perhaps there is considerable wisdom in the human rights documents quoted at the outset, all of which cast the right to be presumed innocent in the light of official accusation.

It might be objected that if the PI is understood to be only a procedural right, then it might be too easily set aside when the authorities deem it vital to convict people whom they believe to be very dangerous or guilty of heinous crimes. When the aim of the authorities is to protect the basic substantive rights of others, or to symbolically stand for them by condemning and punishing the guilty, it might seem altogether too tempting to dispense with fair and rigorous adjudication procedures. Elevating the PI to a substantive right, one that puts it on a par with other substantive rights that the state more reliably aims to secure, might therefore seem a needed antidote to this temptation. However, it is far from clear that labeling something a "substantive" right will better insulate it from official depredation. For instance, few doubt that the right to free speech is a basic human right, but that has not stopped governments from infringing it when the authorities decide that certain kinds of speech are subversive. Calling something a "substantive" right does not magically shield it from official hostility to its exercise or enjoyment. Further, given the PI's central role in helping individuals to resist the unjustified infringement of such undisputed fundamental rights as liberty and property—a role that I explore in considerable detail in chapters 4 and 5—its status as a basic, albeit procedural, right seems unassailable.

The PI as a Right to be Treated as "Above Reproach"

Hamish Stewart suggests a possible response to the doubts raised in the preceding section. He claims that persons have an innate right to be regarded and treated as "above reproach" simply insofar as they are persons.[12] He says that "no person is legally in the wrong just because he or she is a person; to be legally in the wrong, he or she must have done something legally wrong."[13] Even if this is correct, it does not seem to carry us very far. True, no one should be punished just because he or she is a person. Clearly, it is conduct that is the relevant basis for legal punishment and specifically conduct that has been proven to be in violation of the criminal law. But who would have thought otherwise? And why do we need an innate human right to be presumed innocent to capture this insight?

Though Stewart himself does not say so, perhaps the idea is this: Persons should not be viewed as reproachable simply in virtue of their possession of what we might term "status" characteristics, things such as their race, gender, ethnicity, or youthfulness. These are not characteristics over which individuals have any or proximate control. In this respect, conduct is different. Conduct is something that, presumably, individuals have control over and can be punished for if they are convicted of violating the criminal law. One might, therefore, be tempted to say that persons have an innate right to be presumed innocent based on their status characteristics. We could even take this one step further, since it is apparent that an individual's conduct can be judged more negatively based on his or her status characteristics and this, too, seems objectionable. Racial prejudice, for instance, can lead the police to regard perfectly innocent conduct as suspicious, or somewhat suspicious conduct as very much so. Hence, we might say that one has a basic human right to be presumed innocent based on one's status characteristics and to not have one's conduct judged more negatively solely because of one's status characteristics.

However, it is not clear what this important insight really has to do with the presumption of innocence. It might make sense to say that persons have something like a basic and substantive human right to be judged according to an unbiased evaluation of their conduct. Yet such a basic right clearly has implications beyond the criminal context, in the awarding of jobs, promotions, and college admissions, among other things, especially if "conduct" is taken in a cumulative sense to include accomplishments or earned qualifications. True, we do not want police or prosecutors to respond solely or primarily to individuals' status characteristics, if to them at all. The problem is that police and prosecutors often, and probably typically, respond to the apparent criminal misconduct of persons. That, in turn, means that the right to be presumed innocent, if interpreted as above, will have relatively few implications for the criminal justice process in many cases. It would "protect" individuals only insofar as the authorities were reacting, in whole or in part, to their status characteristics. Yet that surely cannot be what proponents of such a right hope for.[14]

Stewart goes on to argue that the innate right to be presumed innocent, in fact, has a vital role to play in the criminal justice process. He claims that it explains why we require the authorities to justify their intrusions upon the rights of suspects and formally accused persons in a progressively more stringent manner as they stop, arrest, detain, investigate, and charge them.[15] Initially, it might not take much justification for the police to stop and question an individual, though the police ought to have and be able to articulate some reasonable grounds (ones linked to conduct) for suspicion. Also, we should insist that the authorities justify each subsequent stage in their actions against individuals whom they suspect of crimes, and the burdens of justification should be increasingly more demanding. The authorities should have "probable cause" to arrest individuals, be required to get warrants to search their houses or businesses, amass evidence that is reasonably likely to produce convictions in order to charge them, and convince a judge that bail or, worse, pretrial detention is proper and necessary. Again, Stewart traces these progressively more stringent requirements to the innate right to be presumed innocent.

However, it is apparent that such requirements do not follow from the status characteristic account of the presumption outlined above, especially if the authorities move against those whom they suspect of crimes based on unbiased assessments of their probable criminal conduct. Fortunately, Stewart does not explicitly endorse the status characteristic account. Unfortunately, he says little to explain how the innate right to be presumed above reproach because one is a person grounds the requirement of such progressively more stringent justifications by the authorities. Again, if the authorities act pursuant to the apparent criminal conduct of persons, they do not treat them as prima facie reproachable simply because they are persons. Stewart's account of the innate right seems to have little applicability to the authorities so long as they refrain from discrimination against individuals based on their mere personhood.

Independently of whether Stewart's right to be presumed innocent insofar as one is a person can ground the successive justifications that he believes are needed, there are various puzzles about how the PI could work to do so. It cannot take much to rebut the PI in the early stages of official inquiry into criminal conduct. The police might need some justification for stopping or arresting persons, but some evidence that they are or have been involved in one or more crimes will usually suffice. Certainly we would not want to require them to have proof beyond a reasonable doubt. But once the PI is surmounted by considerations of sufficient weight, how does it come back into play to require further, and increasingly stringent, justifications as official inquiries proceed? Why, once it is rebutted initially, does it not disappear altogether? Perhaps the idea is that in the early stages of police and prosecutorial inquiry, it is only partially rebutted. Yet partial rebuttal would seem to imply a gradual weakening of the right, not a strengthening of it of the kind needed to explain why, as the authorities proceed, progressively more stringent justifications of their actions are required. Again, in the trial setting, the rules about overcoming the PI are relatively clear: the government bears the burden of proving guilt, and the standard of proof is exacting—beyond a reasonable doubt. Also, the court is focused narrowly on one or more past acts of the accused, in an attempt to determine whether the accused breached the criminal law. If the court determines that the accused has done so, conviction and legal punishment ought to follow. Outside of that context, as we are with Stewart's account, the scope, purpose, and consequences of the PI are decidedly less clear; so are the rules governing its rebuttal and the coherence of the account we can offer of them.

All of that being said, I concede that there is something to the notion that the authorities should have to surmount progressively more demanding justificatory barriers as they move to prosecute individuals whom they suspect of having committed crimes. The question is whether we need a substantive human right to be presumed innocent in order to explain and account for that notion. I contend that we do not. Insofar as persons are equal citizens, they are entitled to enjoy and exercise such basic rights as life, physical and psychological integrity, liberty, and privacy.[16] If rights protect the agency interests of individuals, they cannot be trampled or casually infringed by the authorities, or else individuals will not be, and will not believe themselves to be, secure in their exercise and enjoyment.[17] Granted, the police have to be able to stop and question persons whom they suspect of criminal conduct, and to arrest and possibly detain those persons if the answers they receive do not dispel their suspicions. The police should have articulable reasons for doing these things that refer to the conduct of the individuals in question and should have to provide them if called upon to do so by a judge or magistrate. Since the infringement of citizens' basic rights is, to this point, relatively narrow in scope and brief in duration, the justifying reasons should not have to be very strong. Yet as the authorities move further against individuals—by detaining them for longer periods of time, searching their homes or businesses, charging them with crimes, and requiring them to appear to answer to the charges—they should have to furnish progressively stronger reasons for their actions. On the account I propose, the strength of the reasons should track the extent to which official actions infringe (or perhaps, threaten to do so) the basic rights of individuals. The more official actions infringe those rights, or threaten to do so, the stronger the reasons officials should have to give to justify them. In the case of requests for the pretrial detention of suspects, the government should have to provide strong evidence of the guilt of accused persons on serious charges and convincing proof that no other means exist to ensure that the accused will appear to answer to the charges or refrain from further criminal misconduct until they do so.[18] Pretrial detention is, in many respects, indistinguishable from imprisonment, with its very substantial curtailment of the basic rights of individuals. Given that imprisonment is justified only as a punishment for relatively serious charges that the government has proven beyond a reasonable doubt, the test for justifying pretrial detention should be, it seems, almost as exacting.

Not only is a substantive human right to be presumed innocent not needed to explain why the government should have to provide progressively more convincing reasons for its actions, such a right might have unsettling implications for the activities of law enforcement officials. Admittedly, Stewart does not interpret the right as placing any unusual barriers in the paths of those officials; they can continue to stop suspects, question them, arrest them, and charge them, at least so long as they can provide reasons of the appropriate kind as they proceed. But I wonder whether this can be correct. If individuals possess an innate human right to be presumed above reproach, would not such a right require the authorities to be, at least, somewhat more reluctant to suspect them of crimes or slower to stop, arrest, or charge them? Why would such a right not require the authorities to give individuals the benefit of the doubt when they observe them engaging in suspicious conduct—or worse, to actively search for reasons not to stop, arrest, or charge them? And would not such a right tend to support higher justificatory burdens on the authorities at every step along the way than are currently the norm? Instead of the relatively weak requirement of "probable cause" to justify formal charges, perhaps a substantive right to be presumed innocent would require prosecutors to satisfy the "preponderance of evidence" standard.

Some might embrace these implications of a substantive right to be presumed innocent. They might believe that the authorities are in need of just the kind of restraint for which such a right would provide the grounds. In evaluating the merits of such an approach, we must sift out concerns about the ways in which some contemporary criminal justice systems prohibit too much behavior or punish it too harshly, as well as concerns about discrimination in the enforcement of justified prohibitions.[19] The narrower issue before us concerns whether it would be a good idea to insist, in deference to a substantive right to be presumed innocent, that police and prosecutors be slowed, or perhaps hobbled a bit, in the enforcement of defensible criminal prohibitions.

Importantly, the choice we face is not one between such an approach and one that gives unchecked discretion to law enforcement officials. Even at the earliest stages of the criminal justice process, we can reasonably require officials to have articulable grounds for their suspicions and actions, ones that refer, directly or indirectly, to the conduct of individuals. Nonetheless, we might think it best to set things up so that the initial justificatory barriers to suspicion, questioning, and arrest are kept fairly low, with the hope that as cases against individuals develop, the standards for proceeding further with official action could be made more exacting. In particular, I suspect that when the crimes under investigation are moderately to very serious, the low-initial-barriers model is the most attractive one. I doubt that we want the authorities to be hesitant about acting when armed robberies, kidnappings, or violent assaults appear to be underway or have already occurred.

The PI as Protecting Reputations

Stefan Trechsel and Liz Campbell also seek to extend the right to be presumed innocent beyond the criminal trial. In his explication of a series of European Court of Human Rights rulings, Trechsel explicitly endorses a substantive human right to be presumed innocent. He notes that there is a range of cases in which public officials might be tempted, or required, to issue statements impugning (or appearing to do so) the innocence of individuals suspected of or charged with crimes, though never convicted of them. Prosecutors or police, frustrated with the trial acquittals of persons whom they believe guilty of serious crimes, might publicly say that the accused were "guilty," in effect criticizing the courts for what police or prosecutors believe are mistaken verdicts. Even if police or prosecutors elect not to file charges in certain cases, or do so only to subsequently drop them, they might issue statements casting doubt on the legal innocence of the persons whom they suspected of crimes. This seems mostly likely to occur if the cases fizzled because the courts excluded damaging evidence against the accused, or witnesses suddenly and inexplicably recanted their testimonies or abruptly disappeared.

In addition to these familiar kinds of cases, Liz Campbell cites others that seem troubling. In England and Wales, employers can inquire into whether job applicants' names are on government "watch lists." Such lists contain the names of persons suspected by their former employers of misconduct of certain kinds, though the individuals in question were neither charged nor convicted of any offenses. To qualify for the list, the secretary of state must conclude, to the civil standard of proof, that a particular employer believed a worker to be guilty of misconduct that risked harming a vulnerable adult.[20] Also of concern are Anti-Social Behavioral Orders (or ASBOs). Though ASBOs exist mostly to exclude individuals from certain areas or activities, they can be seen as publicly labeling them as dangerous or unreliable, and this in spite of the fact that the individuals in question may never have been convicted of any crimes.[21]

Trechsel argues that pronouncements of these kinds by the authorities damage what he terms the "reputation-related aspect" of the presumption of innocence.[22] The PI operates in these cases "to protect the image of the person concerned as 'innocent,' i.e. not guilty of a specific offense."[23] Importantly, the damage done by such pronouncements occurs even if it does not, in any way, defeat the abilities of accused persons to get robustly fair trials. It therefore follows, in Trechsel's view, that the presumption of innocence has a significant nonprocedural dimension to it.

It is possible to concur with Trechsel that the PI is not entirely procedural without committing oneself to the proposition that there is a substantive human right to be presumed innocent. As we will see in the next chapter, numerous theorists claim that there are nonprocedural dimensions to the PI, though without invoking a substantive human right to it. Some of them claim that the PI functions as a constraint on the substantive criminal law. Others argue that it should regulate our interactions with our fellow citizens even if they have never fallen under official suspicion of criminal activity. Hence, it seems fair to say that Trechsel's argument for a substantive right to be presumed innocent is pretty thin. But set that point to one side and focus on the question of whether a PI is needed in order to explain why legal officials ought to be circumspect in their statements about the legal guilt of persons who have not been convicted by a court.

As will become apparent in subsequent chapters, any kind of entanglement with the criminal justice system is apt to have lasting effects on the good names and reputations of persons. Arrest, official accusation, and trials are all stigmatizing, and quite intensely so once the criminal process reaches the lattermost stage and the prosecution puts forth evidence, in a public setting, that an individual is guilty of one or more crimes, especially of serious ones. Silence by government officials after a prosecution has been discontinued or failed might be better than public statements by them designed to make the arrested or accused look guilty. But silence hardly amounts to a ringing endorsement of the material innocence of the arrested or accused. Independently of what legal officials say about cases of these kinds, many in the public will continue to suspect that the individuals charged with crimes were involved in criminal conduct and treat them accordingly. As a result, individuals with arrest or charge records might be denied jobs, credit, licenses, and housing, and might be shunned by their neighbors or former associates. Publicly expressed official doubts about their material innocence are, if not the least of the problems such individuals face, only one of them.

Moreover, such doubts on the part of officials will hardly be surprising given that, in some cases, the officials involved will have persisted in their efforts to convict individuals all the way through to trial adjudication. The public will already know or at least reasonably believe that the legal officials involved believed the accused guilty of crimes and that they could prove them so; if the officials did not believe these things, then what on earth were they doing trying to secure the convictions of the individuals in question? Hence, barring such officials from making statements that attribute guilt to the acquitted seems a tepid remedy, one that will do little to restore the reputations of the accused. As we will see in chapter 8, if individuals who are caught up in the criminal justice system, though never convicted of crimes, are to have their reputation-related interests adequately protected and restored—if, in other words, they are to be regarded and treated by their fellow citizens as responsible and law-abiding—then we will have to do considerably more than insist that legal officials refrain from impugning their innocence. We will have to consider various remedies for restoring what the arrested or accused have lost, though whether these remedies will be successful in all cases, or should be, is open to dispute.

None of this is intended to gainsay Trechsel's valuable point that individuals caught up in the criminal justice system have a vital stake in their reputations. Yet a substantive human right to be presumed innocent is not needed to account for why criminal justice officials ought to be circumspect in what they say about the subjects of incomplete prosecutions. To see why this is so, let us circle back to the account sketched in the preceding section, according to which individuals, as equal citizens in liberal democratic societies, are entitled to exercise and enjoy their basic moral and legal rights. Again, if they suspect individuals of criminal conduct and can satisfy progressively more stringent justificatory burdens as they proceed against them, government officials act appropriately in infringing such basic rights by stopping, questioning, arresting, investigating, and charging them. But there is no use denying that all of these official actions by the authorities make persons look guilty, or at least suspect. To insist that the authorities treat or regard the subjects of their criminal investigations as if they were materially innocent would be, I will subsequently argue, pointless and probably counterproductive. To insist that their fellow citizens so regard and treat the subjects of criminal investigations is less pointless, but might be unrealistic and risky.[24] As I will show in more detail in chapter 6, what can be insisted upon is something slightly different and easily confused with a presumption of material innocence—namely, that all of us should refrain from regarding and treating the subjects of criminal investigations as if they are materially guilty or inevitably will be proven legally guilty in a court of law. The early stages of the criminal justice process are fallible, and the outcomes of the process are unpredictable. People are sometimes suspected of crimes, arrested for them, and charged with them, even though it turns out that they are entirely innocent of them. Everyone should bear this in mind. Hence, we should avoid drawing any firm conclusions about the guilt of persons concerning the crimes of which they are suspected or accused until the criminal justice process has taken its full and due course. It is, after all, trials, or perhaps defensible forms of plea bargaining, that provide the crucial test of the government's suspicions or accusations. Until convictions have been achieved, or guilty pleas entered, caution about assuming or pronouncing individuals "guilty" ought to be everyone's guiding maxim.

Criminal justice officials, in particular, should avoid jumping to conclusions about the guilt of suspects or formally charged individuals and refrain from encouraging others to do so. This means that before their suspicions about individuals have been subjected to the rigorous test of charge adjudication, they should not publicly declare the accused to be "guilty." The reasons for such restraint go beyond the possible tainting effects on judges or juries. We give police and prosecutors formidable powers so that they can fulfill their important functions in the criminal justice system. But their functions are not to pronounce individuals "guilty"; that is the function of the courts. Instead, the police exist to detect criminal activity, stop it in its tracks if possible, and investigate crimes when they have occurred, thereby aiding the government in building strong cases against individuals who have been formally charged with criminal misconduct. Likewise, it is not the role of prosecutors to declare the guilt of individuals, but to investigate suspected crimes (with the aid of the police) and then to either convince accused persons to admit their guilt or assemble and articulate cases against them that will persuade an impartial tribunal of their guilt. Public declarations of the guilt of suspects or formally accused persons by such officials, even if they do not jeopardize fair trials, come too close to the censure that is communicated through conviction and sentencing by a court of law. Police and prosecutors are, after all, government agents, and their actions and words are apt to have special import in the community. In the absence of criminal convictions, individuals must be permitted to resume the full exercise and enjoyment of their basic moral and legal rights. Yet police or prosecutorial declarations that some of them are "criminals" will hinder their doing so. Recognizing the fallibility and unpredictability of the charge adjudication process, and their well-defined roles in that process, police and prosecutors should restrain themselves.

It is especially egregious for such officials to impugn "not guilty" verdicts by the courts, for then it is as if they seek to inflict some of the social costs of criminal conviction upon persons whom the courts have determined do not merit legal punishment. Having failed to persuade a court that such individuals warrant the censure and hard treatment of legal punishment, officials who make such statements appear bent on extralegally censuring them and thus further damaging their reputations. The likely if not inevitable effect of doing so is that individuals acquitted of crimes will find it more difficult to resume the full exercise and enjoyment of the basic rights of citizenship. Criminal justice officials should recognize that they are not justified in doing more than they already have done, though in most cases justifiably, to besmirch the good names of the individuals whom they have charged with crimes and subjected to trials.[25] Yet it is on the abilities of the formerly accused to resume the full and equal rights of citizenship that we should focus in scrutinizing the public statements of criminal justice officials, rather than on an alleged substantive human right to be presumed innocent.

The PI and the Relationship between the State and Its Citizens

Although, like Trechsel, Campbell is concerned with statements made by legal officials that cast doubt on the law-abidingness of citizens who have not been convicted of crimes, she wants to develop a case against such statements that does not depend on their consequences for the reputations of the suspected or formally accused. Campbell does not come right out and say that persons have a substantive human right to be presumed innocent, but she does contend that recent ECHR rulings cannot be accommodated by a narrow procedural account of the PI.[26] Her strategy is to argue that legal officials should abjure such statements, especially when they are based on insufficient evidence, because they are fundamentally unfair to those whose law abidingness is thereby called into question, and thus not in accord with the "proper relationship between the state and its citizens."[27] Liberal states must treat their citizens as law-abiding unless or until those citizens are proven to be otherwise in a court of law.

Thus, she contends that the PI is grounded in general values of political morality "deriving from but also preserving and concretising trust and respect between the state and its citizens."[28]

Beyond pretrial or posttrial declarations by the police or prosecutors concerning the guilt of accused persons, Campbell discusses other ways in which government officials express doubts about the law-abidingness of some citizens. For instance, she criticizes the aforementioned practice of the British government maintaining "watch lists" of persons who are suspected of having engaged in criminal misconduct in their employment, though they were never convicted. Campbell sees this practice as problematic because the evidence standards for entering someone's name onto the watch list are quite weak—well short of the reasonable doubt standard—and because persons whose names so appear are not given the opportunity to dispute the allegations of misconduct that led to their names appearing on the lists.[29] In Campbell's view, inclusion on a watch list is stigmatizing, as it implies that the person has engaged in criminal misconduct. However, Campbell asserts that labeling persons in this way does not amount to punishment proper because it does not inflict hard treatment. This seems to be the reason why she is disinclined to insist upon satisfaction of the reasonable doubt standard before such communications by government officials are deemed to be warranted.[30] Stigmatizing communications are bad but not as bad as stigma plus hard treatment; more than slight proofs of criminal misconduct are required if we are to stigmatize, but not proof beyond a reasonable doubt.

What is most puzzling about Campbell's position is her attempt to detach her objections to the kinds of statements by government officials with which she is concerned from their consequences for the reputations of the citizens involved. One can say that such statements are "unfair" or not sufficiently "respectful of the relationship between the state and its citizens," but these explanations seem unsatisfyingly vague. How exactly are they "unfair" or "disrespectful" of the proper state/citizen relationship? More importantly, can we really make much sense of these notions without citing the likely effects of such statements on the good names and reputations of the individuals involved, a point that Campbell herself at times seems to admit?[31] Yes, the kinds of statements with which she is concerned do communicate censure, and the likely consequence of their doing so is that the individuals whose reputations are thereby sullied will find it more difficult to get jobs or credit. Such individuals might also be treated with wariness or distrust by their fellow citizens in ways that will make their lives more difficult. The individuals targeted by such statements will thus suffer many of the social consequences of criminal conviction in the absence of having actually been convicted. Notice, again, that we do not need a substantive human right to be presumed innocent to explain why such statements are an unjustified burden upon individuals. It is enough to note the myriad ways in which the exercise and enjoyment of the basic rights of citizenship will be impeded by such statements and the dubious authority of the officials involved to make them. We could even say that such statements are "unfair" because it is the courts, not police, or prosecutors, or secretaries of state, who are supposed to censure citizens for criminal misconduct. We could also say that such statements are not "respectful" of the relationship between the state and its citizens insofar as they inflict some of the costs of legal punishment on the latter in the absence of proof beyond a reasonable doubt, provided in a court of law, that they have committed crimes.

Not only is a substantive right to be presumed innocent not needed to explain why we should discourage public statements made by government officials casting doubt on the law-abidingness of individuals in the absence of court findings of guilt, it is not clear how it can be made to yield a satisfying account of why we should discourage them. Again, in the trial setting, it is clear who is supposed to be presuming the innocence of whom—jurors (or the judge in bench trials) are to presume the innocence of the accused relative to the charges levied against the accused. Once we move the PI outside of the trial context, however, things become murkier. Given the concerns of Trechsel and Campbell, it would seem that it is police and prosecutors, or perhaps government officials who have special knowledge about specific cases, who are to presume the innocence of the individuals arrested, investigated, charged, and perhaps acquitted of crimes. Let us suppose, for the moment, that such a prescription makes sense, and this in spite of the numerous actions by such officials aimed specifically at securing the convictions of those whom they suspect of crimes. Since the PI is only a presumption, it would seem that considerations of some kind or other are capable of rebutting it. Who, then, has the burden of rebutting it, and what kinds of considerations are to be deemed capable of doing so? Suppose that the relevant officials have the burden of proof and that the presumption is rebutted only if they can produce evidence that is convincing of the guilt of individuals charged with crimes beyond a reasonable doubt. Convincing to whom? Notice that the relevant officials will sometimes have such evidence prior to trials. In fact, in some cases, they will have more evidence than the jury will be permitted to see, since officials might have seen highly incriminating evidence that was excluded by the courts. Yet if and when the relevant officials have such compelling evidence, does it follow that the PI has been rebutted and that any public statements made by them concerning the guilt of the accused are justified? This is not a conclusion that Trechsel and Campbell, given their concerns, will be eager to accept.

They might be able to avoid drawing it by pointing to the fact that such damning evidence, even if it exists in the pretrial phase in some cases, will not have been subject to defense contestation. The relevant officials thus will be in no position to conclude that the evidence against accused but not-yet-tried persons is persuasive beyond a reasonable doubt. Therefore, they should refrain from pretrial statements declaring accused persons to be guilty. Fair enough, except that this argument might not yield a posttrial prescription against legal officials making statements criticizing acquittals and imputing guilt to the accused. For then the officials (and the public) will have seen all of the evidence as well as its contestation by the defense. Hence, an extratrial right to be presumed innocent does not appear to give Trechsel and Campbell all that they want. Such a right also seems to convert the PI into a nonrebuttable presumption, at least pretrial. No one, including legal officials, will have seen the government's evidence subjected to contestation, not yet anyway. So, is it that the human right to be presumed innocent requires legal officials to presume the innocence of individuals until or unless they are convicted in a court of law?

Some theorists will be tempted to endorse such a claim, but such a position seems untenable. It simply cannot be the case that a substantive human right to be presumed innocent precludes suspicion, investigation, arrest, searches, and charges levied by legal officials. If there is a substantive human right to be presumed innocent, it must be defeasible in the pretrial context, or else police and prosecutors will be unable to do their jobs. Set to one side the mystery of how, once the PI is rebutted in order to permit the earliest stages of a criminal investigation, it suddenly re-emerges to require justification for each successive stage. If police and prosecutors are to perform their vital roles, they must be justified in taking actions that make people look guilty. So, is it that, in spite of this, the human right to be presumed innocent bars them from making public pronouncements of the guilt of persons investigated for, formally accused of, or acquitted of crimes? And does it do so even though it might seem that their actions "speak" louder than their words? Perhaps, but it is not clear why we need a substantive right to make sense of such a bar, rather than the kinds of considerations earlier adduced: the prematurity of such statements in some cases given the fallibility and unpredictability of the criminal justice process, and the ways in which they involve a usurpation of the role of the courts by other criminal justice officials.

One last point: Campbell seems prepared to let government officials sometimes make stigmatizing statements about individuals not convicted of crimes, assuming that those officials have stronger evidence than is currently required and the individuals thereby "censured" have been given some opportunity to dispute the evidence against them.[32] Yet in some of these kinds of cases, there will have been no official charges filed or trials during which the evidence against the accused was fully contested. This suggests that Campbell cannot easily make use of the contestation argument advanced earlier to rescue the extratrial PI from the objection that legal officials will sometimes have damning evidence against accused persons and so would be justified in declaring their guilt pretrial. Campbell takes this position because she distinguishes censuring communications from legal punishment, which includes the additional element of hard treatment. But if legal officials can sometimes censure persons whose criminal conduct has not been proven beyond a reasonable doubt subsequent to full contestation by the accused (with the aid of an attorney), then pretrial declarations of the guilt of suspects or formally accused persons by police and prosecutors would seem to be back in play.

The PI and Due Process

Hock Lai Ho contends that the right to be presumed innocent is more than a vital procedural component of fair trials. Ho cites approvingly Trechsel's claim that the right has a "reputation-related aspect."[33] Ho therefore condemns statements by police or prosecutors that impugn the innocence of suspects, the formally accused, or the acquitted even if those statements cannot plausibly be interpreted as impeding their fair trial rights. The state has not shown such individuals to be guilty in accordance with authoritative procedures; thus its officials must not say things that call their material innocence into doubt. Yet as we have seen, refraining from such statements seems a lukewarm remedy once individuals have been arrested, charged, or acquitted, especially if our aim is to preserve or restore a full presumption of innocence to persons caught up in, but not convicted by, the criminal justice system. Also, a substantive human right to be presumed innocent does not seem necessary or all that helpful in explaining why legal officials ought to be circumspect about what they say regarding individuals believed but not proven guilty of criminal conduct.

Fortunately, Ho has other work for the human right to be presumed innocent. He claims that it "is the right to due process: It mandates that the state cannot convict someone of a crime unless and until the prosecution demonstrates her guilt in a process that bears the defining features, including rights and protections, of a fair trial."[34] The defining features of fair trials include the rights to be informed of the charges, have the assistance of legal counsel, confront the government's case, have the government bear the burden of proof, and have the standard of proof be exacting.[35] Ho sees trials as more than fact-finding enterprises. If that is all they were, then they would fail utterly in cases in which individuals were acquitted of all charges. Acquittals tell us that the government failed to prove guilt beyond a reasonable doubt, but without fully clarifying the "facts" of the case. Ho instead maintains that trials serve as vital checks on government power, in particular the power to prosecute persons and inflict legal punishment upon them. Because individuals have a substantive human right to be presumed innocent, they are, on his account, entitled to demand fair and rigorous tests of the government's evidence for the charges it has lodged against them.[36] Only if the government's case passes such a test is the presumption of innocence rebutted and legal punishment of the accused justified.

There is much to admire in Ho's account. True, individuals formally accused of crimes do have the right to demand trials during which the government's case against them is put to a fair and rigorous test. But we do not need a substantive right to be presumed innocent to explain the societal commitment to due process.

To begin with, it seems a bit odd to speak, as Ho does, of trial conviction as having "rebutted" the substantive right to be presumed innocent.[37] Substantive human rights are not usually the sorts of things that can be "rebutted" or, perhaps, "defeated." They can be violated, infringed, curtailed, or perhaps overridden or forfeited, sometimes justifiably. Talk about "rebutting" or "defeating" the presumption of innocence makes more sense if the presumption is viewed as a key procedural component of the right to a fair trial, part of what I have termed the "proof structure" of trials.

Indeed, as Ho himself suggests, it might be a sensible strategy to remind judges or instruct juries that criminal defendants begin trials with a presumption of material innocence.[38] Doing so would help motivate those with the responsibility to render verdicts to set to one side whatever they believe or suspect about defendants and intentionally take up a stance toward them according to which they are presumed citizens in good standing in the community. As Ho elsewhere notes, we would thereby encourage judges or juries to take an initially "protective attitude" toward the accused, so that government proffers of evidence were subject to close scrutiny.[39] Reasonable doubts about the government's case should be resolved in favor of defendants, not the government. Only if the government's case is very convincing (beyond a reasonable doubt in many jurisdictions) should judges or juries come to regard the presumption of innocence as successfully rebutted and convict the defendant. Understood in this way, as an aspect of the right to fair trial, it makes sense to think of the presumption of innocence as something that can be rebutted or defeated. But again, to so conceive the presumption requires only that we view it as a basic procedural right, not a substantive human right.

What of Ho's contention that accused persons have the right to demand a fair and rigorous test of the government's case against them? Must not such a right be grounded in a substantive human right to be presumed innocent, which defendant's "exercise" by demanding trials? I do not think we need such a right in order to make sense of the justified demand for a fair and rigorous test of the government's case. We need only the more familiar basic rights to such things as liberty, autonomy, and privacy, coupled with a vivid recognition of the ways in which the criminal justice process can go awry. Again, if individuals are to be treated as equal citizens in society, they must be secure in their enjoyment and exercise of such basic rights, ones that protect and facilitate the exercise of their capacities for agency. Such rights should not be intruded upon casually by government officials, or by anyone else for that matter. Criminal conviction, with its associated stigma and hard treatment, curtails the exercise and enjoyment of basic rights both during the time individuals are being punished and often for a considerable time afterward.[40] Given the fallibility and corruptibility of the criminal justice process, it makes sense to hold that individuals have a right to demand fair and rigorous trials at which the government's evidence in support of its allegations is tested. Again, we can conceive of the right to a fair trial as a second-order moral right, one designed to protect against the unjustified curtailment of first-order moral rights. Yet such a second-order right is one to a procedure of a specific and rigorous kind. Basic rights to liberty, autonomy, and privacy are weighty enough, all by themselves, to ground a right to such a procedure. A substantive human right to be presumed innocent is not needed to explain why we should be extremely cautious about punishing people; it is sufficient to note the ways in which the lives of individuals are damaged by it, sometimes irreparably.

In fact, many of the individuals charged with crimes do not seem to value, or value much, the right to be presumed innocent, which would be odd if it were a substantive human right on a par with other such rights. In the United States, over 95 percent of criminal cases are resolved through plea bargaining.[41] In England and Wales, the percentage is not that high, though it is close to it in the magistrates' courts and over 70 percent in the Crown Courts.[42] Also, forms of plea bargaining, or at least charge or sentence reductions for accused persons who are willing to admit their guilt, sometimes combined with more perfunctory trials, can be found in many other legal jurisdictions.[43] This raises the question whether trials are the only acceptable means of rebutting the human right to be presumed innocent. Ho does not say they are, though he does speak, at one point, of the right to trial as a "cherished right."[44] However, many of the individuals charged with crimes do not seem to cherish it. They are prepared if not eager to waive it, especially if by doing so they can avoid imprisonment for their confessed crimes and thus the curtailment of what seem to them to be considerably more cherished rights.[45]

In response, Ho might argue that many accused persons readily waive the right to trial because they are threatened by prosecutors or judges with much longer or harsher sentences if they exercise it and are ultimately found guilty. The practice of plea bargaining depends fundamentally on the sentencing differential, the difference between the sentences received by convicted persons who plead guilty and the ones received by persons who are convicted of the same crimes after trials. It is the magnitude of the sentencing differential in countries like the United States that convinces, or perhaps coerces, accused persons to waive the right to be presumed innocent. We should not conclude from this that they do not value the right or that it is not basic and substantive.

Yet it is possible to agree with this critique of certain forms of plea bargaining and reject the claim that we need a substantive human right to be presumed innocent to make sense of it. The problem with permitting prosecutors to manipulate the sentence differential is that plea bargaining then proves an ineffective check on the fallibility of the investigative and charging process. Simply put, such differentials reduce or render irrelevant the evidence that the government has against those it has accused. The solution is to limit the discretion prosecutors have to manipulate the sentence differential and insist that judges find the evidence against individuals convincing to at least a "more probably guilty than not" standard before they accept guilty pleas.[46] Accused persons who pled guilty would then be understood to have waived the right to trial, and with it the presumed innocent deliberative starting point of those tasked with rendering verdicts. Such reforms in plea bargaining can all be understood as measures designed to ensure that it more effectively filters the guilty from the innocent or partly innocent and thus is a defensible procedure for the adjudication of charges.

Proponents of a human right to be presumed innocent might argue that any form of charge adjudication besides trials at which the government's case is put to a stern test, is inconsistent with the right. Such logic would not only rule out plea bargaining, but presumably guilty pleas, even if made in exchange for no charge or sentencing concessions by the authorities. The feasibility of such an approach will obviously be questioned. Equally doubtful is its normative defensibility. The plea-bargaining literature is replete with stories of individuals charged with crimes who are intent on avoiding trials and eager to enter guilty pleas.[47] The charges against them are relatively minor, the evidence against them is strong, and if they enter guilty pleas they can avoid somewhat harsher sanctions. Forcing such individuals to go to trial seems paternalism of a questionable sort and a dubious expenditure of societal resources. It is getting their punishment over with and avoiding sanctions that more substantially curtail their basic rights to such things as liberty, autonomy, and privacy that such individuals care about, not the enjoyment or exercise of a human right to be presumed innocent, whatever that comes to.

Conclusion: Recapitulating the Alternative

In the course of raising doubts about a substantive human right to be presumed innocent, I have offered hints of what an alternative account of the presumption, as a purely procedural right, might look like. I have also indicated how such a procedural interpretation might be coupled with an account of the basic moral rights of persons so as to yield a plausible set of constraints on the actions of legal officials, members of the public, and triers of fact during criminal trials. In concluding, I draw these hints and suggestions together and briefly elaborate them.

Again, we do not need to posit a substantive right to be presumed innocent in order to explain why criminal justice officials should have to justify their actions—minimally at first, but more substantially as the criminal justice process progresses. We need only the basic moral rights to such things as liberty, autonomy, and privacy to ground such justifications, coupled with the recognition that as the process progresses, infringements of those basic rights become more pronounced and so the burdens of justifying them should correspondingly be made more demanding. At the limit, and before legal punishment is imposed, the government should have to satisfy a demanding test of its case, unless accused persons decide to waive the right to that test under properly designed plea-bargaining procedures. When accused persons opt for trial adjudication, the various guarantees of fair trials apply, one of which includes an instruction to the jury that they begin their deliberations from the presumption that the defendant is innocent.

Individuals should not be subject to suspicion, arrest, or charges based solely on their status characteristics, or have their conduct evaluated more negatively through the lens of such characteristics. But such a right against discrimination, if it is a right, has implications beyond the criminal justice context and therefore seems to have little to do with a presumption of innocence. Moreover, a presumption of innocence, so construed, would not survive in cases in which criminal justice officials were responding, in an unbiased fashion, to the conduct of individuals. Indeed, it seems unlikely that police and other criminal justice officials often regard and treat individuals as suspects entirely independently of their conduct. Many of the individuals arrested for and charged with crimes are likely guilty of some form of criminal wrongdoing, and sometimes the evidence against them is strong if not overwhelming right from the start.

It is undeniable that even the earliest stages of the criminal justice process stigmatize individuals, making them appear something other than citizens in good standing in their communities. Yet given a recognition of the ways in which the early stages of the criminal justice process are fallible, and may on occasion be corrupt or malevolent, officials and members of the public should refrain from concluding that those arrested or charged are guilty (though perhaps not that they are likely guilty). All of us should exercise caution and insist that investigations and fair and rigorous charge adjudication take their due courses. All of us should bear in mind that some of those suspected of or charged with crimes might be wholly or partially innocent, and we should refrain from actions that will make it difficult, if not impossible, for them to resume the full exercise and enjoyment of the basic rights of citizenship once they are cleared of any and all charges. Hence, legal officials should not publicly declare the guilt of individuals before charge adjudication has taken its course. It is not the role of police or prosecutors, as distinguished from the courts, to declare people guilty of crimes.

CHAPTER 3 | Nonproceduralism and the Presumption of Innocence

IN THE PRECEDING CHAPTER, the focus was on accounts of the presumption of innocence that construe it as a substantive human right on a par with more familiar liberty and welfare rights. Rather than endorsing the notion that the presumption is a substantive human right, I cast it as a basic procedural right and argued that many of the concerns about the operations of the criminal justice system that substantive rights theorists express can be accommodated in other ways. Police and prosecutors should have to justify their actions as they arrest, investigate, and charge those whom they suspect of crimes. Also, such officials should be cautious and circumspect in what they publicly say about the individuals whom they have arrested and charged with crimes, and perhaps failed to convict. But more familiar substantive rights to liberty or privacy, along with the justificatory burdens they establish for anyone who wishes to interfere with them, can account for these constraints. Also, these burdens become stronger the greater the interferences contemplated. Limits on the public statements of criminal justice officials can be seen as grounded in a recognition of the fallibility and unpredictability of the adjudication process—features of it with which police and prosecutors are or ought to be vividly cognizant—in combination with the powerful interest individuals have in their social reputations. Criminal justice officials should not be permitted to inflict simulacra of legal punishment on individuals whom they suspect of crimes in the event that their efforts to convict them come up short.

Yet the idea that the PI can or ought to do more than shield individuals who elect trial adjudication of the charges against them from too easy conviction is defended in other ways than by asserting that it is a substantive right. Some theorists argue that the PI is the basis for constraints on the content of the criminal law itself.[1] Various familiar provisions of the criminal law are thus seen as prima facie in conflict with the PI. Among them are strict liability and reverse onus provisions. The former threaten individuals with legal punishment though they arguably do not deserve it, since they have not been shown to have engaged in wrongful conduct; the latter force the accused to bear the burden of proving a defense or exception to a substantive criminal law provision, thereby illicitly shifting the burden of proof to them. Also of concern are overbroad criminal provisions that expose the materially innocent to the risk of conviction and might expose the guilty to conviction in the absence of proof beyond a reasonable doubt that they are guilty. At least one scholar goes further than this, casting the PI as a constraint on the process by which criminal law provisions are enacted.[2] Patrick Tomlin holds the intriguing view that the PI is contravened if lawmakers adopt criminal prohibitions that are not justifiable "beyond a reasonable doubt."

A position of a different sort is defended by theorists who suggest that the PI ought to regulate our interactions with our fellow citizens more generally. For such theorists, it does not matter whether our fellow citizens have fallen under any kind of official or unofficial suspicion of criminal misconduct. Thus, Antony Duff argues that as a matter of "civic virtue," we ought to regard and treat our fellow citizens as responsive to moral and prudential considerations and therefore presumptively law-abiding.[3] Similarly, Dale Nance argues for a "principle of civility," which he sees as requiring a cautiously optimistic attitude toward our fellow citizens according to which they are presumed innocent of serious wrongdoing.[4]

None of the scholars who put forward these accounts of the PI directly invoke a substantive human right to be presumed innocent. What unites them is the sense that the PI's import is not limited to the procedures by which criminal justice officials move individuals suspected of crimes through the legal system. Yet as we have already seen, once we move outside the trial context, difficult questions arise about who is to be presuming the innocence of whom in relation to what, on whom the burden of proof of noninnocence falls, and what is supposed to be the standard of proof that rebuts the presumption. Perhaps it is unfair to import the proof structure framework of criminal trials into these other contexts or to expect it to make sense in them. Duff might be correct in suggesting that there are many presumptions of innocence, each of which has its own set of regulative rules.[5] But I nonetheless believe it is instructive to continually pose questions the answers to which are fairly clear in the context of the proof structure of criminal trials. Doing so illuminates the problems and puzzles with which the various nonprocedural accounts seem yet to have fully come to grips.

Discussion in the chapter proceeds as follows: In the first section, I take up what seems to be the least ambitious of the nonproceduralist accounts, that of Victor Tadros (and in one of the articles discussed, his coauthor Stephen Tierney). Tadros is mostly concerned with overbroad criminal provisions, or what he terms "divergent" criminal provisions, ones that lawmakers adopt intentionally in order to punish misconduct that they fear will otherwise escape criminal sanctions.[6] Tadros sees such provisions as in conflict with the PI, though he is careful to distinguish his approach from ones that would impose more robust substantive constraints on the content of the criminal law. Though I agree with Tadros that overbroad criminal provisions risk punishment of the innocent, I argue that this defect is not well captured by asserting that such provisions violate the presumption of innocence.

In the second section, I take up the more ambitious position defended by Patrick Tomlin. Again, Tomlin seeks to import something akin to the proof structure of the criminal trial into the lawmaking process. In addition to outlining the theoretical difficulties with such an approach, I argue for what I believe is a more practicable approach to problems of the criminal law's overreach.

In the third section, I consider whether there is a societal presumption against punishment of the innocent, a notion that seems an implicit commitment of numerous theorists. I agree that there is, though I distinguish it from the presumption *of* innocence. I suggest that the societal presumption against punishment of the innocent is a principle rather than a rebuttable presumption of the kind that the PI is usually understood to be.

In the final section, I discuss the arguments of Duff and Nance. I contend that their accounts are unconvincing for three reasons: First, they tell us only that we should regard most of our fellow citizens as unlikely to engage in violent or predatory behavior toward us, which is not equivalent to viewing them as being fully law-abiding. Second, they ignore real-world contexts in which many individuals have good reason to believe that some of their fellow citizens pose dangers to them. Yet when individuals in unsafe circumstances, or with histories of victimization, act warily toward some of their fellow citizens, their actions do not seem to be failures of civic virtue or in violation of a principle of civility. Third, I contend that there are numerous important differences between the trial PI and a civil one, if it exists. These differences cast doubt on the viability of a civic PI.

Tadros on Divergent Offenses

In a series of articles, Victor Tadros (and in one of the articles, with coauthor Stephen Tierney) has defended a view according to which the presumption of innocence is to be seen as more than a procedural right; it also places substantive constraints on the criminal law itself. In truth, Tadros seems undecided about whether to characterize his position as one according to which the PI morally constrains the substance of the criminal law. He is clear that his position does not preclude the adoption by legislative bodies of provisions that will likely fail any plausible normative test of criminalization. If, for instance, a legislative body wishes to criminalize "swearing in public," it can do so, in his view, without running afoul of the PI. Thus, bad or regrettable criminal provisions might be fully consistent with the PI.[7] On this point, I concur with Tadros. Criminal prohibitions that are objectionably paternalistic or which come to little more than a majority imposing its views about proper conduct on individuals, in the absence of any identifiable harm to others that such prohibitions seek to prevent, can and should be subjected to critical scrutiny. But the grounds for objecting to such criminal provisions will typically be that they do not demonstrate sufficient respect or regard for the rights of individuals to live their lives as they see fit, not that they violate the PI.

Nonetheless, Tadros believes that the line between purely procedural constraints on the criminal law and substantive ones requires rethinking.[8] Also, he wants to distinguish his position from purely procedural ones, according to which so long as the government fully bears the burden of establishing guilt beyond a reasonable doubt of an accused person's violation of a criminal provision, then the provision is consistent with the PI.[9] Hence, he is not averse to characterizing his view as one according to which the PI has "substantive implications for the criminal law."[10]

My focus will be on one of the kinds of criminal law provisions with which Tadros is concerned, ones that he characterizes as involving "divergent offenses."[11] He discusses numerous examples of such offenses. What they all have in common is that they make liability to legal punishment overinclusive in ways that even the lawmaking body that adopts them recognizes. So, for instance, in an effort to criminalize the sexual exploitation of minors, lawmakers might adopt a provision that makes any sexual contact with a minor an offense.[12] Though what the legislature intends to target is the sexual exploitation of minors, mostly by adults but also by other minors in some cases, the language of the provision will make some individuals liable to punishment whom lawmakers probably do not wish to see punished. If, for example, a fifteen-year-old boy kisses his fifteen-year-old girlfriend, with her consent, and kissing amounts to "sexual contact," then the boy could be arrested, charged, and convicted of the relevant offense—and this in spite of the fact that lawmakers very likely would not want his conduct punished. The "target misconduct," as it were, is the sexual exploitation of minors; the conduct of the fifteen-year-old boy is not of this kind. Similarly, lawmakers might criminalize unauthorized entry into a building with the intention of burglarizing it in order to discourage individuals from making such entries. But though unauthorized entry for the purpose of burglary is the target misconduct, the relevant provision might be crafted in such a way as to potentially sweep in some individuals who enter buildings without authorization but who have no intention to burglarize them.

Why might lawmakers adopt such divergent or overinclusive provisions? As Tadros makes clear, they typically do so because they fear that wording the provisions in less inclusive ways will allow some individuals who have engaged in the target misconduct to escape punishment.[13] Most who have sexual contact with minors should be liable to punishment, and lawmakers want to ensure that they get it; the few who should not be punished can be sifted out by prosecutors exercising their charging discretion. Likewise, most individuals who make unauthorized entries into buildings have nefarious purposes; the few who do not should be able to explain themselves to prosecutors. Although the legislature might hope that prosecutors will separate those worthy of charges from those who are not, as Tadros rightly points out, there is no guarantee that this will occur.[14] And importantly, prosecutors are not usually held to the reasonable doubt standard in making charging decisions. It is the court, in the form of a jury or judge, who is supposed to employ that standard once all of the evidence in a case has been presented.

The problem with such overinclusive provisions, Tadros claims, is not simply that they inevitably and foreseeably risk punishment of individuals who did not engage in the target misconduct—individuals who are "innocent" in the eyes of the legislators who crafted the provisions. It is also that they will be convicted because the provisions relieve government officials of the burden of establishing their guilt of the target misconduct beyond a reasonable doubt.[15] All that the government will have to prove beyond a reasonable doubt about the fifteen-year-old boy is that he had sexual contact with his girlfriend, not that he was sexually exploiting her. In Tadros's view, such provisions "interfere with" the presumption of innocence, in the sense that the boy is innocent of the target misconduct but convicted of it in the absence of proof beyond a reasonable doubt that he is guilty.[16] Importantly, it is not solely the innocent who are at risk from such overinclusive provisions. Some factually guilty individuals also might be convicted despite the government's not having to prove their guilt of the target misconduct beyond a reasonable doubt.

At first glance, it is not clear, exactly, how such overinclusive provisions "interfere" with the presumption of innocence. Suppose that individuals are charged with crimes under them. At the outset of their trials, assuming that their cases go to trial, the jury would, we should assume, be instructed that the accused are entitled to a presumption of innocence and that the burden of proof is entirely on the government to prove the guilt of the accused beyond a reasonable doubt. In what way, then, does the overinclusive provision "interfere" with the presumption of innocence?

In places, Tadros seems to suggest that it is lawmakers who have interfered with the presumption of innocence.[17] But this seems a bit otiose. After all, they have not interfered directly with it as they might do if, for instance, they adopted provisions that required the courts to, in the relevant kinds of cases, begin trials by instructing juries to presume the legal guilt of accused persons and to convict unless the accused can prove their innocence, beyond a reasonable doubt. Such provisions would constitute an unquestionable legislative interference with the presumption of innocence.[18] Likewise, if lawmakers adopt certain kinds of reverse onus provisions, according to which in order to avoid conviction accused persons must do more than provide an evidential basis for defenses or exceptions that they assert, such provisions would shift the burden of proof in ways that might be thought to implicate the presumption of innocence.[19] So-called persuasive reverse onus provisions, in effect, require accused persons to do more than raise reasonable doubts about their guilt. They thereby make it easier for the government to bear the burden of proof and rebut the PI. But these are not the kinds of interferences with which Tadros is concerned in his discussion of divergent offenses. It might be suggested that legislators must presume the innocence of citizens in some broad or amorphous sense as they craft criminal legislation, and that overinclusive provisions of the criminal code constitute a failure to do so. Though as we have seen, some theorists advocate just such a preaccusation or, more broadly still, presuspicion presumption of innocence, it does not seem that

Tadros is one of them, or at least that his argument in this context depends on such an account of the PI.

Instead, what Tadros seems to mean by the claim that divergent offense provisions "interfere" with the presumption of innocence is something like this: They foreseeably set things up so that the familiar proof structure of criminal trials—consisting of the presumption of innocence, the burden of proof, and the standard of proof—does not function to reliably separate those guilty of the target misconduct from those not guilty of it and convict persons only when their guilt with respect to the target misconduct is established beyond a reasonable doubt. Granted, we recognize that with respect to any given provision of the criminal law, the proof structure, though it provides a stern test of the government's case against accused persons, might fail to shield the materially innocent from legal punishment. That this is so is regrettable, of course, but probably unavoidable. The problem with divergent offense provisions, however, is different. They foreseeably and avoidably put at risk some individuals who, in the eyes of the legislators who crafted the provisions, are innocent of the target misconduct and whose guilt with respect to it need not be established by the court beyond a reasonable doubt before it convicts them. Again, it is actually worse than this, since the overinclusive nature of the provisions means that some individuals who are guilty of the target misconduct will be convicted of it despite the government's never having to prove beyond a reasonable doubt that they engaged in it.

If this is Tadros's position, it nonetheless remains unclear how it is that adopting divergent offense provisions "interfere" with the presumption of innocence. Again, jurors at the outset of trials of individuals charged under such provisions will still be told to presume the innocence of the accused, which might be interpreted as telling them to presume the accused to be a citizen in good standing with respect to the criminal provision in question. If the accused are being tried by judges, they could also begin trials with the sort of protective attitude toward the accused that I will argue is the essence of the PI. Nothing about the overinclusiveness of the relevant provisions precludes either of these possibilities. Further, the reasonable doubt standard remains the standard of proof that the government must satisfy in order to gain convictions. The problem that overinclusiveness creates is that it will naturally lead jurors to focus not on the target misconduct, but on the proxy for it that is described in the relevant provision. The government might be able to demonstrate, beyond a reasonable doubt, that the defendant is guilty of the proxy misconduct. It is thus the focus of the jury, rather than the presumption of innocence, that is "interfered with."

Granted, lawmakers might know this or be persuaded to recognize it. If they are aware of the problem and decline to revise the relevant provisions, are they then "interfering" with the PI? As a diagnosis of the problem posed by such provisions, this account seems nonperspicacious. Usually, we hope that when provisions of the criminal law are drafted, they focus squarely on the target misconduct that lawmakers want to prohibit and punish. Overinclusive provisions fail to do so and thus foreseeably frustrate the ability of the proof structure to separate the guilty from the not guilty and assign punishment only to those whose guilt of the target misconduct is proven beyond a reasonable doubt. Putting it that way seems more to the point than casting such provisions as "interfering" with the PI.

It might be suggested that Tadros's position should be interpreted as saying that the PI is interfered with whenever lawmakers adopt criminal prohibitions that unreasonably risk the punishment of citizens though they have not been proven guilty, beyond a reasonable doubt, of wrongful, or seriously wrongful, conduct. Yet such an approach would convert Tadros's position into the kind of robustly moral position with respect to the criminal law that he explicitly disavows. He claims not to be saying that the PI is interfered with if lawmakers prohibit conduct that no defensible normative theory of criminalization would authorize.[20] His account is not one focused on the normative content of the criminal law, but on the strategies sometimes employed by lawmakers who are determined to see to it that all of those guilty of conduct that they want to prohibit are duly punished. The problem is that such strategies derail the proper operation of the proof structure by telling the courts to focus on the proxy misconduct rather than the target misconduct.

Incidentally, it is worth noting that there is more than one way for lawmakers to tackle the problem of misconduct that threatens to elude sanctioning by the criminal law. The approach that Tadros focuses on involves adopting overinclusive provisions and then relying on prosecutors or the courts to check their excesses. Alternatively, we could encourage legislators to strive to faithfully and narrowly capture the target misconduct with which they are concerned in the provisions they adopt and thereby avoid overinclusiveness. If the concern is that some malefactors might, as a consequence, elude criminal conviction, the solution would be to encourage prosecutors to charge those who are on the margins of the target misconduct with crimes and then let the courts decide whether to ratify this "stretching" of the provisions. At least the courts would then focus on the target misconduct, rather than some proxy for it, and the courts would have to be satisfied that the reasonable doubt standard was met or exceeded by the government. The worst that could be said about this alternative approach is that it would expose some individuals to criminal liability who believed that they had stayed within the limits of the criminal law. Hence, such an approach would raise "fair notice" issues with respect to enforcement of the criminal law. It is hard to say how much sympathy we should have for the few individuals whom prosecutors could thereby convince a court to convict. Many of them, after all, will surely have known that they were skirting awfully close to the line separating licit from illicit conduct. All things considered, it might be preferable to tolerate some unfairness to such individuals rather than to adopt overinclusive provisions that foreseeably thwart the operations of well-designed charge adjudication procedures.

Grafting Criminal Procedure onto the Lawmaking Process

Patrick Tomlin also believes that the PI has implications for the content of the criminal law. Like Tadros, he eschews the full-on moral interpretation of the relationship between the two, according to which the PI is contravened if lawmakers adopt, and the criminal justice system enforces, criminal prohibitions that a defensible normative theory of criminalization would not authorize.[21] For one thing, Tomlin recognizes that there is no single, agreed-upon normative theory of criminalization upon which he or other legal scholars can call; instead there are numerous such theories with different implications for the content of the criminal law. For another, a fully moral interpretation of the relationship between the PI and the content of the criminal law would likely entail the condemnation of many existing criminal prohibitions, even if those prohibitions have been enacted by democratically elected lawmakers using their duly authorized powers of legislation. Granted, there might be plausible grounds to dispute many of the criminal prohibitions adopted by democratic governments. But again, the plausible grounds will more likely be that such provisions give inadequate weight to the basic rights of individuals to order and live their lives as they see fit, or attach criminal sanctions to misconduct that is not grave enough to justify the censure and hard treatment of the criminal law. Claiming that the problem with such provisions is that they violate or interfere with the PI seems an unhelpful way of characterizing their defects.

Tomlin instead attempts to graft something like the proof structure of criminal trials onto the lawmaking process. He takes it to be uncontroversial that, at trial, the PI requires the government to prove the guilt of the accused beyond a reasonable doubt. Akin to my approach in chapter 5, Tomlin articulates the need for a direct moral grounding of the right in this context, meaning that he is not willing to weaken the protections of the PI even if doing so would produce more long-term utility or a superior ratio of true to false convictions.[22] We make trials stern tests of the government's evidence because we believe that convicting the innocent is a serious moral wrong. Yet, he argues, if punishing those who are innocent, though mistakenly convicted, is bad, it is equally bad to punish persons by criminalizing conduct that should not be criminalized. Tomlin terms this parity between mistaken punishment via trial error and mistaken punishment by exposure to punishment through indefensible criminal law provisions the "equivalency thesis."[23] The way to prevent the latter is thus parallel to the way to prevent the former—to insist that conduct not be criminalized unless its significant wrongfulness is demonstrated beyond a reasonable doubt.

Here, Tomlin encounters a difficulty. Trials in common-law countries are adversary in character and focused squarely on the alleged past conduct of the accused with respect to one or more specific criminal law provisions. The question for the jury or judge is whether the government's evidence against the accused concerning her alleged breach of the criminal law is convincing beyond a reasonable doubt. Lawmakers, concerned to draft a defensible criminal code, have a very different task, one that is prospective in character and apt to involve less structured advocacy by competing parties.[24] Or, if competing views are aired during the legislative process, they are not about the past conduct of specific individuals but about the advisability of adopting one or more criminal prohibitions. It is also less clear, in the lawmaking context, whether there is anything like a burden of proof on lawmakers. Tomlin would likely argue that there is, or ought to be—that lawmakers should have to offer convincing arguments that the conduct they wish to proscribe is wrongful, and wrongful enough, beyond a reasonable doubt. But what, then, is the "evidence" with which lawmakers are to contend? The answer would appear to be competing normative theories of the criminal law. Such theories are the "fodder" for their deliberations about what to include in the criminal code, akin to the evidence presented by the prosecution and defense during criminal trials. Again, Tomlin recognizes that there are numerous normative accounts of criminalization available, no one of which is obviously the correct one. Thus, he suggests that conduct should not be criminalized by lawmakers unless it falls into an area of overlap among competing "reasonable" normative theories of criminalization.[25] Only then will its suitability for criminalization be clear beyond a reasonable doubt. Tomlin seems confident that there will be an overlap and a sufficiently wide one to sustain a viable system of criminal law.

It might seem that Tomlin's equivalency thesis suffers from an obvious defect. When innocents are mistakenly convicted after trials, there is a clear sense in which their unjust punishment could not have been avoided by them. After all, their conduct did conform to the criminal law; the problem is that that the authorities mistakenly perceived the character of their conduct and managed to convince a court that their conduct was criminal. Granted, there might be a few cases in which individuals knowingly skated close to the border between legal and illegal conduct and thus in some sense "risked" misapprehension of the character of their conduct by police and prosecutors, and ultimately the courts. But such cases are presumably rare, and if the individuals in question, in fact, stayed within the law, then their convictions are wrongful. They could have done something to forestall misapprehension of the character of their conduct, but, morally speaking, they should not have had to. By contrast, when lawmakers criminalize conduct that is not wrongful beyond a reasonable doubt, their doing so does give citizens "fair warning" that engaging in the conduct in question will make them liable to legal punishment. Even if citizens strongly object to the criminalization of the conduct in question, they still presumably know that they are subject to prosecution and so can avoid engaging in the relevant conduct. In short, in the unjust criminalization cases, citizens have more control over whether they suffer unjust punishment than in the mistaken conviction cases.

Tomlin addresses this objection to his equivalency thesis by arguing that "fair warning" is not sufficient to distinguish the two cases of unjust punishment.[26] He asks us to imagine a justified criminal provision that is enforced in a racially discriminatory fashion. The targets of the racial discrimination might know that if they go into certain areas they will be arrested and charged with, and likely convicted of, violating the provision, though they are innocent of having done so. They therefore have "fair warning" of their unjust punishment, and could avoid suffering it by staying out of the area in which discriminatory enforcement is the norm. Still, this alone does not make their punishment just.

We might agree with Tomlin's conclusion but doubt that his argument fully disarms the "fair warning" objection to the equivalency thesis. Why is this? Because the discriminatory enforcement in the analogy that

Tomlin describes is clearly outside of the remit of the authorities. True, simply warning individuals that you will treat them wrongly if they engage in some conduct contrary to your wishes does not make treating them wrongly justified if they go ahead and engage in the conduct. If it did, then muggers who warn their victims "Your money or your life" would be justified in harming individuals when they refused to turn over their money. However, duly elected lawmakers are different from muggers and from government officials who act outside of their authority. It is not simply that the provisions adopted by lawmakers give citizens fair warning of the kinds of conduct that will expose them to criminal liability. It is also that lawmakers who adhere to the rules governing lawmaking act pursuant to their authority in enacting (and thus presumably seeing to the enforcement of) criminal provisions. Citizens might not agree with some of the provisions lawmakers adopt and might be tempted to contravene them. But citizens have an alternative to doing so that, at least in democratic societies, we reasonably insist that they take—namely, attempting, through democratic means, to get the relevant provisions changed. No society, not even democratic ones, can tolerate for long citizens deciding to be a law unto themselves. Thus, a society can reasonably enforce the provisions its lawmakers have adopted until or unless they are changed through the appropriate (democratic) means.

In response to this, Tomlin might argue that lawmakers do act outside their remit if they adopt criminal provisions proscribing conduct that is not wrong beyond a reasonable doubt—that is, provisions that do not fall into the convergence zone of competing reasonable normative theories of criminalization. But I doubt that he can save the equivalency thesis in this way. For one thing, such a circumscription of the authority of lawmakers is too strongly normative. As Tomlin would likely have to concede, few if any existing societies impose the kind of stringent normative constraint on the activities of their lawmakers that Tomlin recommends. The "secondary rules" defining the authority of lawmakers in democratic societies might require them to follow certain procedures to ensure that criminal provisions are enacted through the majority rule of duly elected officials, but little more than this.[27] In this way, lawmakers who adopt provisions that fail Tomlin's test continue to act pursuant to their authority in ways that distinguish them from muggers and from police and prosecutors who act outside their remit by intentionally enforcing the laws in a discriminatory fashion.

More to the point, there are reasons to doubt that the constraint on criminalization that Tomlin favors is a plausible or helpful one. As Tomlin admits, an alternative way to discourage the unwise criminalization of conduct is to urge lawmakers to pay more attention to the costs, limited efficacy, and other untoward consequences of overcriminalization.[28] As numerous theorists have argued, the criminal law is a blunt instrument, one that should only be used to proscribe and punish significantly wrongful conduct.[29] Not only do other means of discouraging misconduct of minor kinds exist, they are often less costly to society, and damaging to the life-prospects of individuals, than the infliction of legal punishment on them. This is especially true when legal punishment takes the form of imprisonment, with its considerable costs and life-altering consequences for those made to endure it. It seems more straightforward and thus more likely to be efficacious to ask lawmakers to attend to these features of criminalization than to ask them to adopt Tomlin's PI-based constraint on criminalization.

Also, Tomlin's constraint raises numerous questions that he does not acknowledge or address. Again, the constraint tells lawmakers to criminalize conduct only if it falls into the convergence zone of "reasonable" theories of criminalization. Why Tomlin restricts the purview of lawmakers to "reasonable" theories and what counts as "reasonable" are matters that he does not discuss. Yet even if we go along with him in constraining lawmakers in this way, there are further theoretical and practical difficulties that cast doubt upon the feasibility of his approach. Why think that the mere convergence of numerous competing normative theories on prohibited conduct provides us with proof that the conduct is "beyond a reasonable doubt" appropriately criminalized? Tomlin might argue that if all of the "reasonable" theories support the criminalization of certain kinds of conduct, then this gives us strong reason to believe that the conduct really is significantly wrongful enough to be criminalized. But for one thing, it is not implausible to believe that all of the "reasonable" theories of a given era could harbor irrational prejudices against certain kinds of conduct, as, for instance, many of the "reasonable" theories of earlier eras likely did regarding same-sex sexual relations. For another, convergence is consistent with significant differences among competing theories about (*a*) why certain kinds of conduct are significantly wrongful, and (*b*) just how wrongful they are (and thus, how much they should be punished). Why not require lawmakers to do more than simply look for areas of convergence among the competing theories? Why not instead require them to use the competing theories as resources in developing a coherent, articulated normative theory of their own, along the lines suggested by Rawlsian wide reflective equilibrium?[30] That, it seems, would give them something more like proof beyond a reasonable doubt that the conduct they elect to prohibit is, indeed, appropriately criminalized.

Of course, we might doubt that such an ambitious project is one for which most democratically elected lawmakers are suited, if indeed anyone is. Yet even Tomlin's more limited project seems a stretch for most lawmakers. It would require them to be able to distinguish "reasonable" from "unreasonable" theories, to have some knowledge about and understanding of numerous versions of the former, and then to discern the area of overlap among them. It is hard to see how such an approach would serve as a better check on excessive criminalization than the simpler one that reminds them of the gravity of criminal sanctions, their costs and consequences, and limited efficacy.

Further, we might question whether it is correct to say that lawmakers should criminalize conduct only when it is clear beyond a reasonable doubt that it should be liable to punishment. Lawmakers can criminalize conduct but attach relatively mild sanctions to it. True, criminalization mistakes will still result in unjust suffering, but they need not produce the kind of suffering that harsh criminal sanctions like imprisonment do. Why does this matter? Because misconduct might be conceived as existing along a continuum. At one end will be forms of misconduct that any plausible theory of criminalization will seek to outlaw and stoutly punish. At the other end will be forms of misconduct that societies might seek to discourage through means other than the criminal sanction. In-between, although closer to the less serious end of the continuum than to the more serious one, will be kinds of misconduct that societies might use criminal sanctions to punish or might not. Lawmakers might recognize the costs and limited efficacy of criminal sanctions and be averse to overusing them. But they might believe that some kinds of conduct will be most effectively controlled if at least mild criminal sanctions attach to them, though they might candidly concede that it is not clear beyond a reasonable doubt that this is so. Do such lawmakers act irresponsibly in criminalizing the conduct? Tomlin would have us think so, but it does not seem implausible to believe that the criminal law is an appropriate tool to discourage mildly harmful forms of misconduct so long as (*a*) the sanctions attached to such misconduct remain modest, and (*b*) it is possible, as in democratic societies it presumably will be, to rescind such provisions should a majority of the populace strongly disagree with them. Not only will Tomlin's approach to criminalization be difficult for lawmakers to apply, it seems to inordinately constrain them. Perhaps it does so because Tomlin tacitly conceives of legal punishment in its harsher forms rather than in the variety of forms it can and does take in most legal jurisdictions.

The infeasibility of Tomlin's approach is shown more vividly in his efforts to extend the reasonable doubt standard to official decisions about the sentence ranges to be assigned offense types and the specific sentences to be assigned offense tokens.[31] Tomlin has argued that legislators ought to be convinced beyond a reasonable doubt that the sentence ranges assigned to offense types are appropriate and, in particular, that they do not expose offenders to unjust (that is, excessive) punishment. Similarly, judges, in assigning sentences to specific offenders, ought to be convinced beyond a reasonable doubt that they are not imposing unjust punishment on them. Again, as with legislative decisions about what conduct to criminalize, it is unclear what the "evidence" is that lawmakers and judges would weigh and balance in making these decisions about sentencing. But set that point to one side. We might agree that legislators and judges ought to go about the vital tasks assigned to them carefully and seriously. Legislators, in particular, ought to be more sagacious than they often appear to be in evaluating the limited benefits of criminal sanctions and comparing them with their costs and burdens. Or their decisions about sentence ranges ought to be better informed by fully articulated and defensible accounts of ordinal and cardinal proportionality in sentencing. But given the complexities of the issues anyone who must devise or implement a sentencing scheme has to face, do we really want to insist that they not act until they are convinced, beyond a reasonable doubt, that they have discerned appropriate sentence ranges for the wide array of criminal offenses or appropriate specific sentences for offense tokens? I doubt that. More to the point, the issue, it seems to me, is not how convinced legislators or judges must be that they have made the right decisions, but what kinds of reasons and evidence they employ and how systematically they weigh and balance them.

One last point is worth mentioning. Tomlin's account seems more focused on the reasonable doubt standard than the presumption of innocence. Again, Tomlin wants lawmakers to criminalize conduct only when it is clear, beyond a reasonable doubt, that it is appropriately dealt with by the criminal law. But what, if anything, does this have to do with the PI? Tomlin might respond by arguing that the PI logically entails use of the reasonable doubt standard. The presumption of innocence is not honored, on such an account, unless individuals are proven guilty beyond a reasonable doubt in a court of law. Applied to lawmakers, the idea would be that the PI is not honored if they criminalize conduct that has not been shown to be significantly wrongful beyond a reasonable doubt.

Yet it is far from certain that the initial perspective we instruct judges or jurors to take on the accused, in the form of a presumption of innocence, logically entails the standard of proof that they should use in determining whether the government's case against the accused is sufficiently convincing to warrant convicting them.[32] When accused individuals face lengthy terms of imprisonment if convicted, or other kinds of especially severe criminal sanctions, the case for insisting upon proof beyond a reasonable doubt is impressive. But many criminal provisions are attended with sanctions that are relatively mild, and then it is less clear whether proof beyond a reasonable doubt is the obviously correct standard of proof. Antony Duff has argued that the PI requires the reasonable doubt standard because criminal conviction conveys the community's censure of individuals and this is an especially grave matter.[33] However, how much censure criminal conviction conveys depends crucially on the ways in which the conduct in question is sanctioned. Many widely used forms of sanctions deliver significantly less than crushing blows to the social status and well-being of those convicted of crimes. Admittedly, if a logical gap exists between the PI and the reasonable doubt standard, all that follows is that Tomlin's argument might have to be recast—in terms of what the reasonable doubt standard entails about criminalization, or perhaps in terms of what I have termed the "proof structure" of criminal trials entails about it. But like other legal scholars, Tomlin seems to want to milk more out of the PI, standing all by itself, than it can be plausibly thought to give us.

A Societal Presumption against Punishing the Innocent?

Despite my criticisms of Tadros's and Tomlin's attempts to cast the PI as a constraint on the content of the criminal law, it still might seem that there is something to the notion that the innocent—persons who have not engaged in serious wrongdoing of the kind appropriately proscribed by the criminal law—should not be liable to legal punishment. It is, in other words, plausible to claim that there is a societal presumption against punishing the innocent. Yet if certain kinds of deficiently crafted or overinclusive provisions of the criminal law expose the innocent to legal punishment, it might then seem that they contravene such a societal presumption. Does that not show that the PI has some bite when it comes to the substantive provisions of the criminal law?

I do not think that it does. I contend that the societal presumption against punishment of the innocent it is not really a presumption *of* innocence, not in the way that the framing perspective we instruct jurors to take on the accused at the outset of trials is. For one thing, notice that it is not clear who is to be presuming innocence in the case of the societal presumption against punishing the innocent. Society? But society is a collection of individuals, not an agent who can deliberately take up a perspective toward anyone or anything. For another, it is not clear what could rebut the societal presumption against punishment of the innocent. What *evidence* would rebut it? None that I can imagine. This suggests that a societal presumption against punishing the innocent is more like a principle than a presumption of the kind the PI is supposed to be.[34] We categorically reject punishment of the innocent and can scarcely imagine the kinds of considerations that would convince us to do otherwise. Such a principle should guide us both in devising substantive provisions of the criminal law and in devising the procedures used to enforce it. Even if there are considerations that might convince us to, in some circumstances, discount or set aside the principle, they are apt to be drawn from competing principles of similar weight, such as the principle that we ought to protect the innocent from serious harms.[35] It is in the nature of principles that they have to be weighed and balanced against one another so that we can figure out what course of conduct we should pursue or what procedures we should adopt and by which we should abide. But the logic of principles and the ways in which they can be pitted against one another is distinct from that of presumptions like the PI and their rebuttal; to conflate the two only invites confusion.

It is, I would contend, the principle *against* punishment of the innocent that undergirds opposition to strict liability provisions of the criminal law, not that such provisions contravene a presumption *of* innocence. To see this, we must focus on what "innocence," or its opposite, "guilt," means in the principle against punishment of the innocent. "Guilt" cannot simply mean conduct in violation of the criminal law, no matter what the content of its provisions. If it meant that, then persons could be punished for conduct that was completely harmless or nonblameworthy or both, if lawmakers decided, for some reason, to outlaw such conduct. That would render the principle toothless. Instead, what we want to do is punish conduct that deserves censure and hard treatment because it is significantly blameworthy and harmful to others (or violates their rights). Conduct that does not satisfy these two conditions is "innocent" in the sense of undeserving of the censure of the criminal law.

Seen in this light, what makes strict liability provisions objectionable is that they subject persons to punishment though they are "innocent" in the sense of not having behaved in a blameworthy, or perhaps seriously blameworthy, fashion. Granted, as Antony Duff argues, there might be contexts in which forms of strict or heightened liability are defensible.[36] Some businesses might be legitimately required to adopt special measures to ensure that they safely produce products and keep detailed and accurate records of their efforts to do so. Such heightened liability requirements exceed those placed on ordinary citizens in the conduct of their affairs. Nonetheless, they might be justified because of the risks posed by the production of certain kinds of goods. Yet if we went further, adopting provisions designed to punish businesses no matter how carefully they went about their legitimate tasks, and no matter how carefully they documented their efforts to do so, we would make them liable to censure and hard treatment though their operations were in no way blameworthy.[37] That would be akin to punishing persons who are "innocent" in the sense of not having behaved in ways that are significantly blameworthy and so contrary to the principle against punishment of the innocent.

Moreover, even if we adopt strict liability provisions, individuals charged with violating them would still get the PI if they elected to go to trial. The government would bear the burden of proving that they had violated the relevant provisions and would have to do so beyond a reasonable doubt if their convictions were to be warranted. What the government would not have to prove is that they *culpably* harmed others; that is the real problem with such provisions, not that they conflict with the PI.

The PI as Governing Our Relations with Our Fellow Citizens

Independently of whether the PI makes sense as a constraint on the content of the criminal law, some scholars interpret it as appropriately regulative of our relations with our fellow citizens more generally. If their arguments are convincing, this would show that the PI is not solely a procedural right applicable in the context of official suspicion or accusation.

On Antony Duff's account, we ought to exhibit "civic trust" toward our fellow citizens. Part of doing so is negative—we should not presume that they are "enemies who might attack us."[38] But it is also and more positively to presume that they are "reason-responsive," and, in particular, that they can recognize and guide their actions by moral reasons requiring them to refrain from attacking their fellow citizens.[39] On Dale Nance's account, there is a broad "principle of civility" underlying the PI as it operates in the legal context. That principle requires us to take a cautiously optimistic stance toward our fellow citizens, viewing and treating them as disinclined to engage in serious wrongdoing.[40] As Duff and Nance both make clear, they are not endorsing naive optimism with regard to our fellow citizens. We can reasonably take precautions against being victimized—by locking our doors and installing security systems—especially so long as these precautions are not directed against specific persons, or against certain kinds of persons, without warrant. Indeed, as Duff concedes, the existence of the criminal law itself, with its accompanying enforcement agencies and procedures, is a testament to the unreliability of some of our fellow citizens.[41] In spite of this, we should presumptively regard and treat our fellow citizens as responsive to both moral and prudential reasons and so capable of and, it would seem, inclined to govern their conduct in accordance with the law's strictures. Nance usefully points out that taking a cautiously optimistic attitude toward our fellow citizens has generative social powers: treating persons as reliable and trustworthy might encourage them to be so or to be more so.[42] By contrast, pessimism about the law-abidingness of our fellow citizens not only requires us to invest more of our time and energy deciding which of them can be trusted, it reduces the opportunities we have for socially beneficial interactions. Even guarded pessimism toward our fellow citizens will exact some of these costs.

Neither Duff nor Nance invokes a substantive human right to be presumed innocent as the ultimate ground of his claim about how we should regard and treat our fellow citizens. Duff does say that we are "entitled" to the civic PI, which comes close to suggesting that there are right-generated duties to so act toward our fellow citizens.[43] But his position also might be reasonably interpreted as saying that the failure to be trusting involves some deficiency in our living up to an aspirational standard. Nance's "principle of civility" seems a prescription of some indeterminate weight. He says little about its weight in relation to other principles or the kinds of considerations that might be capable of outweighing it. Yet since he sees it as underlying the PI in both the civil and criminal trial contexts, it seems a principle of substantial import.[44]

However, unmoored from the criminal trial, where the burden and standard of proof are relatively determinate and clear, a civic PI seems somewhat adrift. Duff admits to some crucial differences between the trial PI and the civic one, but elides others.[45] In the trial context, Duff notes that the PI is retrospective and confined. It is confined not only by being temporary but also in its scope, as it is directed toward specific allegations of past criminal conduct. What this leaves out is that the trial PI is actively adopted and taken up in relation to persons about whom those who must render verdicts typically know very little and with whom they are unlikely to interact once the trial is over. In particular, citizens are not are not allowed to serve on juries if they personally know or are otherwise connected with the accused.

The civic PI is different, Duff claims, because it is prospective and general.[46] It is not limited to the duration of a trial, but is ongoing and is not focused on official and specific allegations of past misconduct. We make an enormous variety of judgments about whether and how to interact with our fellow citizens. The civic PI tells us to presume their innocence of legal wrongdoing, or perhaps serious forms of it, such that we can constructively go forward in our interactions with them. What Duff does not mention is that such interactions do not usually depend on, or involve, the kinds of binary, guilty or not guilty, judgments that are the hallmarks of criminal trials. We can interact to a greater or lesser extent with our fellow citizens. Even interactions premised on some doubts about or mistrust of them can remain civil. And if we choose to avoid certain people, or not extend them the benefits of our trust and cooperation, the impact upon them is apt to be much less pronounced than when judges or juries enter "guilty" verdicts against them. Further, we often interact civilly with persons about whom we know quite a bit, not all of it flattering. It is information of this kind that might lead us to be cautious or wary of them. Duff and Nance say relatively little about what rebuts the PI in the civic context.[47] There must be circumstances in which we should abandon it in relation to some of our fellow citizens. If they menace or threaten us, surely we need not persist in presuming them harmless. But how much evidence must we have of others' ill intentions or unreliability before we reasonably can regard them with distrust?

As I will argue in the next chapter, the trial PI is an intentionally adopted stance, one temporarily taken up for a specific purpose. In this regard, it seems quite different from a civic PI. Indeed, there seems something odd about our actively taking up a PI in relation to our fellow citizens, especially when they have not fallen under official suspicion or been accused of any crimes. Imagine walking into the local pub, public library, or shopping mall and announcing that one is "presuming the innocence" of all of the inhabitants. A wag might respond by saying, "Why, has one or more of us been accused of something?" This suggests that the PI cannot be easily detached from its accusatory context. Perhaps the civic PI should be understood as more of a tacit presumption, one that operates passively in the background of our dealings with our fellow citizens, rather than actively, as we want it to do during criminal trials. It is enough if we do not regard our fellow citizens as inclined to do us harm, unless, of course, we have some reason to believe that they are so inclined. It might be too much to demand that we actively and continuously regard our fellow citizens as innocent of legal wrongdoing.

In fact, a more limited and negative account of what seems appropriate in our dealings with our fellow citizens does not seem that far from what Duff and Nance advocate. Again, Duff tells us that we should approach and treat our fellow citizens as if they presumptively are not "enemies who might attack us."[48] Fair enough, but to put it this way hardly amounts to a prescription to regard and treat our fellow citizens as if they are legal innocents. There are lots of criminal acts that do not involve attacking or preying upon others, or doing so in ways that are obvious and threatening—cheating on taxes, misusing prescription drugs or possessing illicit ones, insider trading, ignoring regulatory rules, among many others. Nance casts the principle of civility in terms of a presumption that our fellow citizens are not engaged in *serious* criminal wrongdoing.[49] But this is consistent with our believing or knowing that they are engaged in nonserious forms of criminal misconduct. Many of the crimes processed by the criminal justice system are relatively minor. In the United States, almost 80 percent of all convictions are for misdemeanors, and thus not for crimes that show individuals to be a menace to anyone, except perhaps themselves and a few others with whom they associate.[50] We can constructively interact with others even if we suspect that they skirt the criminal law in ways that do not threaten our interests. In short, a presumption that others will not actively seek to harm us is not the same as a presumption of their full legal innocence.

Further, Duff and Nance do not confront the reality that lots of people live in reasonable fear concerning what some of their neighbors might be capable of. Sure, if one lives in a stable, affluent community, a tacit presumption that the other citizens one is apt to encounter are generally harmless and law-abiding might be safe and reasonable. But many people live in social circumstances where such a presumption is questionable, and some live in social circumstances in which it would be daft. Most contemporary societies contain pockets of social deprivation and exclusion in which the threat of crime is real and ongoing. And some people who live in such areas are apt to be victimized more often than others—women, the elderly, and immigrants. It is not simply where you live that has implications for the reasonableness of your presuming the harmlessness of your fellow citizens, but who you are and, importantly, what your history is. Suppose that you are an elderly person who has been victimized repeatedly by street thugs. You are now walking down the street at night in your decidedly less-than-stable and closely-police-monitored neighborhood and approaching you are several young males who appear indistinguishable from the ones who have victimized you in the past. Of course, you do not know that these young males will accost you. In fact, you have little more to go on at this point than your hunch that they might constitute a threat. Instead of risking further victimization, you duck into a nearby shop and wait for them to pass. Should you be criticized for a lack of "civic trust" or for breaching the "principle of civility?" I would think not. In fact, not acting so as to protect yourself, given your recent history and present circumstances, would seem more the fault, if there is one. Yet these are not unusual histories or circumstances for a significant percentage of persons living in otherwise decent and generally well-ordered societies.[51] Admittedly, the lives of such persons will be stunted or cramped by their wariness of some of their fellow citizens. But it seems wrong to fault them for adopting such postures.

I doubt that Duff or Nance would resist this point. Duff might concede that civic trust requires the existence of reasonably just background social conditions, ones that might not obtain in certain societies or parts of them. Likewise, Nance could argue that the principle of civility holds with full force only in stable and well-ordered societies. But notice how such concessions, once again, point up significant differences between the civic and the trial PI. Not only is the civic PI not really a presumption of full legal innocence, it appears to be reasonably withheld from our fellow citizens at times or in ways that depend on subtle contextual factors, ones that fall well short of providing proof beyond a reasonable doubt that the individuals in question constitute some kind of threat to us. It should be emphasized that in our daily interactions with neighbors, coworkers, relatives, and strangers on the street, we routinely rely on a wide variety of signals, many of which would neither be admissible in a court of law nor collectively yield proof beyond a reasonable doubt about the intentions, proclivities, and focal concerns of those with whom we interact. Rumors, hearsay, fleetingly observed behavior, and limited past interactions are the "evidence" we often draw upon to make decisions of some consequence to our fellow citizens. Duff and Nance might urge us to make such decisions with more care than we often do. However, they are unlikely to urge us to make them with the same degree of care that the criminal courts are supposed to employ in making their binary and more consequential decisions about the guilt or nonguilt of accused persons.

Hence, even if we should not presume, without good reason, that our fellow citizens will actively seek to harm us, this does not amount to presuming them to be innocent of all legal wrongdoing. We can continue to act civilly with persons even if we suspect them of some forms of legal wrongdoing or regard them as mistrustful or unreliable in ways that do not impinge significantly upon our interests. Also, the kinds of reasons that are sufficient to justify caution in our civil dealings seem considerably weaker and less regulated than the ones judges or jurors are supposed to rely upon in rendering verdicts in criminal trials. The fact is, we must live more directly with the consequences of our decisions about whether and how to interact with our fellow citizens than jurors in criminal trials live with the consequences of their verdicts. Put differently, trials are artificial contexts, with their own distinctive purposes, structuring rules, and consequences. The attempt to import the aims of trials and the rules governing them into civil life, with its much more complex circumstances and varied outcomes, seems a dubious enterprise.

Concluding Remarks

There are obvious reasons, ones arguably having little to do with the PI, to be concerned about the scope and content of the criminal law, given the censure and hard treatment it imposes on those convicted of violating its provisions. We should not adopt provisions that subject the blameless or minimally blameworthy to legal punishment. We should reserve the criminal sanction to conduct that is significantly harmful, especially when that sanction takes the form of imprisonment. We must also take care to craft criminal provisions so that they accurately reflect the misconduct that we hope to discourage and punish. Failure to do so will subvert even the most fair and accurate adjudicative procedures, ones incorporating a presumption of innocence for the accused at the outset of their trials. Finally, we should regard and treat our fellow citizens as responsible and law-abiding unless, of course, we have good reasons for suspecting them to be otherwise. Where we have such reasons, how we should treat them depends, further, on whether their lawbreaking poses any kind of threat to us. Lawbreaking comes in numerous forms, many of which are relatively benign and so should not occasion alarm in us, though it might lead us to shy away from interacting with some of our fellow citizens. Circumspection in whom we interact with and how we do so is not tantamount to the infliction of legal punishment upon them, however, and so is not appropriately subject to the strict rules that ought to govern our employment of the criminal sanction.

CHAPTER 4 | The Presumption of Innocence in the Trial Setting

TO THIS POINT, THE conclusions I have urged regarding the PI have had a mostly negative cast. I have argued against viewing the PI as a substantive human right, a constraint on the criminal law, and a useful construct for regulating our everyday interactions with our fellow citizens. More positively, albeit vaguely, I have suggested that the PI is a procedural right whose primary home is the criminal trial. Though few deny that the presumption operates in the trial context, there is disagreement about what it requires of the judges, or more typically, jurors, who are called upon to render verdicts in criminal trials. In this chapter, I flesh out and defend a positive and significant role for the PI, though it is a limited one.

The presumption of innocence is part of the familiar tripartite structure of criminal trials. Those accused of crimes are entitled to a presumption of innocence, the burden of proving guilt is on the government, and the standard of proof that the government must meet is high (typically, beyond a reasonable doubt). There are competing views about why we set up criminal trials in this way and what the relations are among these three main elements.[1] Though these competing views will be the focus of the next chapter, it will help to frame the discussion that follows if I say a little about where I stand on them.

In chapter 5, I defend an account of the criminal trial according to which it is a complex moral assurance procedure for the justified infliction of legal punishment on individuals. On this account, individuals accused of crimes have a second-order moral right (and therefore should have a legal right) to demand that the government's evidence against them survive a rigorous and fair public test before their primary rights—to such things as liberty, privacy, and autonomy—are curtailed by legal punishment. Trials ought to be stern tests of the government's case because only by making them so do we assure ourselves that, when we punish those found guilty, we are justified in inflicting censure and hard treatment upon them. Legal punishment, especially when it takes the form of imprisonment, has potentially life-altering effects on people and for that reason should never be undertaken lightly.[2]

The high standard of proof is the principal means for ensuring that the government's case is put to a demanding test. So long as those who render verdicts do not begin trials with the conviction that the accused are obviously guilty, the burden of proof will be on the government to convince them that the accused are guilty beyond a reasonable doubt. In the absence of any further evidence offered by the government, judges or jurors who are not antecedently convinced of the guilt of the accused will have to acquit based on the reasonable doubt standard. Yet my contention is that the presumption of innocence is a crucial initial starting point for judges or jurors. It matters enormously how far the government has to go by way of convincing those who render verdicts that the accused are almost certainly guilty. More specifically, I draw a distinction between the framing perspective on the accused with which jurors (or judges) should begin trials, and the approach jurors (or judges) should use in evaluating the evidence introduced by the government or by defense counsel. These two tasks have not always been carefully distinguished in the literature on the PI. The perspective on the accused with which jurors begin trials will affect their ability and willingness to give the government's case against the accused the kind of exacting scrutiny that is a prerequisite to the justified infliction of legal punishment upon persons judged to be guilty.

The discussion in this chapter proceeds as follows: In the first section, I survey the possibilities for both the initial framing perspective of jurors and the attitudes with which they approach the evidence. At the extremes will be combinations of the two that are either too friendly to the accused or too friendly to the government. In the second section, I defend a combination of the two that is friendly to the accused, although one that the government will be able to overcome if it can offer decisive proof of their guilt. In the third section, I raise and respond to various objections to the account of the PI put forward in the second section. In concluding the chapter, I emphasize the unique features of the PI in the trial setting and suggest that its clear meaning, scope, and purpose in that context provide a crucial standard against which we can evaluate efforts to extend it beyond that context.

Starting Frame and Evidence Evaluation Options

Jurors are likely to begin criminal trials with a variety of beliefs about the accused, as well as approaches to carrying out the tasks of listening to and evaluating the evidence with which they are confronted. Other scholars who have examined the PI have noted that jurors are not naive and so are probably aware of the winnowing process that results in accused persons appearing before them in the courtroom.[3] The accused would not be where they are if police, prosecutors, a grand jury, or a judge at a preliminary hearing did not believe there was evidence indicating that they had committed one or more crimes. Jurors might also have heard things about the case through the media or conversations in the communities in which they reside. All of this might incline jurors to suspect, if not more firmly believe, that most persons charged with crimes are guilty of something. Knowledge of the winnowing process will likewise incline many judges who are charged with rendering verdicts in criminal cases to suspect that the accused are guilty. Indeed, judges might tend to be more cynical about accused persons than citizen jurors.[4] Judges will know that many accused persons plead guilty and that a majority of those who go to trial are convicted.[5] Hence, if the PI in the trial context is understood as an empirical claim about the likely belief state of jurors or judges at the outset of trials, it is surely off the mark. At best, those tasked with rendering verdicts in criminal cases might not know what to believe about the accused at the outset of their trials, which is not the same as presuming their material innocence.

Fortunately, no one is inclined to interpret the PI as a factual claim about judges' or jurors' beliefs at the outset of trials.[6] The PI is normative in character, prescribing to jurors (or judges) how they should approach or think about the accused, at least at the outset of their trials, and perhaps at various points along the way during them. This would make no sense if jurors could not be educated, or at least influenced by judicial instructions, or if judges could not be trained to set to one side their antecedent beliefs and adopt a perspective on accused persons that is favorable to them. Particularly with respect to jurors, which will be the focus of my discussion, the hope is that a properly devised set of instructions might give them direction and focus when they are otherwise unsure what to think about the accused persons whose fates are in their hands. Judges could be tasked with explaining to jurors that they play the crucial role in vetting the government's case against defendants in the criminal justice system, one that requires them to begin from a frame of reference that might seem a bit strained or artificial, but which is intended to help motivate them to rigorously evaluate the government's case.

What, then, should we tell jurors to use as their starting frame of reference vis-à-vis the persons who stand before them in the dock? It seems clear that we should not tell them to begin with the presumption that the accused are materially guilty, or are very likely so. Such a framing perspective would make it altogether too easy for the government to gain guilty verdicts, even if jurors were also told that the government still had to prove the guilt of the accused to a high standard and so bear some residual burden of proof. Granted, we can imagine circumstances in which defendants viewed as likely guilty at the outset of their trials might nonetheless earn acquittals. Jurors might in some cases be so enamored with the accused, or repulsed by the actions of prosecutors during trials, that almost any defense put forward by the accused will be perceived as raising reasonable doubt. This is the first indication that the framing perspective on the accused with which jurors begin trials is not the only thing that matters; how jurors approach and evaluate the evidence is also important. But set that point aside for now. The more important one is that whatever the presumption of innocence entails, it precludes instructing jurors to begin trials by regarding the accused as materially guilty, or probably so.

Unfortunately, beyond this, there seems little agreement about the perspective that we should encourage jurors to adopt. In laying out the options, I shall simplify matters a bit and focus on what I believe are the five major contenders in interpreting the PI. Other options might exist, but I suspect that most of them are slight variations on the ones discussed.

First, jurors might be told that they are to consciously adopt the posture, at the outset of trials, that the accused is materially innocent.[7] The most plausible way to interpret this option is as follows: Regardless of what the authorities believe, how those authorities have acted, or what they have said, jurors are to begin the trial by viewing the accused as if they are citizens in good standing in their communities. Citizens in good standing have done nothing to merit being punished. Accused persons need not be viewed as morally perfect or even exemplary citizens, only as materially innocent of the charges against them. The burden to establish otherwise is entirely on the government and the standard of proof it must meet is high—beyond a reasonable doubt. Notice how the "citizens in good standing" frame, which I shall abbreviate PI_m, fits comfortably with the notion that the government ought to bear the burden of proof. Citizens in good standing do not and should not have to prove anything. They should be allowed to go on about the business of living their lives until government officials conclusively establish that they have violated the law. However, it is less clear whether the high standard of proof in criminal cases follows directly from the presumption of material innocence. The standard of proof concerns the degree of persuasiveness that the state must satisfy in presenting its evidence of criminal conduct by the accused.[8] In my view, we set the standard of proof high in order to make trials very stringent tests of the government's evidence. Why we do so is a question to which we shall return in chapter 5. For now, what matters is that the combination of PI_m and the high standard of proof will require the government to put on a highly convincing case if it is to gain convictions.

A second option is close to PI_m, though slightly different from it. According to this second option, jurors should be instructed to adopt a neutral perspective on the accused—meaning that they should view the accused as neither materially innocent nor guilty. Instead, they should regard them as individuals about whom innocence or guilt with respect to the current charges is uncertain.[9] Such an interpretation of the presumption of innocence, call it PI_n, is less friendly to the accused than PI_m, because it is consistent with some doubt about whether they have abided by the law. Though PI_n is far from a presumption of guilt or likely guilt, it does not require jurors to begin with a stance according to which criminal defendants are to be viewed as presumed responsible citizens. PI_n thus might be seen as more in keeping with what jurors know or suspect about defendants as individuals whose law-abidingness is somewhat in doubt. Still, the government will have to bring forward strongly convincing evidence to move jurors beyond neutrality or uncertainty to a finding of guilt beyond a reasonable doubt.

A third option takes us farther from PI_m. The third option holds that jurors should be instructed to adopt the attitude that it is equally probable that the accused are materially guilty as innocent.[10] Call this third option PI_{ep}. More than PI_n, it constitutes a considerable diminishment in the believed-good standing of defendants. Citizens in good standing are not usually believed to be equally likely guilty of crimes as not guilty of them.[11] They are instead believed to be materially innocent of them, or at least very likely so. PI_{ep} differs from PI_n because the latter assigns no probability whatsoever to material guilt or innocence. Jurors instructed to adopt PI_n are to take the position that they just do not know whether the accused are factually innocent or guilty. PI_{ep}, by contrast, asks them to believe something positive though ambivalent—that it is equally probable that defendants are (materially) guilty as not guilty. Nonetheless, given PI_{ep} as a framing perspective, the government will have to bring forth evidence showing that the accused are very likely to be guilty if it is to win convictions.

A fourth possible interpretation likewise invokes probabilities, but in a different way than PI_{ep}. Instead of advising jurors to adopt the perspective that the accused is equally likely to be guilty as innocent, this interpretation tells them to adopt the attitude that the accused is no more likely than the average person in the population to commit the crime with which he has been charged. In cases of rare crimes, such as homicide, jurors would be encouraged to regard the likelihood of the defendant's material innocence as fairly high. With other, more common offenses, jurors would be encouraged to regard the likelihood of his innocence as somewhat lower, although not much so. Since this version of the presumption focuses on the average probability of the accused's material innocence or guilt, I designate it PI_{ap}. Notice that PI_{ap} is vulnerable to jurors' beliefs about the frequency of the various types of crimes in ways that PI_{ep} is not. If jurors mistakenly believe that crimes of certain kinds occur much more frequently than they do, then they will regard individuals charged with those crimes as more likely to be guilty of them than, in fact, they are, given the average probability of guilt. The reverse holds as well. Nonetheless, on the assumption that few jurors will regard most people as guilty of the crimes with which individuals have been charged, the government will have to bear a heavy burden of proof to convince jurors that a defendant is almost certainly guilty.

Larry Laudan supports what appears to be a fifth possible interpretation of the presumption of innocence, one that I will call PI_p[12] According to PI_p, jurors are to begin trials by presuming that nothing about the factual guilt of the accused has been established simply by their having been arrested and charged. Initially, PI_p appears indistinguishable from PI_n. However, Laudan seems somewhat indifferent about jurors' antecedent attitudes toward the accused's likely guilt or innocence at the outset of trials. True, he does say that potential jurors who have strong antecedent beliefs in the guilt of the accused should probably be excluded from jury service.[13] But he seems less troubled by the prospect of jurors who suspect that the accused are likely guilty, or believe them to be more probably than not guilty. Perhaps Laudan believes that jurors who are not obviously prejudiced against the accused will be able to set to one side their antecedent beliefs and focus solely on the evidence presented in the courtroom. Hence, I shall interpret PI_p as saying nothing about the framing perspective on the accused that jurors adopt at the outset of trials. Instead, PI_p requires jurors to focus exclusively on the probative force of the evidence presented to them. If that evidence is highly probative of defendant guilt, as captured by the reasonable doubt standard, then jurors should convict defendants. If not, jurors should acquit them. Laudan's view is that jurors should be dispassionate though rigorous testers of the claims made by both the prosecution and defense during trials. Since PI_p is consistent with a range of beliefs about the accused at the outset of trials, I mostly ignore it in the next section, where I focus on the question of whether there are good reasons to prefer one framing perspective to the others.

Earlier, I hinted that the framing perspective with which jurors begin trials, whether PI_m, PI_n, PI_{ep}, PI_{ap}, or even PLG (understood as a presumption of likely material guilt), is not the only thing with which we should be concerned. What else matters? Obviously, the attitudes jurors have toward the evidence presented at trials and the approach they take to evaluating it are crucial. It is conceivable that jurors might begin with the presumption that the accused are likely materially guilty but be too quickly or easily persuaded by evidence of their material innocence, or hostile to the government's efforts to convince them to declare the accused guilty beyond reasonable doubt. These things might even be true if the burden of proof is put on the defense and the standard it has to meet is high. Of course, it is not just the government that has to worry about how jurors approach and evaluate the evidence; the defense also must be concerned about this. Even if jurors can be persuaded to adopt a defendant-friendly presumption of innocence, such as PI_m, this might be of little account if jurors are utterly credulous once the government begins putting forward its evidence.

Juror approaches to the evidence can be arrayed along a continuum. At one extreme, jurors might display credulousness with evidence, or worse, utter credulousness, meaning that they are too prone to believe it without questioning it or assign it more weight than it merits. Again, such an approach might be taken with regard to evidence proffered by the government or by accused persons, presumably through their attorneys. We can even imagine that such an approach might be taken by jurors to evidence presented by both sides, in which case jurors will likely be pulled to and fro during the trial. At the other extreme, jurors might be close-minded with respect to evidence presentations by one or both sides during trials. In that case, jurors would be unwilling to count as probative or exculpatory evidence what they should count as such. Or they might fail to give such evidence its appropriate weight in their deliberations. Somewhat less extreme would be attitudes of strong skepticism or wariness with regard to evidence, especially where this involves a grudging willingness to entertain it or assign it its appropriate weight. In the middle will be something like what we want and expect of jurors, and therefore the kind of approach we might instruct them to take. This involves receptivity to the evidence and arguments presented by both sides, coupled with a readiness to subject those arguments and evidence to the careful scrutiny needed to determine both its degree of cogency and proper weight in their deliberations. That this, or something like it, constitutes the appropriate approach to the evidence put forward by both sides is, I suspect, unlikely to provoke much controversy. Indeed, proponents of different accounts of what the PI in the trial setting requires as a framing perspective might concur on the proper juror approach to the evidence and arguments presented to them.

It might be thought that one advantage of certain framing perspectives is that they entirely rule out one or more of the deficient approaches to evidence evaluation. For instance, it might be claimed that PI_m is inconsistent with juror credulity toward government proffers of evidence. Once jurors take up a perspective according to which the accused are viewed as if they are citizens in good standing, it might be thought that jurors cannot help but scrutinize the government's case closely. A starting frame of PLG, by contrast, might incline most jurors to believe whatever evidence the government brings forward.

It can be conceded that starting frames tend to be linked with certain attitudes toward the evidence, while denying that such links are matters of logical entailment. Again, there might be jurors who begin with a presumption of the material innocence of the accused but too quickly abandon it when presented with evidence by the government that implicates the accused. Alternatively, jurors could begin trials with the view that it is equally likely that the accused is guilty as innocent but stubbornly refuse to adjust their views to the incriminating evidence because they are suspicious of the motives of the authorities. Simply put, framing perspectives and approaches to the evidence seem separable. Talk about the PI might run them together, but it makes more sense to keep them apart and devise jury instructions to address each of them. Even if there is some redundancy in the two sets of instructions, employing both will very likely do more good than harm.

Making the Case for PI_m

From this point forward, I assume that proponents of differing accounts of the trial PI agree that jurors should be receptive to the evidence and arguments presented by both sides during trials, though prepared to scrutinize them carefully. Utter credulity and complete close-mindedness are juror vices, as are their near relatives. Jurors cannot do their jobs responsibly if they are unwilling to listen to and take seriously the evidence and arguments brought forward by the prosecution and defense during criminal trials. Jurors must also sift through the evidence, determine its cogency and weight, and arrive at some reasoned, overall assessment of it. Assuming that they are prepared to do these things, the questions we face are whether or to what extent the framing perspective about the accused with which jurors begin trials will make any difference in their evaluations of the evidence brought forward by government and defense lawyers.

Let me begin with a concession. It might be that juror receptivity to the evidence from both sides, along with the willingness to scrutinize and weigh it carefully, matters more than the framing perspective with which jurors begin. At least, this might be true if jurors begin with the starting points prescribed by PI_m, PI_n, PI_{ep}, or PI_{ap}. None of the framing perspectives captured by these differing interpretations of the PI can be fairly characterized as wholly unfriendly to the accused. In this respect they are unlike PLG and PI_p, especially if the latter tolerates juror belief in the probable guilt of the accused. Though I will argue for PI_m, I do not regard PI_n, PI_{ap}, or PI_{ep} as utterly without merit. Indeed, given some of the evidence about the framing perspectives with which many real-world jurors begin, these alternatives to PI_m would constitute substantial improvements.[14] Nonetheless, I believe that a case can be made for preferring PI_m to PI_n, PI_{ep}, and PI_{ap}. Having jurors start with PI_m at the outset of trials will give them more motivation to scrutinize carefully the government's case. It will encourage them to adopt what Hock Lai Ho has termed a "protective attitude" toward the accused.[15] Since it is the accused's vital interests that are on the line during criminal trials, this is an attitude that we should seek to foster with jury instructions.

To begin to grasp the case for PI_m, consider the following analogies. Suppose that someone with whom you are well acquainted and of whom you have a high opinion is accused of some moral wrong by someone else who you believe is at least a credible person. The accuser comes to you and lays out the case for the alleged wrongdoing. If you believe in the good moral character of the person accused, you are likely to listen to and evaluate the evidence in ways that, initially at least, are charitable to the accused and therefore not-too-quickly accepting of the accuser's story, though you will not be dismissive of that story. What this means is that you will query the accuser closely, actively searching for alternative explanations for the accuser's evidence that cast the accused's actions in a more favorable light. You also will be reluctant to draw negative conclusions about the accused person in the absence of strongly persuasive evidence about her wrongdoing. To put it differently, you will be protective of the accused, leaning toward giving her the benefit of the doubt with respect to any piece of the accuser's evidence that is ambiguous and with respect to the accuser's overall account unless the evidence is pretty clear that your acquaintance has acted contrary to what you believe is her normally good character.

Compare the preceding with a case in which someone with whom you are only mildly acquainted, or not acquainted at all, is accused of some moral wrong by a person whose credibility you have no reason to doubt. You have no sense of the accused's character, and so your starting frame of reference is apt to be different than in the preceding case. Nonetheless, out of a sense of fairness, you might closely probe the evidence presented by her accuser, be hesitant to jump to conclusions, and even search for alternative explanations of the events in question that exonerate the accused. However, your motivation for doing all of these things likely will be somewhat weaker. After all, your willingness to do them or continue them is not backed by the conviction that the accused really is a good person, as it was in the previous case. Granted, if you are exceptionally fair-minded, you might bend over backward to give the accused the benefit of the doubt. But more normally fair-minded people might not be inclined to push the inquiry into the accused's conduct quite as far or adamantly insist upon its rigor. Also, they might be somewhat less inclined to resolve reasonable doubts about any piece of the accuser's evidence, or reasonable doubts about the overall account presented by the accuser, in the accused's favor.

In similar ways, I believe, the framing perspective with which jurors (or judges) begin trials will influence how they approach the evidence regarding a formally accused person's alleged crimes. The framing perspective will influence whether they scrutinize that evidence closely, search for alternative explanations of events that exonerate defendants, hesitate to believe the accusations leveled by prosecutors or prosecution witnesses, examine carefully the links in the evidence chain that the government presents, and at the end of the trial, are willing to give the benefit of reasonable doubt to the accused, if it exists.[16] Obviously, how dogged jurors will be in performing any or all of these tasks will be matters of degree. It might be claimed that fair-minded jurors will execute them regardless of the reference frame from which they begin. Perhaps so, but the question is whether some framing perspectives will provide jurors with additional motivation to do so, and provide them a more useful guide as they do so, than others. And again, we should not assume that all jurors have the skills and dispositions constitutive of exceptional fair-mindedness. The framing perspective from which such jurors begin trials might help some of them to compensate for their shortcomings in that regard.

It must be admitted that there are significant differences between the informal inquiries into someone's conduct described in my analogies and inquiries conducted by the courts during criminal trials. Jurors are explicitly told that they should not convict the accused unless they are persuaded by the evidence against them beyond a reasonable doubt. That instruction might be thought to provide jurors with sufficient motivation to examine and weigh the evidence against the accused diligently. Also, there is considerably more at stake in the outcomes of trial verdicts. Informal inquiries into someone's conduct, undertaken by friends or associates, rarely have the kinds of potentially drastic consequences for the accused as do guilty verdicts in criminal trials. Knowing that they have the liberty, if not lives, of criminal defendants in their hands, jurors might be expected to have more than adequate motivation to bend over backward to be fair to the accused and thus tough-minded with the government's evidence. Finally, jurors will not personally know defendants or have well-founded beliefs about their character one way or the other. Hence, even if the framing perspective with which jurors begin trials matters, it would seem that juror ignorance about the character of defendants coheres better with PI_n, PI_{ep}, or PI_{ap} than with PI_m. PI_m requires jurors to initially adopt a more defendant-friendly stance than they have any reason to adopt.

These are all valid points. However, I do not believe that they refute what can be said on behalf of urging jurors to take the more prodefendant stance of PI_m. Granted, jurors are not in the position to know that defendants have good character or, what is not quite the same, are members in good standing in the community. Thus they will not naturally extend to defendants the myriad benefits that go with a good opinion of them. But it does not follow that they cannot reasonably be instructed to do so or that the benefits of doing so are illusory, even if they consist of no more than a greater initial hesitancy to believe the state's case along with a steeled resolve to analyze the evidence carefully and fully. Jurors who start with the presumption that the accused are citizens in good standing in the community will likely expect and demand more from the prosecution before they reach guilty verdicts than jurors who start from a frame that tacitly concedes that the accused might not be such citizens. And this might be true even if both kinds of jurors are fully aware of the stakes of trials, appropriately receptive to the evidence, prepared to dissect it, and believe, pursuant to jury instructions, that they should not render guilty verdicts unless the evidence is convincing beyond a reasonable doubt. Sure, jury instructions will remind jurors of the significance of their task and provide them with some motivation to carry it out responsibly. It does not follow that altering the framing perspective with which they begin their task will have no effect on where they wind up or how quickly or easily they get there.

PI_m is counterintuitive, in some ways, but that is precisely its point—to shake jurors out of their complacency and force them to confront the possibility that defendants might be responsible citizens who have been falsely accused. One way to think about PI_m is in terms of its consisting of a procedural reset. Though everything that has happened to the accused to this point makes him look guilty, at trial, he not only starts with a clean slate, he gets something more positive: Jurors are urged to view him as a responsible, law-abiding citizen, and to evaluate each aspect of the government's case against him through that lens. To that end, we might offer jurors the trusted coworker or neighbor heuristic, according to which jurors should strive to regard the accused as they would regard someone they knew and in whose law-abiding character they are confident. Again, the idea is to motivate jurors to look for ways to square each piece of the government's case with the presumption, such that in cases of reasonable doubt about any piece of evidence, the defendant gets the benefit of the doubt. Also, when it comes time to assess the overall strength of the government's case, where reasonable doubt exists, jurors must acquit.

Importantly, it does not follow from such an approach that reasonable doubts about any piece of the government's case must translate into reasonable doubt about its overall case. There might be complex relationships among the many elements of the government's case such that one or several less-than-conclusive bits of evidence will overlap or converge in ways that strengthen each other. In circumstantial evidence cases, something like this will often be true: Though any particular piece of evidence might be subject to reasonable doubt, the various pieces might fit together in ways that point ineluctably toward the accused's guilt. So, for instance, if the government is attempting to prove that the accused was at the scene of an armed robbery, a single, somewhat hesitant eyewitness identification of the accused might be inconclusive in ways that should be resolved in the accused's favor. But other pieces of evidence, each of which could also be somewhat less-than-conclusive, might coalesce with the eyewitness identification to make the accused's presence at the scene of the armed robbery seem almost certain.

Though PI_n and PI_{ep} will provide some motivation to jurors to carefully scrutinize the government's case, they nonetheless both signal to jurors that the good standing of defendants is somewhat in doubt. Again, PI_n tells jurors to adopt the attitude that they just do not know whether the accused is guilty or innocent, and PI_{ep} tells them to adopt the attitude that it is equally probable that the accused is guilty as innocent. The heuristic suggested by the former is that of the coworker or neighbor about whom one knows very little, such that one is hesitant to think one way or the other about her likely guilt or innocence. The heuristic suggested by the latter is more ominous—perhaps that of the coworker or neighbor whose good character one has some, albeit far from conclusive, reason to doubt. Granted, neither heuristic is equivalent to one in which jurors are told to view the accused as like a coworker or neighbor whom one has some definite reason to distrust, but neither gives the accused the same initial shield of skepticism about and resistance to the government's case that PI_m does. Also, with respect to each inconclusive piece of the government's case, jurors who are unsure what to believe about the accused, or who adopt the attitude that the accused is as likely to be guilty as innocent, might be less inclined to resolve their doubts in the accused's favor. Why should they do so, after all, since the good standing of the accused is uncertain?

For different reasons, PI_{ap} likewise seems less protective of the accused, though the extent to which that is so might depend on jurors' beliefs about the frequency of the crimes with which the accused has been charged. In particular, if jurors believe that the crimes in question occur more often than they actually do—a not uncommon misperception, one suspects, in societies in which there is considerable concern about crime—then PI_{ap} might do less than PI_m to shield the accused from too ready or easy findings of guilt. Jurors who believe that certain kinds of crimes are commonly committed might accept weaker proofs of an accused's guilt, all things considered. However, it might be that, in the majority of cases, jurors will simply not know the how often the offenses with which individuals have been charged occur in their communities, or will have conflicting beliefs about their frequencies. This means that PI_{ap} offers somewhat murky or variable guidance to jurors concerning how they should regard the accused at the outset of their trials.

The preceding, mostly intuitive case for the superiority of PI_m to PI_n, PI_{ep}, and PI_{ap} is buttressed by empirical evidence concerning the belief-formation and belief-revision tendencies of persons.[17] Two findings from empirical psychology are of special relevance. First, there is the phenomenon known as "confirmation bias," which is the tendency "to seek or interpret evidence in ways that support existing beliefs, expectations, or hypotheses." Researchers have found that we are inclined to search for or overweight evidence that confirms our antecedent beliefs or hypotheses, while neglecting to search for or underweighting evidence that disconfirms them. Also, we better recall evidence confirming our beliefs than disconfirming them, and see confirming evidence as having more value or weight than disconfirming evidence, other things being equal. Further, even if we do not ignore contradictory evidence, we are inclined to work harder to undermine it. Confirming evidence, by contrast, is accepted at face value. Second, there is the closely related phenomenon known as "belief perseverance," whereby people systematically exhibit resistance to changing their beliefs or hypotheses, once they have formed them, even in the face of new evidence that shows such beliefs or hypotheses to be dubious.

The implications of the preceding for trials and the beliefs and attitudes with which jurors begin them are apparent. If jurors begin with a presumption of likely guilt in relation to the accused, or simply believe it is somewhat more likely than not that the accused are guilty, such views will subtly slant them toward the government's case and against the defendant's attempts to undermine it. Confirmation bias will lead them to believe the government's evidence too quickly and easily, or give it too much weight. It will also lead them to be wary or dismissive of evidence supporting the accused's innocence or, at least, lack of guilt. Belief perseverance will incline them to cling to their starting hypotheses even as disconfirming evidence piles up. All of this might make it too easy for the government to prevail—to shoulder the burden of proof and convince jurors that the evidence of the accused's guilt is convincing beyond a reasonable doubt.

Granted, juror instructions according to which they should be receptive to but critical of the evidence and arguments presented by the prosecution and defense might work, to some extent, to counter these tendencies. But the problem is that such belief formation and preservation strategies often work subconsciously and thus in ways that jurors simply do not recognize. One thing that an insistence that they abandon their likely starting points will accomplish—assuming that their likely starting points are that the accused are more probably guilty than not—is move them out of their comfort zones with their evidence-gathering and belief-preservation tendencies. PI_{ep} moves them a short distance out of that comfort zone, from more likely than not guilty to equally likely not guilty as guilty. But my sense is that PI_{ep} might be too close to the framing perspective with which most jurors are apt to begin trials and so is unlikely to effectively counter confirmation bias and belief perseverance. If we want juries to provide a stern test of the government's case against defendants, we must challenge them to set aside their antecedent beliefs and work from a different starting point. PI_m does this most forcefully and dramatically, confronting jurors with the possibility that defendants are innocents wrongly accused and urging them to view and evaluate the evidence presented during the trial through that lens.

However, the preceding line of argument naturally leads to the following question: Do we want jurors to believe in the material innocence of the accused to the extent of exhibiting confirmation bias and belief perseverance on behalf of them? Assuredly not, since both modes of epistemic operation are irrational, whether they are exhibited on behalf of the accused or against them. Again, we should want jurors to be receptive to all of the evidence, though prepared to scrutinize it. In any event, it is not apparent whether a deliberately adopted perspective, which PI_m will be most of the time, can generate confirmation bias or belief perseverance. My point is not that PI_m should do so. It is instead that without a robust presumption of innocence such as PI_m, one that fundamentally challenges jurors' preconceptions about the accused and the evidence evaluation biases that go with those preconceptions, we seem less likely to get exacting evaluations of the evidence from jurors.

It might still be objected that asking jurors to adopt PI_m is unrealistic given that they do not know the accused or anything about their characters. I am not convinced by this objection. PI_m does not ask jurors to pretend that they know things about the accused that they do not, at least not specific things. Rather, it instructs them to adopt a perspective on the accused that already should be familiar to them, one according to which, absent specific knowledge to the contrary, their fellow citizens are to be regarded as members in good standing in the community. To enliven and reinforce this, jurors might be given the trusted coworker or neighbor heuristic. If it is claimed that jurors have credible beliefs about the conduct or character of the accused, or at least reasonable suspicions, to the contrary, then it is important to note that PI_n, PI_{ep}, and PI_{ap} likewise ask jurors to set such beliefs and suspicions about defendants to one side. Even Laudan's PI_p requires them to do so. If conformity to antecedent juror beliefs is what we want, then PLG is probably the best option in most cases.

The PI and the Right against Self-Incrimination at Trial

A further point in support of PI_m, as against PI_n, PI_{ep}, and PI_{ap}, might be noted as well. Up until now, I have said nothing about juror expectations regarding testimony by the accused during their trials. There is considerable controversy about whether persons accused of crimes should be expected to testify at their trials or are entitled to invoke a right against self-incrimination.[18] Part of that controversy, in the contemporary context, concerns whether the prosecution (or judge) should be permitted to comment on the failure of the accused to testify at their trials. Part of it also concerns whether judges presiding over trials should instruct jurors that the accused are under no obligation to testify because of their right against self-incrimination. Without pretending to address these contentious matters fully, I would suggest that how we conceive of the PI might influence how we come down on them. PI_m, I would argue, coheres better with a judicial instruction, at the outset of trials, that the individuals accused of crimes are under no obligation to disprove the accusations against them, including through their own testimony. After all, presumed citizens in good standing are not supposed to have to prove that they have been law-abiding. The burden to support the accusations is entirely on their accusers. Yet with PI_n, PI_{ep}, and even PI_{ap}, the good standing of the accused is, as we have seen, somewhat less clear. Thus a judicial instruction, at the outset of trials, that defendants have nothing to prove or answer to seems more of an arbitrary stipulation than something that follows, organically, as it were, from the PI.

By way of illustration, go back to the two analogies discussed earlier. In the one, you have grounds for believing that the person accused of some wrong has good moral character. Hence, you might initially be somewhat protective of her in the face of the accusation, and appropriately so. It would be odd, it seems, after being apprised of the accusation against her to immediately search for her and question her closely about it. Instead, you would wait for the evidence against her to mount up to the point where confronting her would seem your only option. If the evidence never reached that point, then you might never inquire into her account of the events in question. Your belief in her good character would insulate her from such an inquiry. In the second analogy, you have no evidence about the character of the accused. Still, a commitment to fairness might lead you to question her accuser closely and examine the evidence supporting the accusation carefully. My sense is, though, that you might be more inclined to seek out the accused earlier, or based on somewhat weaker evidence having been furnished by her accuser, to hear her side of the story. This might especially be true if you not only do not know much about her character but actually have reason to believe that there is some chance that she might have done what her accuser claims, or if you believe that misconduct like hers is fairly common.

However, even a belief in the good character of the accused will not insulate her from expectations that she address the accusations against her if the evidence that she has behaved badly is sufficiently compelling. Those who believe in the futility of an instruction to jurors that the accused are under no obligation to testify are probably correct in some cases.[19] If the evidence against the accused is overwhelming, jurors will, quite reasonably, want and expect the accused to address it. But from this it does not follow that such an instruction is never or usually pointless. Jurors explicitly instructed to take up the framing perspective according to which the accused are materially innocent might delay the point at which they come to expect the accused to testify, or never reach it. Defendants presumed materially innocent should not be expected to defend themselves if the government's evidence against them does not approach satisfaction of the reasonable doubt standard. By contrast, if jurors begin trials with frames of reference according to which the material innocence of the accused is taken to be less clear or in doubt, it seems plausible to believe that weaker proofs of their guilt by the government might generate expectations on the part of jurors that accused persons ought to answer the government's case against them.

Linking the PI to the Proof Structure

The discussion so far might be thought to bring us to the following question: Why should we instruct jurors to adopt the kind of counterintuitive stance toward the accused that PI_m consists in and equip them with a heuristic that motivates and enables them to reason from it as the evidence comes in? As I have already indicated, I view PI_m as part of a complex moral assurance procedure, the other two main parts of which are the burden of proof on the state, and the high standard of proof it must meet. It is likely that trials will always be ordeals for those charged with crimes. But the proof structure of trials makes them ordeals for the government as well. We ought to insist on the kind of moral assurance trials provide because legal punishment has the potential to cripple if not ruin individuals' lives.[20] We should therefore be exceedingly cautious and circumspect about its imposition—indeed much more so than we often are.[21] The reasons for structuring our procedures for determining legal guilt in this way are familiar; thus I shall only briefly summarize them at this point. Many of them will be revisited in subsequent chapters.

First and foremost, police and prosecutors make mistakes in arresting and charging people with crimes.[22] Sometimes these are honest mistakes, sometimes they are not. Even if the vast majority of the individuals charged with crimes who make it to the trial stage are guilty of one or more of the offenses with which they have been charged, some are not. Moreover, some are guilty of fewer or less serious crimes than the ones with which they have been charged. Properly structured trials offer the innocent or partially innocent their last, best hope for exoneration, especially if the appeals process is weighted toward affirming convictions, which it often is.[23]

Second, in the majority of criminal prosecutions, the government has a clear resource edge and typically has a rhetorical edge. Most criminal defendants are indigent. In some countries, this will not matter as much because their indigent defense systems are robust.[24] But no one who has examined the US indigent defense system, for instance, is inclined to characterize it in glowing terms.[25] Though prosecutors and police have limited resources and many cases with which to deal, they still have more resources on which to call to prepare cases against defendants than most defendants have to prepare defenses for their trials. Government officials will also have a rhetorical advantage during trials. Prosecutors (and the police who testify for them) are servants of the public. Defense attorneys, by contrast, are hired (or appointed) guns who have only their clients to answer to. When push comes to shove, it seems likely that prosecutors are more apt to be believed by jurors than defendants or their attorneys. There will be some exceptions to this, of course, but probably not that many.

Third, it is plausible to believe that the proportion of innocent or partly innocent accused persons who go to trial is greater than it is in the set of individuals formally accused of crimes. Most of the individuals accused of crimes plead guilty in exchange for charging or sentencing concessions by government officials. The few who insist on trial adjudication are not all innocent, of course. Indeed, most of them are likely guilty of something. But the mere fact of their being willing to contest the charges, when so many other accused persons decline to do so, should give us pause. Few accused persons against whom the government's evidence is a slam dunk will proceed to trial. As Albert Alschuler has noted, the cases in which the government's evidence is not decisive are precisely the ones that we should insist on being subject to trial adjudication.[26]

In addition to the preceding, contingent reasons for making it difficult for the government to prove guilt, a rights-based reason for doing so also can be identified. It invokes a particular view about the fundamental moral rights of individuals and the conditions under which they can be infringed. Legal punishment typically curtails, sometimes quite drastically, the basic moral (and legal) rights of individuals—to liberty, property, autonomy, and privacy.[27] According to a fairly common strand of thinking about such moral rights, they are not supposed to be the sorts of things of which individuals can be easily or casually deprived.[28] Basic moral rights secure vital interests or capabilities of individuals, ones without which they cannot live decent lives on their own terms.[29] If the government is to infringe such weighty interests or capacities, it must demonstrate to an impartial tribunal that it has powerful evidence that individuals have exceeded their rights in ways that the law (appropriately) prohibits. Indeed, it could be claimed that individuals' basic moral rights ground a secondary moral right to demand such a public, impartial, and rigorous inquiry, a point that I elaborate in the next chapter. Criminal trials, with their exacting proof structures, constitute one way in which that secondary moral right might be honored by the government.[30] And notice that such a secondary moral right might be appropriately exercised by individuals accused of crimes independently of whether or not the authorities have made mistakes in arresting and accusing them.

Further Objections and Replies

Larry Laudan offers numerous arguments against interpreting the presumption of innocence during criminal trials in terms of PI_m. As we have already seen, he believes that PI_m is at odds with what jurors reasonably believe or suspect at the outset of trials, namely, that defendants would not be in the position they are in except for considerable evidence that they are, in fact, guilty of one or more crimes. However, PI_m should not be dismissed simply because it does not cohere with what jurors antecedently believe or suspect, for that ignores the possibility that its function is prescriptive, part of an elaborate moral assurance procedure for the imposition of legal punishment. Moreover, Laudan's preferred alternative, PI_p, is, as we have seen, consistent with jurors beginning trials with beliefs about defendants' likely guilt that will make it too easy for the government to satisfy the standard of proof. Laudan might want to make it easier for the government to convict individuals charged with crimes, but such a position requires more defense than citing the lack of congruence between PI_m and jurors' antecedent beliefs and suspicions.[31]

Laudan also argues that PI_m plays no real role in criminal procedure.[32] It is not needed at the outset of trials. Instead, all that is needed is for jurors to understand that the government's levying of charges against persons proves nothing, along with a firm commitment to heeding and properly evaluating the evidence. Moreover, jurors who acquit defendants need not and cannot plausibly be interpreted as finding defendants materially innocent. Acquittals say only that jurors did not deem the government's case convincing beyond a reasonable doubt. Indeed, jurors might believe, post-trial, that the accused were factually guilty; they simply did not believe that the state had proven them to be so beyond a reasonable doubt.

However, insisting that jurors should begin trials with a provisional view that the accused are materially innocent is fully consistent with their believing, at the conclusion of trials that yield acquittals, that defendants are likely, and perhaps very likely, guilty. Jurors might gradually come off the presumption that defendants are materially innocent because of the powerful evidence presented by the government.[33] This is precisely what we want them to do if, after subjecting the government's case to careful scrutiny, they can no longer maintain their framing perspective according to which the accused are materially innocent. Yet jurors might nonetheless conclude that the government's evidence falls short of being convincing beyond a reasonable doubt, so they acquit. True, they are not finding defendants materially innocent at that point, but that does not show that starting with such a presumption is illogical or unwarranted. It might be warranted if it provides accused persons with an additional measure of protection against premature or facile findings of guilt.

Laudan also argues that jurors cannot be made to voluntarily take up a belief in the material innocence of the accused, which they will have to do if they are given a PI_m instruction.[34] Beliefs of this kind are the results of observations or other evidence that individuals encounter; they cannot be prescribed. This is an important objection, because it forces us to clarify how PI_m is to be understood. If it is understood as a provisional belief, and persons cannot will themselves to believe things, then PI_m will seem untenable. However, we need not interpret the PI_m instruction as an attempt to impart beliefs to jurors about the accused. We can instead interpret is as an instruction to them to take up a rebuttable perspective on the accused, one that they are to use as they evaluate the government's proffers of evidence. In effect, the instruction tells jurors to evaluate the government's case against the accused as they would evaluate evidence of wrongdoing against persons in whose law-abidingness they are confident. To help jurors grasp that perspective, judges might provide the trusted friend or coworker heuristic. Granted, the accused is not a trusted friend or coworker, but the heuristic should enable jurors to grasp the viewpoint on the accused that we want them to take up at the outset of trials.

To illustrate this, suppose that we have reason to believe that a police officer is racially biased in his treatment of individuals. He suspects members of races that he dislikes of more or worse criminal conduct and acts accordingly. It might do little good to advise the officer to believe that individuals of other races are no more crime-prone than those of his race. But it might make sense to ask him to evaluate the conduct of members of other races as he evaluates the conduct of members of his own race. If he is prone to harsh assessments of the activities of youths of other races, for instance, we might usefully instruct him to try to view their activities as he would view the activities of his own teenage children or other teenagers of his own race. The hope would be that by doing so, we might subtly reorient his approach to the policing of individuals of other races. In similar ways, PI_m should be interpreted not as telling jurors to somehow magically come to believe in the material innocence of the accused, but as telling them to view the government's case through the lens of the accused's presumed material innocence.

Finally, suppose that it is accepted that PI_m will make it more difficult for government officials to convince jurors of the guilt of defendants who elect trial adjudication. It will be objected, by some, that whether this counts as an argument on its behalf depends on the optimal ratio of errors of mistaken convictions to mistaken acquittals that we hope to achieve in devising charge adjudication schemes. If it becomes harder for government officials to gain convictions, this will probably mean that fewer materially innocent defendants will be convicted. We will therefore avoid what are known as type-1 errors. But it likewise means that fewer materially guilty defendants will be convicted and punished, therefore increasing the number of type-2 errors. Whether PI_m constitutes a benefit to society depends on the ratio of the two kinds of errors we seek and whether PI_m moves us closer to it or further away from it. At the very least, this means that the "jury is still out" with respect to whether or not PI_m is preferable to its competitors.

Some legal scholars take it to be obvious that the design of criminal trials is to be evaluated solely by reference to our interest in the distribution of type-1 and type-2 errors.[35] Earlier, I sketched an alternative normative account of the proof structure of criminal trials, one that I elaborate in the next chapter. According to it, individuals accused of crimes have a secondary moral right—one derived from their more basic moral rights—to demand public, independent, and rigorous evaluation of the evidence against them before legal punishment is imposed upon them. The tripartite proof structure of criminal trials arguably honors this right, which is not to say that alternative charge adjudication procedures would inevitably fail to do so. But in evaluating charge adjudication procedures, our focus should be on their capacities for providing fair, rigorous public trials, not on optimizing the ratio of mistaken acquittals to mistaken convictions. In short, we should not water down the protections afforded criminal defendants during trials in order to achieve more convictions, even convictions of individuals who are likely to be violent recidivists. We should instead invest more societal resources in preventing their crimes or investigating and prosecuting them when they occur. These are matters to which I return in the next chapter.

Concluding Remarks

My focus in this chapter has been on the PI in the trial context. I have urged a robust interpretation of the presumption as a framing perspective for the jurors (or judges) who must reach verdicts in criminal cases. Such an interpretation of the PI is predicated on making trials the stern tests of the government's case that they are supposed to be. Other interpretations of the presumption will, I have argued, yield weaker tests of the government's evidence, even if they are combined with a commitment by jurors to evaluate that evidence in a rigorous and fair fashion.

In the next chapter, I elaborate my account of the proof structure of criminal trials as a complex moral assurance procedure for the justified infliction of legal punishment. Before doing so, however, it will prove useful to step back from the account of the PI in the trial context defended in this chapter to reiterate certain familiar, though crucial, features of it. First of all, it is clear, in the trial context, who is supposed to be presuming the innocence of whom. Jurors (or judges in bench trials) are to presume the innocence of the specific individuals on trial. Second, what it means to presume the innocence of the accused has a specifiable meaning. Jurors are to evaluate evidence proffers by the government through the lens of the accused's presumed innocent and to thereby determine whether it is possible to square their presumed innocence with that evidence. Third, the presumption is, on the account

I have defended, a deliberately adopted perspective in relation to the accused, one taken up in response to judicial instructions. Fourth, and related to the preceding point, it is a presumption that is adopted for a discrete period of time, namely, the duration of the trial. Fifth, it is a perspective whose purview is limited by official inquiry into one or more acts of alleged past criminal misconduct. Sixth, in the trial context, it is clear what rebuts the presumption—proof beyond a reasonable doubt. Seventh, the prescribed outcome of its rebuttal is clear, namely, conviction of the accused on one or more counts, followed by sentencing by a judge and the imposition of that sentence.

Why dwell on what might seem some rather obvious points about the PI in the trial context? Because collectively they give us an account of the PI that is clear, coherent, and precise, and thus a compelling standard against which to judge proposals to extend the PI beyond the trial. As we have already seen, and will see again in subsequent chapters, most such proposals fare poorly by comparison.

CHAPTER 5 | Justifying the Proof Structure of Criminal Trials

IN CONTEMPORARY LEGAL SYSTEMS, individuals accused of crimes are entitled to public trials during which they enjoy a presumption of innocence, the burden of proving guilt is on the government, and the standard of proof that the government must meet is high—typically, "beyond a reasonable doubt."[1] This "proof structure" of criminal trials seems designed to make it hard for the government to convince judges or juries of the validity of the charges it has lodged against individuals. It is natural to believe that the purpose of the high standard of proof, in particular, is to prevent errors of mistaken conviction. In doing so, however, the standard also makes likely the occurrence of errors of the opposite kind, that is, ones of mistaken acquittal. And it might produce many more of the latter kind of errors than it precludes the former kind. If the two kinds of errors were equally serious, it would be puzzling why we ought to set the standard of proof so high and insist that the government bear the burden of meeting it. But according to long-standing tradition, it is thought worse, and perhaps far worse, to wrongly convict the innocent than to wrongly acquit the guilty.[2] Hence, support for this proof structure, including its high standard of proof, remains firmly entrenched.

In the preceding chapter, I developed an account of the PI in the trial context according to which, at the outset of criminal trials, those tasked with rendering verdicts should adopt a framing perspective that makes them initially resistant to the government's evidence against the accused. I indicated that, so understood, the PI is a vital part of a moral assurance procedure for the justified infliction of legal punishment. Because such a procedure requires the legal officials who act on our behalf to establish the guilt of the accused in a public forum to a high level of certainty, we can act with considerable confidence that we are justified in inflicting potentially life-altering criminal sanctions on persons. In this chapter, I elaborate and defend this account of the proof structure of criminal trials, and contrast it with the more widely accepted "error distribution" account sketched in the preceding paragraph.

The error distribution account makes the case for a rigorous proof structure a contingent one. If we could achieve a more optimal distribution of the two types of errors that trials produce by altering the proof structure, then on the error distribution account, alter it we should. That, in turn, might mean that legal punishment would be inflicted on persons against whom the evidence of their guilt was weaker. Indeed, some scholars working with the error distribution account have questioned the defensibility of the proof structure. They have argued that errors of mistaken acquittal are quite bad, even if not as bad as errors of mistaken conviction, especially if the individuals wrongly acquitted have continuing violent criminal proclivities.[3] Also, true convictions can be shown to have clear societal benefits.[4] It has therefore seemed to them a pertinent question to ask whether the proof structure of criminal trials is socially optimal. If, for instance, by lowering the standard of proof we could gain significantly more true convictions, at the cost of only a few mistaken ones, should we not consider doing so? Two further questions have been raised as well: What is the optimal ratio of errors of the two kinds, and how can we tell whether the proof structure of criminal trials is actually yielding it or something close to it?

It is my contention is that the error distribution account misconceives the purpose of the proof structure of criminal trials. The account I defend builds on the notion that legal punishment is one of the most significant and direct exercises of state power over the lives of individuals. Not only does it have the potential to curtail some of the most fundamental rights of citizens, the censure it communicates damages their reputations in ways from which it will be difficult for them to recover. Yet the legal officials who have the tasks of detecting, investigating, and deciding whom to charge with crimes are not only fallible, they are also corruptible. Hence, all of us have vital interests in seeing to it that the institutions that impose legal punishment operate fairly and accurately. Those accused of crimes have the most direct stake in the outcomes of the investigation and adjudication of criminal charges. As a result, they ought to have the final say about whether to demand trials or waive the right to them. We acknowledge this important point by granting the accused the right to a fair trial.

On the account I defend, this is a second-order right, one designed to prevent unjustified curtailment of primary rights to such things as liberty, privacy, and autonomy. But we must take steps to ensure that the exercise of this secondary right is both voluntary and appropriately constrained by the purposes for which we have institutions of legal punishment in the first place.

Importantly, I do not attempt to show that the familiar proof structure of criminal trials is the only or best way for us to have the moral assurance that our use of legal punishment is justified. My contention in this chapter is the more modest one that the proof structure is the kind of procedure that we should provide accused persons before we impose censure and hard treatment upon them. It treats the curtailment of the basic rights of the accused with the moral seriousness that it merits. However, it is possible that other forms of trials exist that likewise accord the basic rights of individuals the respect and concern they deserve and thereby ensure all of us that state power is being exercised responsibly and carefully.

Before developing this alternative justification of the proof structure of criminal trials, I briefly delineate some of the by-now familiar difficulties faced by error distribution accounts of the proof structure. Discussion of the error distribution approach could occupy several chapters. My aim is to do no more than list some of the ways in which it appears unpromising if our goal is to erect a secure foundation for the proof structure. In the second section, I elaborate my alternative account before turning, in the subsequent sections, to various complications with and objections to that account. Chief among these is the concern that the moral assurance account does not give enough weight to avoiding errors of mistaken acquittal and thus to the value of true convictions. I contend that there are other and more effective things society can do to increase the number of true convictions besides tinkering with the proof structure of criminal trials. In the last part of the chapter, I address the contention that the right to a fair trial requires the government to do everything it can to avert errors of mistaken conviction, no matter what the costs of doing so might turn out to be.[5] I argue that such a stringent account of the government's fair trial obligations would undermine its ability to secure basic rights of equal, if not greater, significance. The government fulfills its obligation to citizens to avoid the infliction of unjust punishment upon them so long as it adopts and abides by procedures designed to provide a rigorous and independent evaluation of the government's accusations against them.

Briefly, the Problems with Error Distribution Accounts

Again, some take it to be nearly axiomatic that our purpose in setting up the elaborate proof structure of criminal trials is to achieve some optimal set of outcomes, particularly with respect to the distribution of errors of mistaken acquittal and mistaken conviction over a series of trials. However, beyond this, there is little agreement about how to characterize the optimal set of outcomes or whether the traditional proof structure of criminal trials yields it.[6]

First, there is little agreement on the optimal ratio of mistaken acquittals to mistaken convictions to which we should aspire. Though mistaken convictions seem worse, and some would say much worse, than mistaken acquittals, that insight alone does not yield any precise ratio. Some argue that the conventional ratio of ten to one, suggested by the venerable William Blackstone, is far from obviously correct, especially if the individuals falsely acquitted of crimes have continuing criminal proclivities and the crimes they will subsequently commit are quite serious.[7] Is it really the case, for instance, that we should prefer to let ten guilty murderers or rapists escape conviction and punishment rather than falsely convicting one person of murder or rape, especially if those guilty who escape punishment go onto to commit numerous other murders and rapes? Such a proposition seems an unpromising one to defend. Yet would an eight to one or five to one or three to one ratio be preferable? These are matters concerning which the error distribution literature is either silent or deeply divided.

Second, even if the ten to one ratio is selected, it is not clear whether the reasonable doubt standard, usually cast as .9 certainty on the part of the tribunals who issue verdicts, will yield that ratio in a sufficiently long run of criminal trials. Whether it will do so depends, in part, on the mix of guilty and innocent defendants who go trial, a mix concerning which we lack reliable data. It also depends on the strength of the evidence against defendants, and the ability or willingness of fact-finders to rationally evaluate the evidence.[8] Moreover, some argue that if the value of true convictions is given its proper weight, then something less, and perhaps considerably less, than .9 certainty will yield the desired ten to one ratio.[9]

Third, the difficulties with determining the desired ratio have led some to suggest the alternative of setting the standard of proof by determining which standard will yield the highest expected utility in the outcomes of criminal trials.[10] Doing so would require us to solve the formidable problem of assigning utility values to the four possible outcomes of criminal trials (i.e. true convictions, true acquittals, false convictions, and false acquittals). Assuming we can do that, and no one, to my knowledge has gone beyond listing some of the pros and cons of each of the outcomes, we would then be in a position to aggregate the values for each possible standard of proof and compare them. But doing that would require us to know or at least reasonably predict the outcomes produced by the alternative standards of proof across a range of similar cases. For only if we knew the likely distribution of trial outcomes for each of the candidate standards of proof would we be able to say which of them yields the greatest expected utility. The problem is that it seems doubtful that we know or can reasonably predict the likely distributions.

Fourth, there is a marked tendency on the part of error distribution accounts to focus exclusively on the standard of proof, as if it were the sole or primary determinant of trial outcomes. Yet what I have termed the "proof structure" also includes the presumption of innocence, which criminal defendants are supposed to enjoy, and the burden of proof, which is to be borne by the government. It seems implausible to hold that these two elements play no significant role in determining trial outcomes. If, for instance, jurors in criminal trials must begin with the presumption that nothing has been established about defendants' guilt from the mere fact that they have been charged, it will be harder for the government to make its case than if jurors start with a presumption of the probable guilt of the accused.[11] Likewise, if the accused are expected to shoulder some of the burden of proving their innocence—perhaps by requiring them to convincingly demonstrate any affirmative defense that they wish to make to the charges against them—this would likely affect the distribution of trial outcomes.[12] Yet if alterations in the presumption of innocence or the burden of proof affect trial outcomes, then attempts to devise charge adjudication procedures that achieve the socially desired ratio of false acquittals to false convictions (whatever that ratio is), or maximize the expected utility of trial outcomes, will prove more challenging than they already are.

Fifth, and perhaps most tellingly, error distribution accounts of the proof structure suggest that the status of the standard of proof is contingent. As society's concerns about crime change, or as its concerns about the powers that government officials wield to investigate and combat crime change, so too the standard of proof might have to be strengthened or weakened if we are to maximize expected utility or achieve the socially desirable distribution of errors. Presumably such fluctuations in societal attitudes could also affect the presumption of innocence and the burden of proof. Yet if one is accustomed to thinking that the appropriate proof structure of criminal trials is more fixed and invariant than this, then the inability of error distribution approaches to account for that is troubling.

The Moral Assurance Alternative

The moral assurance account of the proof structure begins with two observations: First, legal punishment is not only an exercise in state power, it is among the most direct and significant exercises of the state's power over the lives of its citizens. Legal punishment typically curtails several of the fundamental rights of persons.[13] Depending on its severity, its curtailment of rights can be dramatic and enduring. Yet basic moral rights to liberty, privacy, and autonomy are not supposed to be curtailed easily or else their considerable moral weight is not given its proper due. Such rights are usually portrayed as "urgent," "peremptory," or even "conclusive" in our deliberations about how to act.[14] This makes sense if they secure the capabilities that persons use to pursue a wide range of ends, purposes, or activities.[15] To deny or frustrate rights is not simply to fail to satisfy desires or preferences that individuals have, even strongly felt ones. It is instead to deprive them of the prerequisites of human agency or the opportunities through which they exercise it. Indeed, according to many rights theorists, rights are not the sorts of things that can be traded off against aggregates of desire or preference satisfaction, though they might be, in some circumstances, traded off against each other.[16] Even thoroughgoing utilitarian accounts of basic rights construe them as interests very high in utility, such that they can only be outweighed by impressive aggregates of desire or preference-satisfaction.[17] Thus, it is widely accepted that basic moral rights are strongly constraining considerations in the design of social, political, and legal institutions and practices.

It follows that we should be cautious about setting up institutions that have the potential to curtail rights. To make matters worse, institutions of legal punishment do more than curtail basic rights for the duration of the sentences they employ. Legal punishment also communicates censure, thereby tarnishing the reputations of persons in ways that will typically extend beyond the duration of their sentences.[18] Also, when legal punishment takes the form of imprisonment, its long-term effects can be devastating. Imprisonment scars persons psychologically and socially, and diminishes their abilities to find decent, well-paying jobs.[19] A serious criminal record relegates persons to the social and economic margins of society.

Second, it is apparent to anyone who pays attention to the actual workings of criminal justice systems that the officials who make decisions about whom to arrest or investigate, whom to charge and with what charges, and how to proceed with the adjudication of charges, are fallible and sometimes malevolent. The list of ways in which criminal investigations can go awry is long and worrisome, even if the officials who err do so with the best of intentions. Police jump to conclusions about suspects and tunnel vision prevents them from considering other suspects; suspects "confess" to crimes under prolonged and intense interrogation; eyewitnesses are coached by the police or prosecutors or they simply make mistakes; individuals with their own wrongdoing to conceal or downplay implicate others; evidence is tainted in the process of gathering it, mistakenly analyzed, or used despite expert doubts about its validity; prosecutors adopt a conviction mentality that convinces them that a plea to something is better than a dismissal, even if they recognize that the evidence against accused persons is frightfully thin.[20] And, of course, some errors by criminal justice officials will not be unintentional. In what is hopefully a small number of cases, the police concoct or plant evidence in order to implicate individuals whom they suspect of crimes or whom they just do not like. Or they take bribes to ignore certain kinds of offenses or offenders and focus on others. These realities of the criminal justice process should chasten us. Recognizing that they occur, and perhaps occur with some frequency, we should insist upon rigorous procedures for the imposition of legal punishment. Errors in conviction are most costly to the individuals who suffer wrongful convictions. But they are also costly to the taxpayers who support the institutions of legal punishment and who are not protected when the real perpetrators of crimes go unpunished. Further, legal punishment is carried out in the names of all citizens; the prospect of mistakes should gall us and make our support for exacting charge adjudication procedures unstinting.

Fortunately, the proof structure of criminal trials appears to offer such an exacting procedure. It requires the government to put forward its case in a public setting, overseen by an impartial judge, and to convince a jury that the accused are guilty, beyond a reasonable doubt. Jurors are to begin trials by viewing the accused as materially innocent, thereby putting the onus on the government to convince them otherwise. If the government can persuade them not only to abandon the PI but to come to believe that the accused are almost certainly guilty, then it will have done what it must do to show that the infliction of legal punishment upon them is justified.

Error distribution accounts of the proof structure of criminal trials have part of the story correctly. Trials, with their elaborate proof structures, are vital mechanisms for filtering out official error or malfeasance. To deny individuals access to independent tribunals that carefully evaluate the accumulated evidence devalues their rights, making them too easily cast aside when the authorities have a mind to punish those whom they suspect of crimes or simply do not like. Yet error distribution accounts mislead, in my view, by making it seem as if the proof structure of criminal trials is nothing more than an attempt to maintain an appropriate balance between the kinds of errors that charge adjudication produces. Such accounts therefore seem consistent with altering or abandoning the proof structure if doing so will produce a more optimal distribution of errors. They thereby sleight the role of the proof structure as constituting the kind of procedure that respect for basic human rights requires as a prerequisite of their curtailment.

To the preceding, it might be objected that we permit criminal justice officials, in particular the police, to intrude upon the basic rights of citizens in various ways long before they are actually convicted at trials incorporating such a well-defined proof structure. If providing accused persons the right to challenge the government's accusations against them is a prerequisite to the curtailment of their rights, then how can arresting persons, detaining and questioning them, or executing search warrants on their property or records be justified on the moral assurance account? Part of the answer to this objection is that the arrests of individuals and the investigation of charges against them intrude upon their rights in limited ways and do not yet convey official censure for proven misconduct. This is not to deny, of course, that arrest, investigation, and charges are stigmatizing. They are, but they do not amount to a court's conveyance of official censure for proven wrongdoing. Also, as we have already seen, we should require the authorities to have and provide reasons for such intrusions, in order to rebut right-based presumptions against them. The more extensive the intrusions upon individuals' rights, or the longer their duration, the stronger those reasons should have to be. At the pretrial limit, and it is a controversial one as we shall see, law enforcement officials might request that a court detain those formally charged with crimes. Even if such detention can be defended, it seems clear that the strength of the justifying reasons in support of it must be significantly greater than those provided in support of brief police stops and questionings. Why should this be so? Because pretrial detention drastically curtails individuals' basic rights to liberty and freedom of association, among others, and is too often indistinguishable, in practice, from imprisonment for proven offenses. On the account I defend, the more the authorities seek to intrude upon or interfere with the basic rights of citizens, the stronger the reasons they must give in order to justify doing so. Also, the more intrusive official actions become, the stronger the case will be for advance authorizations of them, by independent judicial officers.[21] Such authorizations will help to ensure that the reasons police or prosecutors have are not mere pretexts for harassing citizens or intimidating them, but are instead reasons of the appropriate kinds, ones backed by convincing evidence of past (or perhaps future) misconduct that is within the purview of the criminal law.

Some Complications with the Moral Assurance Account

Given the account of the proof structure as a moral assurance procedure outlined in the previous section, it might not seem clear why we should permit the decision whether to go to trial be the accused person's to make. On the moral assurance account, all of us, and not just accused persons, have substantial interests in seeing to it that basic rights are not curtailed casually. In particular, members of the public should want to ensure that crime investigative and charge adjudicative processes are working properly to convict and punish offenders. Mistaken punishment is costly to the public, and not simply by its needless infliction of sanctions on the innocent. Why, then, cast the right to trial as the accused's to exercise or not, as he or she sees fit? Why not, instead, require all accused persons to submit to trials with their demanding proof structures?

To begin with, though the public (not to mention the victims of crimes) have significant interests in the appropriate investigation and adjudication of charges, it is the accused themselves who have the most direct stake in the outcomes of the investigation and adjudication of criminal charges. It is their liberty, reputations, property, and, in some cases, lives that are on the line. As a result, we might believe that their decisions about whether to go to trial are fairly reliable indicators concerning whether police or prosecutors have made mistakes or are acting capriciously or malevolently. If the accused are not inclined to challenge the government's case against them in order to prevent their basic rights from being unjustifiably curtailed, why should we insist that they submit the government's case to the test of the proof structure? To this it might be added that, though police and prosecutors make mistakes and occasionally act with less than good intentions, it does not follow that they always or usually do so. In many cases, they will have the actual perpetrators of crimes in their grips and the evidence to convict them. Knowing this, as surely they do, many persons charged with crimes see little point in prolonging the inevitable by insisting on trial adjudication of the charges against them.[22] It seems doubtful that we would want them to act otherwise in such cases.

It therefore makes sense to view the right to trial as a second-order moral right of accused persons. As such, it is a right that exists and is exercised at the discretion of the individuals whose basic rights are threatened with curtailment by legal punishment. To this it might be objected that we should not trust accused persons to act in their own and society's best interests in deciding whether to exercise the right to trial. In some countries, prosecutors, and sometimes judges, are permitted to exert various forms of pressure on accused persons to waive the right to trial and enter guilty pleas. Plea-bargaining practices crucially depend on what is known as the "sentencing differential," which is the difference in sentences assigned accused persons who plead guilty to charges and the sentences assigned accused persons who exercise the right to trial and are convicted of the same or similar charges. The concern is that official manipulation of the sentencing differential undermines the voluntariness of trial waivers. As a result, it is thought that some accused persons might plead guilty though they are innocent, or not provably guilty.

It is possible to concede this point while holding to the notion that the right to trial ought to be the accused person's to exercise. As already noted in chapter 2, part of the solution to inflated sentencing differentials is to adopt measures to substantially limit their magnitude.[23] If accused persons do not stand to gain much of a reduction in the sentences assigned to them by falsely pleading guilty, then we will have more assurance that pleas signal their likely guilt on the charges against them. Another part of the solution is to try to limit the "process costs" of going to trial.[24] Such costs might also induce some innocent persons to waive the right to trial and plead guilty. This seems especially likely in cases in which individuals who already have criminal records are charged with relatively minor offenses. Such individuals have little to gain by way of protecting their reputations and might elect to get on with their punishment, and thus more quickly resume their lives, by tendering guilty pleas.[25] We can reduce the temptation to do so by, among other things, eliminating or at least strongly discouraging the pretrial detention of individuals charged with minor offenses.

A further constraint on waivers of the right to trial should be implemented as well. Before any accused person is permitted to plead guilty, a judge should determine that there is at least a preponderance of the evidence supporting the charges against the person.[26] If a judge determines that this evidence sufficiency standard is not met in a given case, she should refuse to accept an accused person's guilty plea. Such a constraint on the plea process would serve two distinguishable purposes. First, it would provide some backup assurance that accused persons are not pleading guilty solely to minimize process costs or receive the modestly reduced sentences that a defensible plea concession scheme would permit. Second, and more importantly, requiring judges to examine the evidence in guilty plea cases would enable them to determine whether and to what extent police and prosecutors are acting in accordance with the overall aims of the criminal justice system. To facilitate this determination by judges, they should be provided full evidence dossiers ahead of the hearings at which accused persons are scheduled to enter pleas. This would enable judges to detect and, hopefully, discourage illicit forms of charge and fact bargaining, both of which have the potential to distort the character of the crimes committed by individuals and thus the punishment those prepared to waive the right to trial wind up receiving.[27] Judges should be permitted to question prosecutors about the charges they have filed and accused persons about the crimes they committed and their reasons for admitting their guilt. I would also permit the victims of crimes, if there are any, to file affidavits with the court if they believe that the charges levied against individuals by prosecutors distort the offenses committed against them. This is common practice in many countries that permit guilty pleas, albeit under more restricted conditions than are the norm in countries with more freewheeling forms of plea bargaining.[28] In short, granting accused persons the pivotal role in deciding whether or not charges against them should be put to the test of the proof structure of criminal trials is perfectly consistent with adopting measures to ensure that waivers of the right to trial occur under conditions designed to protect the myriad interests of accused persons, victims, and the public.

Suppose that accused persons exercise the right to trial and thus to put the government's case against them to the test of a trial's proof structure. Trials are not only elaborately structured, they are public, and this is true even if some accused persons might prefer them not to be. It could be argued that this publicity requirement is invariably in the interests of accused persons. Yet some scholars argue that such a position is dubious when the charges are of certain kinds (e.g., involving prohibited sexual conduct).[29] Hence, if the right to trial is the accused's to exercise or not, should we consider allowing the accused to elect nonpublic trials if that is what they want?

The first point I would make in response to this line of argument is this: While it is true that the presentation of the evidence at trials can be highly embarrassing to the accused, so is the announcement of charges and verdicts of "guilty" by the courts. No one seriously doubts that these other two bookending events are properly public. Once they are publicized, it might seem that the accused have little residual interest in nonpublic trials. However, consider trials that result in acquittals. It could be argued that if trials were nonpublic, at least the accused would not have had to endure the public dissemination of the government's evidence against them, with its possible tarnishing effects on their reputations. Fair enough. Still, this provides only minimal support for nonpublic trials, for there are well-known dangers to such trials. One thing the glare of publicity does is to help ensure that criminal justice officials behave properly before and during trials, according to established procedural and evidentiary rules. Knowing that the public, or perhaps a subset of the public, is watching them, police, prosecutors, and judges will be more inclined to abide by the rules of full and fair due process. We might worry that without such oversight, some of them will be more inclined to cut corners, especially when the accused have long criminal histories and the evidence against them in the extant case seems convincing. Even judges are known to be skeptical about accused persons' claims that they are not guilty.[30]

In response, it might be argued that other criminal justice officials, higher in police or prosecutorial bureaucracies can be expected to exert the needed oversight of those below them in the event of nonpublic trials.[31] Perhaps so, but this assumes, rather too conveniently in my view, that the overseeing officials will be disposed to correct what they perceive to be mistakes or biased judgments on the part of those under their purview. They might, instead, acquiesce in them, to maintain solidarity in their ranks or advance their careers by burnishing their reputations as "team players."[32] One suspects that the temptation to "go along and get along" will be especially strong when the crimes in question are notorious and the accused are known offenders.

Even if it cannot be convincingly shown that the accused have (or always have) decisively weighty interests in the publicity of trials, there are others who have interests in them, and these can be brought in to cement the case for public trials. In countries such as the United States and England, the vast majority of accused persons elect to forgo trials.[33] As I have already noted, we ought to be concerned about the conditions under which the accused make these decisions. But given the rarity of trial demands, when they do occur, it is reasonable to wonder whether the government officials involved in bringing charges have behaved appropriately. Have the accused been harassed by the police, or unfairly targeted by them or by prosecutors? Have they been falsely accused of crimes for which they might suffer unjust punishment, with its substantial costs to them and to the public which must pay for it? These are important questions to which public trials can help provide answers. Nonpublic trials would make it difficult, if not impossible, for citizens to monitor the behavior of criminal justice officials when it is arguably most needed.[34] Also, the victims of crimes have a stake in public trials, because such trials enable them to see whether and to what extent police and prosecutors have taken the crimes committed against them seriously and worked to achieve appropriate penal outcomes.

Doubts Concerning the Reasonable Doubt Standard

My contention is that the familiar proof structure of criminal trials is an appropriate moral assurance procedure for the infliction of legal punishment. Again, that proof structure, suitably interpreted, is a powerful remedy for official error, overreaching, or corruption. Suppose it is conceded that the basic rights of individuals give us more than adequate grounds for positing a second-order right to fair trials. It might nonetheless seem unclear whether such a right requires us to adopt each of the elements of the familiar proof structure of criminal trials, or the entire panoply of them. Why believe that only that proof structure, but no other one, no matter how functionally equivalent to it, can secure effectively the vital interest individuals have in fair trials? Again, my aim in this chapter is to defend the limited claim that the proof structure appears a good candidate for securing those interests. Other ways of securing them might exist, though one would have to spell them out and demonstrate their feasibility in this regard (just as one must do so with the more familiar proof structure). It is easy to say that other ways of satisfying the right to a fair trial exist; the challenge is to elaborate them and show that they are likely to do the job. Also, even if we add to the proof structure other elements that are widely recognized to be essential to fair trials—the right to be informed of the charges and the evidence against one, to challenge that evidence and provide exonerating evidence, and to do all of this with the help of competent counsel—there remains considerable room for variation in the forms fair trials might take.

To go a bit further with this, it is apparent that Anglo-American jury trials, with their strongly adversarial character, reliance on citizen jurors, and unanimity or strong majority verdict requirements, are not the only or necessarily the best mechanisms for ensuring realization of the right to a rigorous and independent evaluation of the evidence against persons accused of crimes. One has to demonstrate these claims and do so while comparing such trials with their counterparts in civil law systems.[35] When it comes to the makeup of the independent tribunal, the procedural rules according to which evidence is presented, and the roles of the various main participants in criminal trials, there is considerable room for debate about how best to structure trials. Indeed, it seems likely that there is no one best structure, but a number of defensible ones. Still, these diverse trial forms arguably all preserve a common proof structure in the form of the presumption of innocence, the burden of proof, and the standard of proof. Whether that core can be altered, while honoring the right to a fair trial, is a further question. Even with respect to it, we should concede that the answer might be "yes."

The preceding remarks will be thought by some to evade the more pertinent question—whether the right I have articulated requires use of the reasonable doubt standard in whatever proof structure is adopted in a given society. One plausible interpretation of that standard is that it is met if the government can present multiple, independent lines of evidence establishing the guilt of the accused and rebut all evidenced alternative explanations of the events in question according to which the accused are not guilty of the relevant charges.[36] As we have seen, it is the standard of proof on which error distribution accounts focus. Some who favor such accounts have questioned its retention. How and to what extent does my alternative account support the standard? As I conceive it, our concern in setting the standard of proof ought not to be one about preserving some optimal distribution of trial outcome errors. Instead, our focus should be on honoring accused persons' rights to rigorous, independent evaluation of the government's case against them. Why might honoring that right require the reasonable doubt standard? The answer cannot be that the standard is entailed directly by the element of "rigorousness" in the statement of the right, for saying so comes too close to circular reasoning.

To address this challenge from error distribution theorists, recall why it seemed important to insist that accused persons have a right to demand a rigorous and impartial evaluation of the government's charges against them. The rights that might be curtailed by legal punishment are not mere interests of persons, if by this we mean desires that they happen to strongly wish to be satisfied. Instead, they are interests that are foundational in individuals' lives, in the sense that their realization makes a variety of activities and pursuits possible and thereby enables individuals to craft decent lives of their own choosing. Interests as foundational as these should not be easily curtailed. This gets us some way toward insisting that if the government is to curtail them, it must satisfy a demanding test of its evidence.

But why not think that the appropriate test of rigor is, for instance, a "more plausible than the alternatives" test? On such a test, the government should prevail if its account, according to which an accused person has committed one or more crimes, is more plausible than the accused person's account, according to which he has not.[37] Though I believe that we should reject this weaker test, it must be conceded that the case for the more stringent, reasonable doubt standard depends, to some extent, on the seriousness of the criminal allegations in question. In cases in which the crimes alleged are felonies that carry with them the possibility of imprisonment, it seems clear that the individuals on trial stand to lose a great deal if convicted. But what if the crimes of which individuals are accused are less serious, such that the legal sanctions they face will consist mostly of minor burdens or inconveniences? Erik Lillquist has suggested that although the reasonable doubt standard might be defensible for serious offenses, a lower standard of proof might be sufficient for less serious ones.[38]

It is, I would admit, difficult to understand why we would insist on elaborate trials, replete with the reasonable doubt standard, for offenses that carry with them no more than the threat of modest fines. Still, some sort of hearing at which the government is required to present its evidence and the accused are given the opportunity to dispute it would seem to be in order in such cases, and substantial doubts about the guilt of the accused ought to be resolved in their favor. The preceding concession to opponents of the reasonable doubt standard does not carry us very far, however. Any criminal charge for which the accused might face a term of imprisonment, even if for only a brief period, threatens a significant curtailment of their rights. Accordingly, the grounds for insisting that the government's evidence must be strongly convincing to an independent tribunal seem impressive. This means that most all felonies and some misdemeanors ought to be covered by the reasonable doubt standard. Also, misdemeanors convictions for which the available sanctions are modest can have implications for future sentencing decisions. Many jurisdictions permit or require sentencing judges to take convicted persons' prior records into account in assigning them sentences for their most recent convictions.[39] Thus, just about any significant criminal conviction is a serious matter with implications for the rights of individuals and therefore activates their second-order right to demand a rigorous, independent evaluation of the government's evidence.

A further objection begins with the observation that in tort law, the standard of proof in trials is much lower—a preponderance of the evidence—and yet a finding of liability can result in significant infringements upon the property rights of tortfeasors, who might be required by the courts to pay substantial compensation to those they have injured. If the law permits infringement of the rights of citizens based on a mere preponderance of the evidence in tort cases, why should it have to adopt a much higher standard when it comes to the imposition of criminal sanctions?

The answer to this question is that criminal convictions have considerably more adverse implications for the rights of individuals than do findings of tort liability. Legal punishment censures individuals for their conduct and imposes hard treatment on them in the form of losses or deprivations, some of which might substantially curtail their basic rights to liberty, privacy, and autonomy for lengthy periods of time. The expressive character of legal punishment also sets offenders apart from the law-abiding public and stigmatizes them as wrongdoers. Findings of tort liability might be embarrassing to individuals, but the aim of tort law is compensation for victims, not censure of tortfeasors.[40] Further, though required tort compensation limits the rights of tortfeasors, such losses tend to pale in comparison with those imposed by criminal sanctions, especially when such sanctions take the form of imprisonment. Tortfeasors can generally go on living their lives, though required compensation payments might cramp their abilities to do so. Those censured by the criminal law and sent to jail or prison cannot go on living their lives, at least not during the time of their incarceration and likely for some time afterward. Also, their criminal convictions are apt to dog them—marking them as violent, predatory, or unreliable in ways that findings of tort liability seem less apt to do. Finally, individuals can indemnify themselves against tort compensation payments by purchasing insurance. In the event that they are found liable for others' injuries, their insurance companies pay most of the damages, leaving tortfeasors free to go on about their lives. Criminal offenders cannot similarly evade the losses imposed on them by criminal sanctions. It thus makes sense to require the government to meet a higher standard of proof before criminal sanctions are imposed.

The Moral Assurance Account and the Guilty

The moral assurance account might seem curiously insensitive to the negative consequences of the tripartite proof structure of criminal trials. I have suggested that the structure exists as one plausible way of effectively securing the second-order moral right to a fair trial. I have thus parted ways with more familiar accounts that cast the proof structure as a mechanism for optimally distributing the two kinds of trial outcome errors, or maximizing the expected utility of trial outcomes over a sufficiently lengthy period of time. The account I have offered is one-sided in its focus on accused persons and the obstacles that the state must surmount to justifiably curtail their rights. Yet to some, it will seem foolish to suggest that we should craft rules of criminal procedure without thinking about how they will impact our ability to convict the guilty.

The approach I defend is, however, fully consistent with granting government officials formidable powers to apprehend and punish those guilty of crimes. The rights of citizens, and in particular, the second-order right of those citizens accused of crimes to fair trials, are best conceived as constraints on the government's crime-fighting function. Importantly, if we believe that government officials are not able to do their jobs effectively, there are numerous things we can do to help them. We can supply funds to hire more police officers and criminal investigators and equip them with better technology or provide them with better training. We can also employ more prosecutors, staff more criminal courts, and build more prisons. There are costs to doing all of these things, of course, and the burdens will be borne by taxpaying citizens, as presumably they should be, for such citizens are the ones who stand to benefit from an increased emphasis on crime detection and sanctioning.

We could also make the crime-fighting jobs of government officials easier by converting the presumption of innocence to a presumption of guilt, placing the burden of proof on those accused of crimes, or lowering the standard of proof. The costs of such measures will generally fall on the accused, and especially those among them who are wholly or partially innocent, though law-abiding citizens will also bear the costs of wrongful convictions. Unlike error distribution accounts, which would have us balance such costs against the costs of mistaken acquittals, the approach I defend eschews such balancing. If too many of the guilty are escaping conviction, the solution is to spend more on apprehending and convicting them, not diluting protections afforded the accused aimed at ensuring that their basic rights are not unjustifiably curtailed.

It will be objected, however, that how we set up the proof structure of criminal trials affects the rights of others in society beyond the individuals accused of crimes. When individuals are falsely acquitted because of the reasonable doubt standard, their victims (assuming that their crimes had victims) will not have their rights symbolically reaffirmed by the government.[41] Worse than this, individuals mistakenly acquitted because the government could not satisfy the reasonable doubt standard might go on to commit further and sometimes serious offenses. When the harms suffered by the victims of such crimes are substantial, they might equal or exceed those suffered by the mistakenly convicted. If our aim is to protect rights, then we should consider trading off the rights of the accused against the rights of the past or future "victims" of the reasonable doubt standard. Larry Laudan, for instance, focuses on known recidivists accused of crimes and cites disturbing figures about their likely future offenses, in an attempt to convince us that the reasonable doubt standard is far from intuitively defensible given its high costs in such cases.[42] Suppose that certain violent recidivists can be predicted to commit ten to fifteen crimes per year. If wrongly acquitted at trial because of the reasonable doubt standard, they might escape several years of imprisonment. Laudan invites us to multiply those years by the estimated number of the offenses they will commit each year to gain a clearer appreciation of the enormous costs—to the rights of innocent citizens—of the reasonable doubt standard. Surely the approach I defend is unattractive if it tells us to ignore those costs and focus solely on the rights of the accused.

Laudan's argument casts the error distribution approach to the proof structure of criminal trials within what has been termed a "utilitarianism of rights" framework.[43] According to that framework, we should try to figure out which proof structure will produce the maximum (or optimal) overall satisfaction of the various rights claims that individuals have. True, individuals accused of crimes might have the right to demand rigorous, independent examinations of the evidence against them before their basic moral rights are curtailed by legal punishment. But their right-claims have to be weighed against the claims of the victimized to the vindication of their rights by the government and the rights of individuals who, if the accused have violent criminal proclivities, they might victimize in the future. Once we are prepared to weigh the rights of the accused against the rights of their past and possible future victims, it is suddenly less clear that the proof structure of criminal trials as we know it, with its high standard of proof, maximizes the satisfaction of the respective rights claims, especially in cases in which the accused have long and violent criminal histories.

The invitation to weigh and balance moral right claims in this way might be refused. Some theorists interpret moral rights as categorical side-constraints or as trumps against collective goals of various kinds.[44] As such, they are not to be understood as susceptible to being traded off against considerations of general utility or even against one another, except perhaps in extreme and unusual circumstances. But rather than insisting on such a controversial account of rights, it seems better to try to address Laudan's argument on its own terms. I believe that there are enough problems with it to discourage most proponents of rights consequentialism from abandoning the high standard of proof in criminal cases.

Laudan's argument focuses narrowly on violent recidivists accused of new crimes and the standard of proof that the government must meet to convict them. Yet once one adopts a consequentialist approach to the various rights that might be in play, there is no reason why one should not reconsider the presumption of innocence and the burden of proof. Why not tell jurors at the outset of trials of known, violent recidivists that they should view the accused as likely guilty and as having to prove their innocence? Perhaps such an approach with such defendants would produce the optimal results, as compared with granting them the PI at the outset of their trials and requiring the government to bear the burden of proof. Laudan could embrace this implication of his argument, though it does raise the concern that the deck is being stacked rather heavily against such defendants. My point is simply that there is nothing about the logic of the consequentialist approach that precludes having to consider alterations in the proof structure beyond lowering the standard of proof. Laudan does not pursue these complications in his discussion.

His focus on known, violent recidivists makes sense in one way but is puzzling in another. It makes sense if one is concerned about the rights of future victims and the possible impact of the standard of proof in extant cases. But it is puzzling if one focuses on the victims of the current, alleged crimes (assuming there were victims) and their claims to have their rights vindicated by the government, for why should it matter whether those who violated their rights are violent recidivists or not? Victims presumably want their rights vindicated regardless of the past history of the individuals who violated them. Perhaps Laudan is unimpressed by such rights-claims of recent victims, believing them to be too suspect or weak to justify lowering the standard of proof. Or perhaps he recognizes that, instead of lowering the standard of proof and thus better securing the rights of future victims (though at some cost in terms of convictions of more innocents), there are other, and maybe better, things society can do to "stand for" the rights of crime victims. For instance, society could publicly condemn their victimization quite independently of punishing anyone for it, or better still, provide them (or their surviving family members) with compensation for their injuries or losses.[45] But then, as I have already noted, there are other, and maybe better, things society can do to try to protect future victims besides diluting the standard of proof in criminal trials. Hiring more police and providing them with better crime-detecting and investigative technologies will also reduce the number of future victims, and it will do so without having to sacrifice the rights of criminal defendants. Similar things might be said about improving the educational and economic opportunities of the most downtrodden in society, providing adequate mental health care to all citizens, and making prisons more humane and less debilitating. Laudan assumes that sending individuals to prison is an unproblematic crime-reduction strategy. But while imprisonment might temporarily incapacitate offenders and thereby reduce their crimes, current harsh forms of it might also make them more violent and crime-prone.[46]

Laudan's focus on known recidivists makes the rights-balancing argument more convincing than it otherwise might be. Why is this? Because by doing so he makes the costs of the high standard of proof seem more probable, where these costs are understood in terms of unjustly acquitting individuals who will go on to commit violent offenses. Lowering the standard of proof in the trials of all defendants would seem a dubious strategy for preventing lots of violent crimes, since many of those accused of crimes will not go on to commit subsequent violent offenses if they are acquitted on the current charges. Only violent recidivists seem likely to do so. Yet Laudan ignores the evidence that recidivists accused of crimes might be among those most in need of the protections afforded by the proof structure of criminal trials. Numerous legal scholars have noted that when the police are unsure about the perpetrators of crimes, they focus on known offenders.[47] Such "usual suspects" policing is worrisome, especially when the police or other investigators shift their focus from investigating known offenders to developing cases against them, sometimes through dishonest or other questionable means.[48] Also, prosecutors will be reluctant to believe known offenders' protestations of innocence, more or less regardless of the quality of the evidence against such individuals.[49] Hence, though Laudan is right to argue that mistaken acquittals of recidivists are socially costly, he does not seem concerned enough about the dangers of lowering the standard of proof in cases involving them.

Laudan also pays little attention to the risks of subjecting some criminal defendants to different standards of proof for their alleged crimes. Even if it is possible to rigorously define the criteria identifying the defendants who will be subject to the lower standard of proof, prosecutors and judges might seek to expand the pool of defendants eligible for the relaxed standards or implement the criteria in ways that subtly or not so subtly discriminate against the poor or socially marginalized. It might be better, in other words, to have a single, uniform standard of proof than different standards for different defendants.

Further, Laudan's argument gains considerable traction from the notion that a significant number of violent recidivists are unleashed on society because of the high standard of proof. But there are reasons to doubt this. As we have seen, in the United States, about 95 percent of the individuals charged with crimes ultimately plead guilty rather than insist on trial adjudication of the charges against them.[50] Prosecutors in the United States have been given daunting powers by legislators and the courts to "persuade" individuals charged with crimes to plead guilty, and this with no more than what are widely believed to be perfunctory determinations by judges that there is a "factual basis" for guilty pleas. Among the powers accorded to prosecutors is largely unfettered charging discretion, which means that prosecutors can routinely overcharge defendants in order to menace them with extraordinarily long sentences should they risk trials and be convicted.[51] Prosecutors also can offer substantial charge reductions and lenient sentencing recommendations in exchange for pleas, thus opening up vast sentencing differentials between trial and plea-bargained outcomes. Also, accused persons who foolishly resist entering pleas can be threatened with trial penalties, in the form of harsh posttrial sentencing recommendations on any charges of which they are ultimately convicted.[52] Further, legislators have empowered prosecutors by enacting sentencing schemes with substantial sentence ranges for the various offense types.[53] Prosecutors then employ threats of sentences at or near the tops of these ranges in order to extract guilty pleas, even if they do not believe that the crimes in question merit such sentences. To all of this, add the fact that, at least with respect to those charged with felonies, the government wins an estimated 80 percent of the cases that go to trial.[54] Even on the assumption that the vast majority of those who go to trial are, in fact, guilty of some or all of the charges against them, some of them would not be eligible for the reduced standard of proof because they are not violent recidivists. Given all of this, it does not seem plausible to hold that significant numbers of violent recidivists are being mistakenly acquitted due to the reasonable doubt standard.[55] Few such individuals charged with crimes will go to trial; fewer still will gain acquittals. Only someone whose glass is well more than half empty can look at the United States criminal justice system and conclude that diluting that standard in a relatively few cases will yield a more favorable overall balance of rights claims.

Should We Do "Everything Possible" to Avoid Mistaken Convictions?

Laudan is more persuasive when he chastises legal scholars who insist that "everything possible" must be done to avoid convictions of the innocent. Labeling them "garantistas," Laudan lists the many things that we could do, but have not done, to prevent convictions of the innocent. Among the "reforms" we could adopt to reduce errors of mistaken conviction are excluding all confessions by suspects or defendants, prohibiting the use of inculpatory evidence from accomplices where that evidence has been procured by plea deals, employing a "beyond all doubt" standard of proof, and unconditionally excluding all evidence about defendants' past criminal histories.[56] If garantistas balk at adopting these and other reforms, as Laudan believes they should, then they are conceding that we should not be doing everything possible to avoid errors of mistaken conviction.

I have not claimed that the second-order right of criminal defendants to fair trials implies that the government, or society, must do "everything possible" to avoid mistaken convictions. Nevertheless, it will be useful to make clear why my position does not entail such a proposition. The reason it does not do so is straightforward enough: Though rights generate duties on the part of other persons to not interfere with the associated capabilities, and in the case of government officials, to protect individuals and help them realize those capabilities, it does not follow that anyone has a duty to do "everything possible" to secure them.[57] Take the right to liberty, for instance. Though the government must undertake reasonable measures to secure it for persons, such as passing laws that prohibit interferences with it and enforcing them, it is not clear what it would mean to say that the government must do "everything possible" to protect the liberty of individuals. Granted, there will be circumstances in which the government might do more to protect liberty rights than it is doing. But there will always be something more it could be doing to reduce unjust infringements of citizens' liberty rights. It could hire more police, provide twenty-four-hour surveillance of neighborhoods and homes, and monitor more closely the activities of known offenders. Yet at some point, we must accept that further societal investments in protecting liberty are unwarranted, in part because expending more resources on protecting it will mean that other important rights are left insufficiently secured.

In the case of the secondary right to a fair trial, I have claimed only that the government must, if it is to overcome the presumption against curtailing the basic moral rights of its citizens, provide a public forum in which there is a rigorous, independent evaluation of the evidence against defendants. There is room for debate about exactly what the government must do to satisfy this requirement, and there is likely more than one way in which it can do so. But having to provide such a forum and ensuring that it is structured to reliably separate the defendants regarding whom the government has highly persuasive probative evidence from defendants regarding whom it does not is one thing. Having to do "everything possible" to avoid errors of mistaken conviction is quite another.

Just to be clear, I am not saying that existing governments should not be doing more to protect the innocent. As most everyone who has examined it acknowledges, the indigent defense system in the United States is appallingly underfunded.[58] But fixing that system need not be cast as part of an effort to do "everything possible" to prevent conviction of the innocent. Instead, doing so can be defended on the more modest grounds that providing effective assistance of legal counsel is part and parcel of ensuring that those accused of crimes get fair hearings. After all, a fair trial will not be possible for defendants who do not understand the crimes of which they are accused, the rules of criminal procedure or evidence according to which they will be tried, and who therefore are effectively stymied in their efforts to challenge the admissibility of evidence or raise pertinent questions about it during the course of a trial.

Concluding Remarks

One of the principal functions of the state is to secure the rights of its citizens to such things as liberty, physical and psychological integrity, autonomy, and property. In order to do so it must prohibit certain kinds of conduct and enforce those prohibitions. In the process of doing so, it will inevitably intrude upon and ultimately curtail the rights of some its citizens to act as they see fit. Yet it would be an odd system of right-enforcement if the state was permitted to curtail the rights of citizens in the absence of a clear, authoritative, and public showing that they have exceeded the bounds of their rights. Rights would not be worth much to us if they could be taken away or curtailed because some officials believe that we have exceeded them, especially when those officials are far from trustworthy or unbiased in the formation of their suspicions about the conduct of their fellow citizens. We thus permit individuals accused of crimes to insist that the evidence developed by state officials against them be put to a rigorous and dispositive test. We make the test a stern one because so much is at stake for those accused of crimes.

The familiar proof structure of criminal trials is indisputably a demanding test of the state's evidence. Whether alternative proof structures can provide such a test is debatable. Those who believe that they can should try to convince us of their claims. However, we should reject arguments for alternative proof structures premised upon making it easier for the state to amass convictions of the guilty. Such arguments betray a misunderstanding of why we make it hard for the government to prove the guilt of criminal defendants. We do not do so in order to attain some optimal ratio of mistaken acquittals to mistaken convictions. Instead, we do so in order to assure ourselves that when we punish our fellow citizens, we do so justifiably.

CHAPTER 6 | Do We Need a Pretrial Presumption of Innocence?

TO THIS POINT, I HAVE argued against accounts of the PI that are more ambitious and in favor of one that assigns it a significant, albeit limited, role in the context of criminal trials. Some scholars might concur with my critique of the more extravagant claims made about the PI but challenge the narrowness of my own account. Even if the PI is not appropriately construed to be a substantive human right, a constraint on the content of the criminal law, or appropriately regulative of our more informal dealings with other members of society, there is one context in which it might seem to apply that my account does not appear to accommodate. As we have seen, numerous human rights documents proclaim a right of individuals suspected of or formally accused of crimes to be presumed innocent until proven guilty in a court of law.[1] These documents are lauded by legal scholars, many of whom hold that the PI is an important pretrial procedural constraint. These scholars find many tasks for the PI to perform in the pretrial context. For some, the presumption is needed in order to discourage the authorities from inflicting punishment upon individuals, or publicly declaring them to be guilty, before their guilt has been authoritatively determined.[2] For others, a pretrial PI is needed to protect the fair trial process; individuals widely and publicly depicted as guilty before their trials occur seem more vulnerable to conviction by judges or citizen jurors.[3]

Beyond protecting fair trial rights, some scholars, as we have already seen, contend that a pretrial PI is needed to protect the "reputation-related interests" of individuals.[4] By discouraging public depictions of their guilt by legal authorities, the PI shields the good names and reputations of the accused, thereby making it easier for them to resume their lives in the event that the charges against them are dropped or they are acquitted. There is also the contention that a pretrial PI is needed in order to explain why police and prosecutors must justify each successive stage of their intrusion into the lives of individuals whom they suspect of crimes as they investigate them.[5] Because individuals are presumed innocent, police must have reasonable grounds to stop and question individuals or to arrest them. Police must also get warrants to search their property, and bear the burden of convincing a judge or magistrate of the necessity of holding suspects in custody until formal inquiries into their conduct have been completed. Beyond this, it is held that a pretrial PI is needed to limit the use of pretrial detention.[6] Finally, some argue that the presumption underlies the right to silence and widely accepted restrictions on coercive interrogations.[7]

In spite of the seemingly formidable case for a pretrial presumption of innocence, there are those who challenge the notion. The US Supreme Court has dismissed the contention that the presumption of innocence applies to the pretrial stage, insisting that it is applicable only in the context of a criminal trial.[8] It seems fair to say that the Court's arguments to this effect are rather brief, more in the way of assertions than carefully crafted arguments. Fortunately, some scholars of the law have stepped into the breach. In particular, Larry Laudan has argued that it is difficult to square a pretrial presumption of innocence with the treatment of arrested and formally accused persons.[9] Those suspected or accused of crimes can be stopped by the authorities, questioned, arrested, detained, their property searched, fingerprints and blood samples can be taken from them, and they can be compelled to give up records (including diaries) that incriminate them. Further, grand jury or preliminary hearing indictments of individuals suggest, and quite vividly, that the authorities do not regard the persons under investigation as innocent. Indeed, it would be odd to insist that police and prosecutors must regard them as such, for how could they go about doing their jobs if they did?[10] The public might not know quite what to believe about the arrested and accused, but the reasonable conclusion for it to draw is that the individuals in question are likely guilty of something.[11] The presumption of innocence might make some sense in the trial context, as a vital part of the tripartite proof structure, the other two parts of which are the burden of proof on the government and the standard of proof. Yet the trial is a special setting, one in which jurors might be usefully given instructions about how to regard the accused at the outset, so that they can rigorously test the government's case. Outside of the trial context, however, a presumption of innocence is alleged to make little sense.

It is natural to suspect that supporters and critics of a pretrial presumption of innocence are, to some extent, talking past one another. In particular, what a pretrial presumption of innocence means, who must subscribe to it, what rebuts it, and what are the consequences of its rebuttal are questions in need of much clearer answers than they are often given. Delineating some of the ways in which these questions might be answered will be my focus in the first section. In the second section, I develop an extended argument against a pretrial presumption of innocence, especially insofar as this is taken, as I contend it must be, as a pretrial presumption of material (or factual) innocence. Like Laudan, I believe that such a presumption is difficult to square with the many things we do to and require of suspects and formally accused persons in the pretrial context. Something weaker—a pretrial nonpresumption of material or probative guilt—might make sense in that context. However, even that alternative seems to inadequately and misleadingly characterize what it is we want and reasonably can demand of police and prosecutors in the pretrial phase. Granted, such officials must be steadfastly committed to having fair and rigorous due process take its course. So must members of the public and even the victims of crimes. Yet all of this is, I argue, consistent with there being reasonable doubts about the material innocence of the individuals under investigation. Admonishing legal officials or members of the public to not have such doubts makes little sense, although it does make sense to insist that they remain patient and withhold final judgment about the accused until due process has taken its course.

In the third section, various arguments for a pretrial presumption of innocence are examined. My strategy will be to concede that most of these arguments capture important truths about how legal officials, and sometimes members of the public, should conduct themselves in the pretrial phase. However, I contend that they do not show that such officials, or members of the general public, must regard and treat the accused as materially innocent. In the concluding section, I recapitulate the main lines of argument in the chapter and then take a brief look back to chapter 4. Even if the presumption of innocence makes little sense in the pretrial phase, it might nonetheless have a vital role to play during criminal trials when we ask jurors to set aside what they believe or suspect and perform the important task of putting the government's case to a stern test.

Before proceeding, one important point should be noted. I have spoken so far of a "pretrial" presumption of innocence. Yet it is common knowledge that in many legal jurisdictions, trials are rare, with most criminal charges resolved through some form of plea negotiation.[12] It might therefore be better to speak in terms of a "preadjudication" presumption of innocence. Of course, if my arguments in what follows are correct, there is really no such presumption and, if there are few trials, little role for the presumption to play in the majority of criminal cases processed in many legal jurisdictions. Some will be deeply troubled by this implication. In any event, I ignore the complications raised by plea bargaining for appropriate charge adjudication and, along with most others who write about the PI, pretend that trials are the norm in charge adjudication.[13] Little that I say about the presumption of innocence in what follows will be affected by the fanciful nature of that pretense.

Some Preliminary Distinctions

As we saw in chapter 1, it is important to distinguish between the material guilt or innocence of those accused of crimes and their probative guilt or innocence.[14] The former concerns whether they are, in fact, guilty or innocent of the offenses of which they are suspected or formally charged; the latter concerns whether the government can prove their guilt, to the relevant standard, in a court of law. If it cannot, then they are legally or probatively "not guilty" and so "innocent." There is a crucial difference, in other words, between what is true and what legal authorities can prove decisively. A finding of probative guilt by a court does not definitively establish material guilt, though it might establish it probabilistically. An acquittal by a court, and thus a failure to establish probative guilt, does not establish an accused person's material innocence or even, perhaps, her probable material innocence.

We must also distinguish among the various parties who might be required to presume the innocence of suspects and formally accused persons. First, there are the police and prosecutors directly involved in a given case. These legal officials likely will have seen considerable evidence against the accused—or at least what they reasonably take to be such evidence—and might have heard full and complete confessions from some of them. Such officials therefore will be in a different position with respect to the accused than other government officials and members of the public. Those not directly involved in the investigation and prosecution of crimes might have seen or heard a few things about specific cases, but they are less likely to be immersed in the details of them. A third group is rarely discussed in the literature on the PI: The victims of crimes, especially the ones who (*a*) know who victimized them, and (*b*) are certain that the person or persons accused are the ones who did so. Granted, many crimes lack direct victims, and those crimes that have them will include individuals who are not sure who stole from, assaulted, or otherwise injured them. But in more than a few cases, victims will have special knowledge and vivid awareness that the accused are the individuals who committed crimes against them.

A further point is important as well: Presumptions, as we have seen, appear to come in different strengths.[15] It is natural to think, first, of the PI in the trial setting. In that setting, the presumption is a particularly strong one, rebuttable only if the government can adduce evidence that is powerfully convincing to an independent tribunal—the relevant standard of proof being "beyond a reasonable doubt" in many countries. Yet if there is to be a pretrial PI, it cannot be so stringent or else police and prosecutors will be hobbled in doing their jobs. Granted, the authorities should have (and be able to articulate to a court that enquires into their conduct) some justification for arresting and charging individuals. But such justifications are apt to take much weaker "probable cause" or "reasonable suspicion" forms. Since presumptions appear to come in stronger and weaker versions, we must consider what degree of stringency any one of them is supposed to have in a given context if we are to avoid confusion. We must also ponder whether and to what extent such weaker presumptions amount to presumptions of innocence at all.

Lastly, does the PI govern solely the conduct of legal officials, members of the public, or victims? Or is it also supposed to govern their beliefs or, more plausibly, the perspectives they take on suspects or formally accused persons? It might be claimed that it does not matter what beliefs, attitudes, or perspectives police or prosecutors have about those they suspect or have accused of crimes; it matters only how they treat them or whether they abide by certain procedural rules as they process such individuals through the criminal justice system.[16] So long as legal officials refrain from punishing the accused before their guilt is authoritatively determined, and refrain from public statements concerning their guilt, nothing more is required of them by the PI. Analogously, consider legal rules that prohibit discrimination in hiring based on race, gender, or sexual preference. At some level, we do not care what attitudes those who make hiring decisions have toward job applicants or what they think about the legal rules forbidding discrimination. It is enough if they simply abide by the relevant rules in making hiring decisions. Similarly, it might be argued, what attitudes toward suspects or formally charged persons the police have, or what perspective on those who have become entangled in the criminal justice system prosecutors take up should not concern us. All that matters is that criminal justice officials abide by the rules of due process and avoid actions that unnecessarily cast suspects and the formally accused as guilty before their guilt has been authoritatively determined.

Attempts to portray the PI as concerned exclusively with the conduct of criminal justice officials seem unconvincing for a number of reasons. First, what the authorities believe about suspects or accused persons, or what perspective they take on them, surely might affect how carefully or thoroughly they investigate their alleged crimes. If legal officials adopt the attitude that most of the individuals who fall under their purview are probably guilty and deserving of punishment, then those officials will be more apt to discount their assertions of innocence and, what is more worrisome, decline to investigate at all or very carefully alternative theories about the crimes in question. Notice that hostile or indifferent attitudes by employers toward rules prohibiting discrimination will likewise affect whether they abide by the rules in spirit, as opposed to by the letter, and might also affect whether they actually conform with the rules rather than seek to evade their import. Second, and more to the point, the PI seems different from legal rules that proscribe conduct, for it is typically stated and portrayed in ways that imply the need for an intentional attitude or perspective on the accused. We, or at least some of us, are to *presume* their innocence, not just act toward them in certain ways or avoid acting toward them in certain ways. In this respect, the PI seems different from other legal rules that only govern conduct.

In particular, with members of the public, the presumption's requirements would appear to have more to do with how they regard the suspected or accused, since there might be few opportunities for interaction with them and thus little scope for prescribed conduct toward or in relation to them. Granted, if the formally accused are released back into their communities until the charges against them are resolved, it might matter how they are treated by their fellow citizens. Also, there might be things members of the public can do, by way of conduct, that will support or, alternatively, interfere with the proper and authoritative determination of the accused person's guilt or lack thereof. But part of the point of insisting on a presumption of innocence seems to be to encourage the adoption of a specific perspective on the accused, one that will then inform and guide conduct in relation to them. Of course, which such perspective makes the most sense is a question that will be addressed in the coming pages.

Doubts concerning a Pretrial Presumption of Innocence

Important as the preceding distinctions are, few who discuss the pretrial PI attend to them and thus clarify the sort of innocence it is held to involve, who is supposed to presume it, and what sorts of considerations are capable of rebutting it.[17] Let us begin with the kind of innocence involved—material (or innocence$_m$) or probative (or innocence$_p$). As we saw in the first chapter, it seems implausible to interpret the presumption of innocence as involving innocence$_p$. For this would require the legal officials directly involved in the arrest and prosecution of crimes to regard and treat the accused as probatively—that is, proven—innocent, or perhaps as likely to be proven innocent. Neither of these is a plausible prescription. Police and prosecutors arrest suspects, investigate them, charge them, and pursue charges to their resolution precisely because they believe that the individuals in question can be proven guilty, or can be induced to admit their guilt if enough evidence against them is accumulated. It is hard to imagine how or why such officials would carry on as we want them to if they presumed that the innocence of those whom they suspect of crimes was proven or was likely to be. It might make more sense to require such officials to regard and treat accused persons in some neutral way with respect to their provable guilt—to be agnostic, as it were, about whether their guilt is or will be proven. But such an attitude also seems at odds with the important functions such officials perform in the criminal justice system. We want them to assiduously investigate crimes, determine who committed them, and bring them to justice. If such officials have reasonable grounds for suspecting individuals of crimes, but doubt that they have evidence sufficient to establish their guilt in a court of law, we do not want them to presume the best about suspects and simply leave off their investigations, at least not when the crimes of which they suspect individuals are serious. We want them to doggedly continue their investigations, to unearth more evidence, if they can. We also do not want police or prosecutors to be reluctant to believe in the guilt of suspects or resistant to efforts to find more evidence, as we might want jurors, during trials, to be at least initially resistant to the government's proffers of evidence against formally accused persons. Also, it would be strange for police or prosecutors to regard the burden of proving the guilt of suspects as being on their accusers or (alleged, we should say) victims. Reports of crimes by victims or members of the public should spark investigations; once they are underway, we expect police and prosecutors to continue them to their completion. All of this is consistent, of course, with police or prosecutors deciding that the reports they have received are false or, what is different, not possible to confirm.

It likewise seems doubtful that members of the general public are to presume the innocence$_p$ of those who been arrested for or charged with crimes. Members of the community likely regard and expect the accused to be proven guilty. Would it make sense to admonish members of the public to presume innocence$_p$? Not really, since whatever the ultimate outcome of charges in criminal cases, proven innocence is almost never one of them. Even if charges against individuals are dropped by prosecutors or dismissed by judges, or defendants gain acquittals after trials, their probative innocence is rarely established. It is not the aim of the criminal justice system to prove people innocent; why, then, should we direct members of the public to presume that it will do so?

Similar considerations hold with respect to victims of crimes who know that it is the accused who victimized them. They neither expect nor want the criminal justice system to prove the innocence of the accused; indeed they fervently want it to prove their guilt. In any event, it would be bizarre to instruct victims to presume that the probative innocence of the accused is or will be established.

Fortunately, I doubt that proponents of a pretrial presumption of innocence have probative innocence in mind. Instead, it appears that it is the material innocence of suspects and formally accused persons that is to be presumed. But by whom, and what does such a presumption require of them? Start with police and prosecutors. One problem, right off the bat, is that their actions toward suspects and formally accused persons seem to belie any presumption of innocence$_m$ on their part.[18] Again, the police stop or arrest individuals whom they suspect of crimes, detain them for questioning, obtain search warrants to gather more information about suspects, and turn the results of their investigations over to prosecutors if they believe charges should be filed. Along the way, suspects might have been required by the courts to submit to searches of their homes, businesses, and records. They might also have been required to give blood or urine samples. Prosecutors might question or investigate suspects further, and ultimately charge them with one or more offenses. They might also request bail as a condition of release or request remand in cases in which they fear that the accused will abscond, interfere with the course of justice, or commit further pretrial offenses. All of these actions seem decidedly at odds with a pretrial perspective on suspects and formally accused persons according to which they are materially innocent, unless such a presumption is a weak one, easily overcome by evidence well short of the reasonable doubt standard.[19] And if it is that weak, we might wonder what real purpose it serves.

Is it that, in spite of the actions police and prosecutors have taken that strongly imply the guilt of persons, such legal officials are nonetheless to strive to regard and treat them *as if* they are innocent$_m$—"so far as possible"—as it is sometimes put?[20] The "so far as possible" qualifier cannot be taken literally, as it is *possible* for the authorities never to arrest, investigate, or charge anyone with crimes. Instead, it must be understood within the context of the official duties police and prosecutors perform: They must treat (and perhaps regard) the accused as innocent$_m$ "so far as possible" given that their jobs are to apprehend lawbreakers, gather evidence against them, and see to it that they are punished for their crimes. The question we now face is what such a requirement could come to.

Consider the PI, as I have elaborated it, in the trial context. I claimed that jurors (or judges in bench trials) should evaluate government proffers of evidence through the lens of the accused's material innocence. This means that jurors should initially adopt a protective attitude toward the accused such that they strive to view the evidence presented by the government as consistent with the accused's innocence, at least until they can no longer do so because the government's case is deemed overwhelming. Such a perspective on the accused in the trial context has a clear purpose and limited scope. Its purpose is to enable jurors to put the government's case to exacting scrutiny; its scope does not extend beyond or outside of the trial context. It is also a perspective that might become unsustainable in the face of decisive evidence against the accused.

Would we want police and prosecutors to similarly approach the detection and investigation of crimes, and the adjudication of charges against those whom they have formally accused of them? I strongly doubt that we want this. The tasks of police and prosecutors in the criminal justice system are markedly different from those of jurors. Jurors have the task of evaluating the cogency of the government's case against accused persons once it has been fully assembled and publicly presented. Police and prosecutors have the very different tasks of detecting crimes, amassing evidence against those whom they suspect of them, pressing charges against the accused, and, in the trial context, urging the courts to convict them. Start with the police. Surely we want them to be somewhat proactive in the detection of crimes—to be, in other words, on the lookout for them in ways that would seem to rest uneasily with a presumption that all citizens are responsible and law-abiding. Indeed, the more serious the crimes in question, the stronger our desire is apt to be for the authorities to prevent them before they are well underway. If the police observe suspicious behavior (e.g., a person running from a bank wearing a mask and carrying a gun), would we want them to view such behavior through the lens of the suspicious person's presumed material innocence? In other words, should the police be expected or encouraged to try to square the observed suspicious conduct with the presumed material innocence of the agent in question? The question answers itself, I believe. Further, if the suspect is detained and questioned but denies having robbed the bank, should the police be inclined to believe him and thus cease further investigation of him, based on a presumption of his material innocence? In other words, would we want the police to have the kind of complacency about criminal wrongdoing that a presumption of material innocence would seem to encourage? I do not think so. Instead, we want the police to be more than a little suspicious of certain kinds of persons and their conduct and to act on their suspicions.

Keep in mind that many of the persons with whom the police deal on a daily basis have lengthy criminal records of which the police are cognizant.[21] This raises another issue: Would such persons be entitled to the same presumption of material innocence, when they are observed engaging in suspicious conduct, as citizens who lack such records? I doubt that also. Is the idea that a pretrial presumption of innocence_{m}, because it is only a presumption, is at some point rebuttable? Perhaps so, but again, given the role of the police in the criminal justice system, it would have to be fairly often and easily rebuttable. And then we might reasonably wonder what significant role, if any, it plays if it is so quickly dispatched by a little bit of evidence that citizens are involved in offending.

Prosecutors might initially appear to be differently situated, with respect to the PI, than the police. Prosecutors have more complex roles in the criminal justice. They are supposed to be both advocates for the public in the enforcement of the criminal law and ministers of justice.[22] Maybe when the police bring cases to them, they should initially presume the innocence of those whom the police suspect of crimes, have arrested for them, and have gathered evidence against. Like jurors, prosecutors might be encouraged to view the evidence that the police have gathered against suspects through the lens of their presumed material innocence. I do not doubt that prosecutors often do something like this, though I suspect that they most likely do it in anticipation of whether the case will pass the reasonable doubt standard needed for conviction. They might also examine the evidence to see if it seems strong enough to elicit guilty pleas from the accused, which is not the same as determining whether it is convincing beyond a reasonable doubt. In any event, the similarities between what prosecutors do and what jurors do stop there. For one thing, if prosecutors determine that the evidence against a suspect is insufficiently strong, they do not "acquit" the accused, as jurors do in criminal trials. Instead, they might strongly urge the police to find more evidence or undertake doing so themselves. Such actions by prosecutors would appear to sit uneasily with a presumption of the material innocence of suspects. Granted, in some instances, prosecutors might refuse to file charges against suspects or drop them if they have been filed. But such actions on their part do not amount to acquittals and might not foreclose future investigations and charges against the individuals in question. Further, prosecutors can file charges based on weak proofs of the guilt of suspects. No one believes that the "probable cause" threshold is a formidable one.[23] Even if one believes that prosecutors should have to satisfy a more demanding evidence standard before they file charges, given the stigmatizing effects of their doing so, it seems unlikely that an enhanced standard will come anywhere near the reasonable doubt standard. This means that prosecutors can publicly accused persons of criminal misconduct without proof beyond a reasonable doubt that they have engaged in it. And that, in turn, seems hard to reconcile with the notion that prosecutors should regard and treat those who have become entangled in the criminal justice system as if they are materially innocent.

Importantly, it does not follow from the preceding that police and prosecutors can commence punishment of those whom they believe are guilty of offending. Punishment must await an authoritative finding, by the courts, that accused persons are guilty of the criminal misconduct of which police and prosecutors suspect and have charged them. But that is because due process must be allowed to take its course, not because police or prosecutors must treat or regard accused persons as innocent$_{m}$. Likewise, the requirement that such officials remain circumspect in their public statements about suspects and defendants might be little more than a prophylactic designed to ensure that the accused get fair trials. Police and prosecutors should not say things about the accused that will taint the jury pool, or improperly influence trial judges.[24] Still, we might doubt the value of such a prophylactic. What does it really matter what police or prosecutors say publicly about cases when their actions already bespeak, in clear and forceful ways, their views about the likely guilt of the accused?[25] Moreover, if protecting the right to fair trial in this way is all the pretrial presumption of innocence comes to, its role will turn out to be vanishingly slight, since the vast majority criminal cases are adjudicated without trials.

Could it be that persons other than the legal officials directly involved in the prosecution of crimes are to presume the material innocence of the formally accused—say other government officials or members of the general public? All of these individuals are on the "outside," as it were, and thus not privy to the (often) damning evidence (and in some cases, freely offered confessions of individuals) with which officials directly involved in cases are acquainted. Set to one side victims who are certain that the persons who preyed upon them are the ones charged with having done so. Surely it would be untenable to insist that such victims regard or treat the accused as materially innocent, whatever that means, even if it is appropriate to insist that they should support letting due process take its course. There will still be lots of other people who might be usefully instructed concerning how they should regard and treat individuals who have, to this point, only been arrested for or accused of crimes.

One problem with this suggestion is that the actions of police, prosecutors, and even judges in relation to the accused will typically and not unreasonably be taken by members of the public to signal something significant about the accused—namely, that their law-abidingness is in question.[26] Also, if members of the public know anything about the actual operations of the criminal justice system, which they might, they will know that many of those charged with crimes are eventually convicted.[27] We might nonetheless, somewhat quixotically perhaps, insist that members of the public regard and treat the accused as materially innocent ("so far as possible"?), in spite of what they reasonably suspect. But it is not apparent why such a presumption on their part matters all that much. It is the decisions and actions of the legal officials directly involved that imperil the accused. So long as members of the public refrain from vigilante action and let due process take its course—neither of which presupposes that they presume the accused to be materially innocent—what difference does it make whether members of the public suspect most accused persons of being materially guilty?

One concern might be that members of the public will react cautiously, or worse, contemptuously, if they encounter accused persons before the charges against them have been authoritatively resolved. Such behavior on the public's part might be deemed inappropriate or premature, so they might usefully be instructed to presume the material innocence of accused persons. Yet I doubt that cautious treatment of the accused is inappropriate, though whether and to what extent that is so depends on how serious the charges are against them or lengthy and disturbing their criminal histories. The good standing of the accused is in question, after all, so some reluctance to treat them as "hail fellows well met" seems warranted. Open contempt or ridicule does not seem appropriate, but mostly because nothing authoritative about the conduct of the accused has yet been established. Reminding the public of that, though, is a far cry from instructing them to regard and treat the accused as materially innocent.

Perhaps the idea is that members of the public should think better of their fellow citizens, even the ones who have been arrested and charged with crimes.[28] Indeed, doing so might be laudable, but it is hard to see why such a hopeful view of one's fellow citizens should be translated into the kind of legal demand of which the PI is alleged, by some, to consist. It might be virtuous of us to presume the goodwill of our fellow citizens until their lack of it has been established in a court of law, but the enforcement of virtue is not something that is normally thought to be within the criminal law's purview. Moreover, as we have seen, whether it is virtuous, naive, or outright foolish to presume the law-abidingness of one's neighbors might depend on such things as the neighborhood in which one lives, how recently or frequently one has been victimized by one's neighbors, or one's knowledge that the neighbors who have been accused of crimes already have lengthy criminal records. If civic trust is the ground of a pretrial PI, it would seem to be one that yields a weak and highly contingent presumption, at best.

Making a Fresh Start: What We Can Reasonably Require in the Pretrial Phase

If neither a presumption of probative nor material innocence makes much sense in the pretrial context, regardless of whom we require it, with what, if anything, are we left? Let us make a fresh start. Police and prosecutors might be confident, in any given case, that they not only have the culprit but have the evidence to convict her. But they must also recognize that they could be mistaken on one or both of these counts. They might not have sufficient evidence to convince a court of the accused's guilt, or she might be, in fact, innocent of (some or all of) the crimes of which they have accused her. Maybe instead of saying that legal officials should, pretrial, presume the material or probative innocence of suspects or accused persons, we should say something different—that they ought not presume the probative or material guilt of the accused. Police and prosecutors should recognize and acknowledge that their confidence that the evidence against the accused will be sufficient to convict them might be misplaced. Juries in criminal trials might not interpret the evidence the way they do; judges in bench trials might likewise confound their expectations. A nonpresumption of probative guilt is thus a sensible posture for police and prosecutors to adopt.

More than this, police and prosecutors should be encouraged to recognize and acknowledge their own fallibility. They might have jumped too quickly to conclusions about the material guilt of suspects and then, in various more or less conscious and dishonest ways, contrived to build cases against them.[29] These days, it should hardly come as news to the authorities that they can make mistakes, sometimes dreadful ones.[30] At least until verdicts or guilty pleas are in, they should steer clear of presuming the material guilt of the persons arrested and charged with crimes. Such officials do not have to regard or treat them as materially innocent, but they should be alive to the possibility that they might be. This will mean, among other things, that such officials ought to listen to and heed their own doubts about the material guilt of the accused. They should also be encouraged, if not required, to bring in other officials to give cases a "fresh look," especially when the charges in question are serious and the accused decline to admit their guilt. Only when the accused are convicted or enter guilty pleas might it be appropriate for police and prosecutors to adopt (rebuttable) presumptions of the material guilt of the individuals involved.

Such nonpresumptions of probative and material guilt also seem more appropriate where the general public is concerned. We can plausibly say to the public that, though things look bad for the individuals arrested for and charged with crimes, it is important to keep in mind that (*a*) they might be materially innocent of all or some of the charges against them, and (*b*) their probative guilt has not been established and might never be. Members of the public might be usefully reminded that the charge adjudication process is sometimes a long and complicated one and always a fallible one. Caution in drawing conclusions about accused persons is fully warranted; so is supporting the full and fair determination of the charges against them. Even if most of those charged with crimes are both guilty and will be convicted, not all of them are or will be. Granted, it might make little sense to urge a nonpresumption of material guilt to victims whose victimizers have been appropriately charged with crimes.[31] But we can still encourage them to adopt a nonpresumption of probative guilt until the charge adjudication process takes its full course.

So, have we hit upon something sensible, even if it is not what proponents of a pretrial PI appear to want? Yes and no. Though pretrial nonpresumptions of probative and material guilt are more defensible than pretrial presumptions of probative or material innocence, I also believe that they somewhat distort what we want, especially of the legal officials directly involved in criminal prosecutions. Police and prosecutors confront a wide variety of cases. In some of them, perpetrators are caught in the act, or shortly after they have committed crimes, and make little effort to deny what they have done. In more than a few instances, perpetrators fully admit to their crimes, or the physical and other evidence against them is overwhelming from the start, and the only question remaining concerns what charge or charges to which they will plead guilty. I am not sure what sense it makes to say, in such cases, that the legal officials involved should not *presume* the probative and material guilt of the accused. Sure, presumptions that some of those charged with crimes are guilty and will be proven to be so might have to be abandoned or modified, but it is in the nature of presumptions that they can be overcome. Only if such presumptions of probative and material guilt were exceedingly strong—rebuttable only by very convincing evidence of the accused's absence of guilt—would they be inappropriate. Yet there seems little reason to hold that all presumptions are of this strength. Indeed, proponents of a broad, pretrial presumption of innocence must concede that it is not so stringent as to preclude the authorities from arresting, investigating, and charging individuals with crimes, though these actions call their probative and material innocence into doubt. In short, in some cases, police and prosecutors do not seem to act inappropriately if they presume that the accused are materially guilty and that their probative guilt will soon be established. Accused persons will still have the option of putting the government's case to the test of the proof structure. Police or prosecutors' presumptions do not preclude that; neither should they affect, in any way, the instructions given to jurors about their having to presume the innocence of the accused.

In other kinds of cases, however, matters are more complicated. Suppose that the authorities are less certain about who committed a crime or whether one was even committed. Whatever behavior, evidence, complaints by alleged victims, or reports by alleged witnesses sparked the suspicions of the authorities in such cases will have to be investigated further. As their investigations proceed, officials might begin to form working hypotheses about the events in question—who acted in what ways and for what purposes. Such working hypotheses will be little more than educated guesses about the events in question, but they will suggest further avenues of inquiry that might or might not pan out. When they do not pan out, investigators might have to abandon their working hypotheses and develop new ones. Nonetheless, in some of these kinds of cases, the damning evidence will eventually emerge. I am not sure why, if and when it does, we should think it inappropriate for the officials involved to believe, with some confidence, that certain individuals did commit crimes and that their criminal misconduct can be proven—that is, to presume the material and probative guilt of those they have come to charge with crimes. Again, so long as such presumptions remain rebuttable, why should we object to the authorities adopting them?

Admittedly, there will be cases in which the authorities come to believe, and quite firmly, that an individual is materially guilty of an offense, though they doubt that they can prove her guilt in a court of law. Presumptions of material and probative guilt need not always go hand in hand. It might be thought that the authorities, in the kind of case just described, act inappropriately by presuming the material guilt of an individual in the absence of confidence that they can establish her probative guilt. Perhaps so, but that all depends on why it is that they are not sure that they can establish her probative guilt. Suppose that highly incriminating evidence against the individual was excluded by a judge on the grounds that it was illegally acquired. In such cases, it does not seem inappropriate for police and prosecutors to presume the material guilt of a defendant though they do not presume her probative guilt.

What seems worrisome about allowing police and prosecutors to form and act on such presumptions, rebuttable though they might be, is this: They might form them too quickly and be inclined to stick with them in the face of conflicting evidence. Worse than this, they might form such presumptions prematurely and then employ all manner of questionable tactics to make adjudicative outcomes conform to them. The list of ways in which police and prosecutorial conduct can distort the search for the truth about the cases under their purview is long and disturbing—among them, harsh interrogations, manipulation of lineups, reliance on eyewitnesses that have been coached, the shading of testimony by police, investigators, or experts in ways designed to make defendants look guilty, and suppression of exonerating evidence. Such tactics are notoriously prone to producing unreliable adjudicative outcomes. But all this shows is that what we should demand of police and prosecutors is an unwavering commitment to seeking justice, not simply convictions. They should doggedly search for the truth concerning the events under their investigation and continue to do so even after they have formed presumptions about the material or probative guilt of those they have charged with crimes. It should not take something like proof beyond a reasonable doubt for them to abandon their presumptions. Any substantial grounds for doing so should suffice and should lead them to question their conclusions and re-examine the evidence in support of them. But such unwavering commitments to full and fair due process have little to do with presuming the material or probative innocence of accused persons. And though encouraging legal officials to adopt nonpresumptions of material and probative guilt comes closer to capturing what we want of them, it nevertheless seems to oversimplify and in some ways distort how we should want and expect them to go about their important tasks.

Granted, when it comes to members of the general public and their stance toward those suspected or accused of crimes, it makes eminent good sense to encourage them to adopt nonpresumptions of probative and material guilt. But the truth of the matter is that there might not be much harm in their presuming the material or probative guilt of most of the individuals charged with crimes, at least so long as such presumptions remain subject to revision. The public is largely unaware of and uninvolved in the vast majority of crimes processed by the criminal justice system. Only a few very serious crimes or noteworthy offenders garner the public's attention.[32] Even in such cases, what the public presumes might not matter all that much so long as they support full and fair due process for the accused and respect its outcomes. Strident assertions that members of the public must presume the innocence of those charged with crimes assumes a more knowledgeable or involved public than exists in run-of-the-mill criminal cases.

In short, what we want to discourage in the pretrial context is a rush to premature or conclusive judgments concerning the material or probative guilt of suspects and formally accused persons, along with what might go with such judgments, conduct by the authorities (or in some cases, by other citizens) that thwarts full and fair due process, or worse, inflicts legal punishment on persons before they have been convicted by a court of law. It might be suggested that the notion of the presumption of innocence is useful shorthand for the complex of desired attitudes and conduct by the authorities and members of the public that we wish to nurture and sustain. What can it hurt, after all, if we mildly distort what we want of officials and members of the public, especially if by doing so they are thereby stimulated to conduct themselves accordingly? In particular, it might be thought that we need a little rhetorical overkill to forestall the premature (i.e., before an accused person's guilt has been demonstrated beyond a reasonable doubt in a court of law) infliction of legal punishment upon individuals.[33]

However, I believe that we would be better off reminding police and prosecutors of the numerous specific ways in which investigations can go awry, and of the fallibility, and sometimes the corruptibility, of their judgment. Instructing them to presume the innocence of those whom they suspect of crimes and against whom they have seen damning evidence is, at best, unhelpful and, at worst, likely to be cynically dismissed.

Arguments in Favor of a Pretrial Presumption of Innocence

Numerous arguments have been advanced concerning the need for a pretrial presumption of innocence. My aim in this section is to show that none of them is convincing. My strategy will be to argue that either the alleged need for a pretrial PI is nonexistent, or pretrial nonpresumptions of guilt, along with commitments to full and fair due process, will suffice to satisfy it.

As we have seen, one common argument is that we need a PI to explain why police, criminal investigators, and prosecutors must mount progressively stronger justificatory barriers as they arrest, detain, interrogate, search the property of, charge, and demand bail or pretrial detention of suspects.[34] It is held that a pretrial PI is the ground for these justificatory burdens: Because individuals have it, the authorities should be made to overcome it. Notice again, however, that such a presumption, if it exists, cannot be a very strong one or else the authorities will be hampered in their efforts to arrest, charge, and convict offenders. The police do not and should not need anything remotely approaching proof beyond a reasonable doubt to stop and question suspicious individuals, or to arrest and briefly detain them. Similarly, prosecutors need only satisfy the relatively weak requirements of having "probable cause" or a "reasonable prospect of conviction" to charge them.[35] This hardly seems a formidable PI. Also, it is unclear how a pretrial PI grounds the progressive justificatory burdens. Once the presumption is initially overcome (or rebutted) by, for instance, a justified police stop and questioning of an individual, how does it come back into existence to ground subsequent justificatory burdens? In other words, once the presumption is rebutted by the first justified official inquiry into conduct, why does it not entirely lose its normative force? More puzzling still is how the presumption would re-emerge as the ground for successively stronger justificatory burdens.

As I have already suggested in chapter 2, an alternative and more plausible ground for such progressive justificatory burdens exists in the form of basic rights to such things as liberty, privacy, and autonomy.[36] Given the fundamental moral importance of such rights, they should not be too easily infringed by the authorities in their pursuit and prosecution of criminal offenders. Minor infringements of them, in the form of the police stopping and questioning individuals, should have to be justified. But given the limited extent to which such actions by the police infringe basic rights, it should be relatively easy to justify them. However, as the authorities move to detain, interrogate, search the property of, and charge individuals, they intrude upon their basic rights in more profound ways and should have to provide correspondingly stronger justifications for doing so. At the pretrial limit, if the authorities request the detention of those they have charged with crimes, they should have to provide quite powerful proofs that such detention is necessary. Notice that if we posit rights to liberty, privacy, or autonomy as the ground of the successive justificatory burdens, the strength of those burdens can be tied directly to the extent to which official actions intrude upon the associated rights.

Another argument in favor of a pretrial PI is that it is needed to protect the reputational interests of persons.[37] Pretrial, police and prosecutors should be circumspect in their public comments about those whom they suspect of or have charged with crimes, or else the reputations of individuals will be sullied further than they already are by their having been arrested and charged. Proponents of a pretrial presumption of innocence for reputation-related purposes contend that prohibitions on public declarations by the authorities do more than help to ensure fair trial rights. Such prohibitions also prevent unnecessary damage to the good names and reputations of the accused. This damage will be hard to fix in the event that the accused are acquitted or the charges against them are dropped.

In evaluating this argument for a pretrial PI, it is useful to begin with a couple of sobering observations about the criminal justice system. First, as we have already noted, many of the individuals arrested and charged with crimes are "repeat players."[38] They already have criminal records, sometimes quite lengthy ones. Hence, their good names and reputations are already besmirched, perhaps beyond repair. It is doubtful that what police or prosecutors say about such individuals pretrial will have much impact on their reputations, or if it does, it will do little more than make bad reputations worse ones. Nonetheless, further tarnishing of their reputations might be regrettable and something to be avoided. Second, in the vast majority of cases, police and prosecutors will not be disposed to issue public comments about the accused. In the United States, for instance, close to 80 percent of the offenses processed by the criminal justice system are misdemeanors.[39] Few in the public care about the disposition of such cases, and the legal officials involved will have little incentive to talk about them publicly. For better or worse, the workings of the criminal justice system produce considerable anonymity for most accused persons. Only in relatively rare cases of more serious or notorious crimes might police or prosecutors be tempted to comment upon the probative or material guilt of suspects or formally accused persons. Ironically, it is not clear what point there is to their doing so, unless it is to assure an anxious public or concerned victims that the perpetrators will be brought to justice. The actions of police and prosecutors in such cases will already betray their views about those they have arrested and charged. The public will surely know or presume that the officials involved believe such individuals to be materially and probatively guilty. Indeed, it does not seem a stretch to say that the public will believe that the legal officials involved "presume" the material and probative guilt of those they have arrested, investigated, and charged.

Setting the preceding points to one side, it is not clear why we need a PI—especially in the form of a presumption of material innocence—to protect the reputational interests of accused persons. Police and prosecutors ought to be circumspect about what they say in the pretrial context because, until a court has declared the accused "guilty" or "not guilty" (or, perhaps, "not proven" to be guilty), full and fair due process has not yet taken its course.[40] Accused persons have not been convicted and might not be. Again, the charge adjudication process is not entirely predictable (though not entirely unpredictable either), and police and prosecutors, of all people, ought to know this. The judges or juries who determine verdicts might confound their expectations. Police and prosecutors also know, or ought to, that the investigation of cases and the adjudication of charges are fallible processes. Admittedly, many police and prosecutors might find it difficult to believe or admit that they make mistakes, but such beliefs or attitudes should be strongly discouraged.[41] In short, it is simply premature of police and prosecutors to publicly declare the accused probatively or materially guilty, whatever their own private beliefs or (hopefully rebuttable) presumptions. Moreover, it is not their job to declare guilt; that is the role of the courts.

Arrest and indictment are bad enough for anyone's reputation, though as we have just seen, worse for some people's than others. In the event that the charges against individuals turn out to be mistaken or unproven, the accused must be permitted to try to go on with their lives—to resume the full enjoyment and exercise of their basic rights as citizens. This will prove difficult for many of them, as perhaps it should in some cases. After all, it would be naive to believe that all or even most of the accused who are not convicted are, in fact, innocent of the crimes of which the authorities suspected them. Members of the public presumably know this and might react with caution or distrust toward the formerly accused, regardless of adjudicative outcomes favorable to the accused. It seems doubtful that such attitudes by the public are always unreasonable, though the public too should be reminded of the fallible nature of the criminal justice process. Pretrial public declarations of the guilt of the accused by the authorities will compound the difficulties some of the formerly accused, but not convicted, face. Such declarations will have the likely effect, if not the purpose, of imposing informal social sanctions on the formerly accused, when the courts have determined that they do not merit legal sanctions. The imposition of such social sanctions, whether intentional or not, clearly exceeds the remit of legal officials. Though legal officials should be reminded of this and strongly urged to be cautious and circumspect in their pretrial statements about the accused, none of this requires them or us to presume the material or probative innocence of the accused.

A further important argument for a pretrial PI is that it serves as a vital ground for resisting the pretrial detention of accused persons.[42] Precisely because the accused are to be presumed materially innocent, so the argument goes, it should be exceedingly difficult to justify depriving them of their freedom and subjecting them to other indignities. Indeed, pretrial detention is (too often) nearly indistinguishable from legal punishment proper, which is most assuredly unjustified at this juncture. Pretrial detainees are usually housed in (typically squalid) local jails alongside individuals already convicted of crimes. It would seem that the admonition to regard and treat the accused as innocent is directed primarily to the legal officials who might otherwise seek to detain the accused before trial. Also, the presumption involved is, in the minds of some legal scholars, close to absolute, at least where the reasons for detaining the accused turn on the belief that the accused is materially guilty.[43] Some scholars allow for pretrial detention in the interests of ensuring that official inquiry into the alleged actions of the accused, in the form of a criminal trial, can take its full course. Thus, if it seems clear that the accused might abscond, threaten witnesses, or otherwise interfere with the course of justice, then and only then is pretrial detention permitted.[44]

I examine pretrial detention at some length in the next chapter. Thus, my comments here will be relatively brief. There are numerous reasons to strictly limit pretrial detention, though they have little to do with a prescribed PI. First and foremost, those only charged with crimes should not be subjected to what amount to punishment-like conditions. But that is because their probative guilt has not yet been established, not because they are presumed (by anyone) probatively or materially innocent. Even if we made pretrial detention conditions considerably nicer and less restrictive, which we surely ought to do, such detention would constitute a significant and lasting intrusion upon the basic rights of persons, one that ought to require stringent justification. Indeed, it ought to require almost as stringent a justification as we require for inflicting legal punishment upon them. The charges against individuals should have to be serious, the evidence against them powerful, the threat they pose to others or to the course of justice should be manifest, and the government should have to show that no other means, short of pretrial confinement, will suffice to contain the risks posed by the accused.[45] Even in cases in which all of these conditions are satisfied, the government might be required to periodically demonstrate that it is doing all it can to prepare for trial, with the goal of limiting the duration of pretrial confinement.

Second, it is clear that pretrial detention interferes to some extent with fair trial rights, by making it more difficult for the accused to meet with and aid their attorneys in preparing defenses.[46] Not only are leisurely and secure conversations with their attorneys more difficult for those held on remand, but detainees will find it harder to track down witnesses who might attest to their innocence. Detainees also will likely lose their jobs, if they had them, and thus the income needed to hire higher-quality attorneys to assist in their defense.

Third, it is undeniable that pretrial detention increases the pressure on the accused to accede to guilty pleas, even in cases in which they are wholly or partially innocent of the crimes of which they have been accused.[47] The difficult conditions of much pretrial detention provide powerful incentives to many accused persons to cut their losses and plead guilty, especially if they can thereby assure reduced punishment for themselves. This will be especially true for innocents or partial innocents who already have criminal records and are accused of minor offenses. It is not uncommon for prosecutors to agree to sentences of "time served" in pretrial detention in exchange for guilty pleas from individuals, thus effectively converting time on remand into punishment. Again, what is troubling about this is that those held on remand have not yet been convicted of anything. Still, they are being punished, or perhaps "prepunished," and their detention is used as a bargaining chip to "persuade" them to admit their guilt. We should have grave doubts about whether such a process yields veridical convictions, but such doubts have nothing to do with a pretrial PI.

Thomas Weigend claims that the presumption of innocence is needed in order to resist the temptation to presume the guilt of persons charged with crimes and thus to commence punishing them before the charges against them have been authoritatively resolved.[48] This temptation will be powerful given the many infringements on their basic rights that the accused are made to endure in the pretrial period. On Weigend's account, it is as if these official depredations have a kind of momentum that leads us to prematurely punish those whom we presume will wind up being convicted. Yet it is not clear why resisting this momentum requires us to presume what in many cases, as Weigend admits, is unlikely to turn out to be true.[49] Instead, it seems sufficient to insist that government officials, and the public, ought to support and insist upon full and fair due process taking its course prior to the imposition on anyone of criminal sanctions. Further, we could remind everyone that the charge adjudication process (*a*) is somewhat unpredictable and (*b*) is fallible. Doing so should provide more than sufficient grounds to await the final disposition of charges before we start punishing people.

Finally, it has been claimed that there is a link between the presumption of innocence and the right against self-incrimination.[50] Because those accused of crimes are presumed innocent, the burden of proving their guilt ought to be entirely on the government. The accused should neither be expected nor forced to prove their innocence. Hence, in the pretrial phase, they can justifiably refuse to answer questions about the crimes of which they are suspected by the authorities, invoking their "right to silence." Without the presumption of innocence as a theoretical underpinning, it is alleged that important pretrial prohibitions against harsh interrogative techniques or worse, the use of torture, would make little sense.

Obviously, we should prohibit the use of coercive interrogative techniques in the pretrial phase of criminal proceedings. However, we do not need a PI, especially in the form of a presumption of material innocence, to make sense of why we should do so. The use of such techniques is symptomatic of all that we should want police and prosecutors to avoid as they investigate crimes, typically motivated, as they are, by sloth or premature judgments concerning the guilt of suspects. The use of coercive interrogation techniques is notoriously unreliable, a point that even cynical legal officials, aware of the fact that many of those suspected or accused of crimes are guilty, should be strongly encouraged to bear in mind.[51] Many of the most troubling cases of mistaken convictions have relied on confessions gained through their use. If anything, it is a nonpresumption of material guilt that partly undergirds prohibitions on the use of such tactics. Independently of that nonpresumption, harshly coercive or manipulative interrogation tactics are an affront to the dignity of suspects, even guilty ones. All suspects should be treated with respect for their rights of physical and psychological integrity, except when doing otherwise is necessary to stop them from engaging in imminent unlawful actions. We should not permit investigators to strike, threaten, intimidate, or subject suspects to sleep or other forms of deprivation to gain confessions from them, even truthful ones.

It is also worth noting that in many legal systems, even if those accused of crimes cannot be made to literally speak against themselves either before or during trial, they can be required to do all manner of other things that reveal their guilt, often against their will. They can be required to submit to searches and seizures of their property, turn over records, including diaries, and provide voice, urine, or blood samples.[52] Again, all of these seemingly justified intrusions into their lives are difficult to square with a pretrial presumption of material innocence.

Concluding Remarks

My account will appear too steeply deflationary to many scholars of the criminal law. My rejection of a pretrial PI will be seen as going too far against the grain of certain accepted truths within legal and popular culture. We are used to hearing of the "presumed innocence" of individuals who have been arrested for and charged with crimes. The media proclaim this, even as they relentlessly detail the alleged crimes of individuals based on initial police reports, the testimony of alleged eyewitnesses, or what often amount to little more than rumors. Presumably, the media are, in issuing such reminders, following the lead of legal practitioners, scholars, or informed observers of legal culture. By way of illustration, this seemingly elementary proposition about the legal system was invoked recently by a National Football League player whose teammate had been arrested and charged with rape right before an important playoff game. The player admitted that it was difficult to cope with the charges against his teammate. His mood lifting somewhat, he then proceeded to say, "I do believe that in this country that you are innocent until proven guilty."[53] How can an account, such as my own, that conflicts with this pervasive sentiment possibly be correct?

Yet consider what had already happened to the football player in whose presumed innocence we are being exhorted to believe. He had been arrested and charged with a serious offense. Right off the bat, this made him look like something other than a citizen in good standing in the community. Also, he had been required to submit to a medical examination, as the alleged victim claimed that she had scratched him while attempting to fend off his assault. Such examinations are not usually required of the presumed innocent, or so it would seem. Further, the accused was required to post bail and wear a GPS ankle bracelet, the latter so that the authorities could track his whereabouts. Again, these are not the sorts of things that we require of the presumed innocent but of persons whom we have reasonable grounds for believing have something for which to answer. The accused also will be required to appear at subsequent hearings and eventually at a trial, if it comes to that. In the meantime, he has been suspended by his team. He is not permitted to practice with or play with the team until the charges against him have been fully resolved. The details of the accusations against him have also been trumpeted by the media. To say that his status as an upstanding citizen has been, for the time being at least, significantly diminished seems an understatement.

Granted, proponents of a robust, pretrial presumption of innocence might object to the media coverage of his case. More to the point, they might criticize one or more of the steps taken against the suspect by the authorities and his employer. But I doubt that they would object to all or even most of them. As we have seen, proponents of a pretrial PI do not usually reject requiring accused persons to post bail when their alleged crimes are serious. Neither can proponents of a pretrial PI easily object to required court appearances by persons formally accused of crimes, or court-ordered investigations of their persons or property. Proponents of a pretrial PI might caution employers against prematurely suspending or dismissing employees accused of crimes. But they might have to accept such actions by employers in cases in which the crimes of which individuals have been accused are grave. I doubt that employers reasonably can be expected to let persons accused of murder or rape continue in their jobs until the charges against them have been fully adjudicated.

It might be claimed that a pretrial presumption of innocence simply consists in the nonpresumption of material and probative guilt, combined with a commitment to full and fair due process. If so, then my contention would be that what we want of criminal justice officials, and members of the public, is being misleadingly packaged. More than this, I believe that we would be do better to be more specific and precise, not to mention more realistic, in stating what it is we want from everyone: Caution in jumping to conclusions, circumspection in gathering, analyzing, and drawing inferences from the evidence, and patience in letting due process take its sometimes tedious and halting course. Further, with respect to police and prosecutors and their pretrial conduct, we should forcefully and repeatedly warn them about tactics that are well known to produce errors in investigating crimes and convicting persons of them. We should also take steps to actively discourage or prevent them from employing such tactics.

Once accused persons go to trial, assuming they do so, a full-blooded PI instruction to the jury on their behalf should be provided. Again, at that point, the aim is to reset the criminal justice process, at least in the minds of those tasked with rendering verdicts. All that they believe or know has gone before should be set to one side, and the government's proffers of evidence should be examined in the light of the accused's presumed innocence. The presumption is rebuttable, but only by powerful evidence that the accused are guilty of the crimes with which they have been charged.

CHAPTER 7 | Pretrial Detention and the Presumption of Innocence

INDIVIDUALS CHARGED WITH CRIMINAL offenses are sometimes detained until their trials or until the charges against them are resolved through plea bargaining. Such detention is the norm for individuals accused of serious crimes and, sometimes, not-so-serious ones, especially if the accused are deemed dangerous or if they are simply too poor to pay bail. Most everyone who has examined this practice has found aspects of it to be objectionable. One concern is that the conditions of pretrial detention are no better than, and often worse than, those experienced by individuals imprisoned for criminal convictions.[1] Since pretrial detainees have not yet been convicted, it seems incomprehensible why they should be treated as if they have been. Further, pretrial detention is often justified by government authorities on the grounds that those charged with crimes pose threats to others in the community.[2] Yet there are reasons to doubt the ability of government officials to predict, with much accuracy, the future offending of individuals.[3] This, in turn, means that many of those charged with crimes will be deprived of their liberty when, in fact, they pose no real threat to others in society. Also, given that pretrial detention disproportionately befalls the poor, and thus individuals who are already at a serious disadvantage when it comes to retaining quality defense counsel, detention compounds their woes by making it harder for them to meet with and help their attorneys to mount credible defenses to the charges against them.[4]

Beyond these specific concerns, there is an overarching one concerning whether pretrial detention is consistent with the presumption of innocence.[5] As we have seen, the PI is taken by many scholars to be a fundamental guiding norm of the legal, and specifically criminal justice, system. Individuals suspected of or formally accused of crimes are to be presumed innocent unless or until they are convicted, by a court of law, of one or more offenses. Yet not only does pretrial detention come rather too close to punishment prior to conviction, it is stigmatizing, in that the individuals subject to it are deemed too untrustworthy or dangerous to be allowed to live freely in the community while the charges against them are being adjudicated. They are thereby presumed and marked as probably guilty, or so it would seem.

Surprisingly, in spite of these and other problems with pretrial detention, some of pretrial detention's harshest critics defend its use in certain limited contexts. In particular, numerous scholars argue that pretrial detention can be justified when individuals charged with crimes are believed to be at risk to abscond or interfere with the course of justice by, say, threatening witnesses.[6] Yet these grounds for pretrial detention are sharply distinguished from detention for "mere dangerousness," which it is believed is rarely, if ever, justified. If mere dangerousness justifies pretrial detention, then it would also appear to justify detaining individuals who seem dangerous but who are not currently charged with any crimes; it might even justify detaining some individuals who have been acquitted of the charges against them if the authorities still deem them to be dangerous.[7]

Like others who have examined pretrial detention, I am dismayed at the casual approach to justifying and implementing it found in numerous legal jurisdictions. The chapter begins with an examination of the conditions of pretrial detention. I contend that individuals not yet convicted of crimes should not be treated like those who have been, even assuming that contemporary forms of imprisonment can be justified.[8] Specifically, I maintain that we ought to do much more to make pretrial detention as little like imprisonment as we can, consistent with its crime prevention aims. Though I am doubtful that reforms of the kinds I propose are in the offing, that fact, if it is one, has implications for the criteria to be employed in utilizing pretrial detention. Simply put, the more like ordinary imprisonment it is, the harder it should be to justify. This leads into the discussion in the second section of the chapter, in which I argue that we should tighten up the criteria for employing pretrial detention and strictly limit its duration. Simplifying a bit, I argue that individuals should be assigned to pretrial detention only if there is strong evidence that they have committed serious crimes and that they pose a substantial risk to others or are likely to abscond or otherwise interfere with the course of justice. Individuals charged with minor offenses will rarely satisfy these conditions and so should not be detained pretrial, though they might be reasonably required to pay bail. Even persons charged with more serious crimes might not satisfy them.

The first two sections prepare the way for the heart of the chapter's discussion. Not surprisingly, given my view that the PI is to be conceived narrowly, as a crucial component of the proof structure of criminal trials, I am skeptical about claims that pretrial detention conflicts with it. I contend that we can explain what is worrisome about pretrial detention—in particular, its profoundly disabling and stigmatizing effects—without invoking the presumption of innocence. Moreover, if pretrial detention conflicts with the PI, then so will many of the other forms of preconviction rights infringement routinely engaged in by legal authorities. It is possible, although it would be disastrous, to reject them all. The wiser course is to demand progressively more stringent justifications of such infringements of liberty, privacy, and autonomy, depending on their scope and duration. Pretrial detention is the most extreme form of justified right infringement short of conviction and punishment, especially where the latter involves imprisonment (or worse, death). For that reason, the burdens of justifying pretrial detention should be substantial. However, I believe that sometimes they can be shouldered by the authorities and that pretrial detention, whether to prevent other serious crimes or ensure the course of justice, can be defended. I therefore part ways with those scholars who reject pretrial detention outright and, more importantly, with those who seek to restrict it to accused persons who are deemed risks to abscond or interfere with the course of justice.

In the fourth section, I argue that absconding or interfering with the course of justice are not distinctive rationales for pretrial detention, contrary to the claims of numerous legal scholars. As with other future crimes, the authorities' concerns that some accused persons will abscond or otherwise interfere with the course of justice are only predictions. Thus, my position is that it is not plausible to draw a sharp distinction between pretrial detention for preventive purposes and for purposes of ensuring the course of justice.

In the fifth and final section, I consider other arguments against pretrial detention. Some scholars argue that pretrial detention amounts to depriving persons of their liberty merely because they are deemed dangerous. They also argue that we have limited abilities to predict future criminal misconduct. I argue that sufficiently demanding criteria for the justification of pretrial detention would require the authorities to demonstrate that an individual's dangerousness has been recently manifested and is likely to manifest again before the current charges against him or her have been resolved. Also, though our predictive abilities are far from perfect, the probability that a person will commit further crimes is not the only factor worth considering; also important is the seriousness of the crimes he or she might commit.

Institutionalizing a Distinction between Pretrial Detention and Legal Punishment

There is widespread agreement that pretrial detention should not be the equivalent of legal punishment. The US Supreme Court insists that pretrial detention is a "regulatory" practice, meaning, apparently, that it is not punishment but instead an effort by the government to ensure the safety of others in society until the charges against criminal defendants can be authoritatively adjudicated.[9] But in practice, there is little difference between pretrial detention and punishment proper. Pretrial detainees are usually kept in local jails and thus, like convicted prisoners, deprived of their liberty.[10] The material conditions of confinement for pretrial detainees are often worse than those for convicted offenders serving their sentences in state or federal prisons. Local jails are usually overcrowded, there are few, if any, work or educational opportunities, and visitation by family members and friends is difficult. Thus, pretrial detention brings with it the disabilities and deprivations attendant to imprisonment and then some. Further, it seems undeniable that pretrial detainees are stigmatized by their confinement. Even if government officials state repeatedly and publicly that pretrial detainees are "innocent until proven guilty," the fact is that detainees would not be where they are if they were deemed to be responsible or reliable members of society. It is hard to see pretrial detention as anything other than prepunishment—that is, as a preliminary for the real or further punishment of the accused that is believed to be more or less inevitable.[11]

It might be claimed that pretrial detention, unlike legal punishment, does not involve the official censure of individuals for their proven criminal conduct.[12] If punishment consists of both censure and hard treatment, then pretrial detention is not punishment. Perhaps, but pretrial detainees will likely suffer the strong suspicion of guilt in the public's mind, and their detention will mark them as something other than members in good standing in the community. Worse than this, it is well known that time served in pretrial detention is effectively converted to prison time through plea bargains in which prosecutors agree to suspended sentences or noncustodial ones in recognition of defendants already having been confined for some period of time.[13] Indeed, federal law in the United States requires that time in pretrial detention count toward the service of a custodial sentence.[14] The insistence that pretrial detainees are not (yet) being censured for their proven crimes, while correct as a matter of logic, seems dubious in light of such practices and the larger social reality in which they exist.

It is therefore easy to dismiss pretrial detention on the grounds that it amounts to the punishment of individuals before their guilt has been authoritatively demonstrated. Too easy, I believe. Pretrial detention does not have to resemble punishment so closely.[15] Assume for the time being that it is, in some cases, justified and that its sole justification is to prevent the commission of further crimes, whether they involve absconding or interfering with the course of justice, or offenses of other kinds. There is no good reason why pretrial detainees should be kept in the same or similar facilities as convicted prisoners. In fact, given their status as not-yet-convicted of anything, it seems clear that they should be kept in very different kinds of facilities—more like decent hotels than squalid local jails. Even if it can be shown that austere living conditions are a justified aspect of imprisonment for serious criminal convictions, such conditions seem unjustified for individuals who have only been accused of crimes.[16] Nothing about the preventive function of pretrial detention requires individuals to suffer cramped living quarters, near complete loss of privacy, isolation, poor-quality food, or predation by other detainees.

Also, pretrial detainees should not have to endure the many disabilities that attend imprisonment for criminal convictions. These include the loss of work and the income that goes with it, the loss of access to family members and loved ones, and the loss of leisure or recreational activities. Take work, for instance. At least some individuals accused of crimes and assigned pretrial attention will have been gainfully employed prior to their having been arrested and charged. The income they earned will have been used to support themselves and those dependent upon them. Why should pretrial detention preclude individuals from working if it is possible for arrangements to be made to facilitate its continuation? Or if such arrangements cannot be made, why should they and their dependents be expected to endure the loss of income that attends the inability to continue working? If we are not actively seeking to punish pretrial detainees, but only to prevent them from committing further crimes, the answers to these questions are elusive. This suggests that pretrial detainees whose work cannot be facilitated ought to be paid compensation for their lost income so that they can continue to fulfill their responsibilities to others and provide for their own needs and comfort above the level provided by the government (and to pay for private defense counsel, if they so choose). Of course, not all of the individuals accused of crimes and kept in pretrial detention will have been gainfully employed at the time of their alleged crimes. Some may have earned all or most of their income illegally. But others might have been actively searching for legal work, and some might have been on some form of public assistance. But for their detention, they might have found work and their public assistance would have continued. My sense is that these detainees also ought to be compensated, though perhaps not at the levels of the gainfully employed. Indeed, compensation at some minimal level might be the default position, with the onus on the government to show that detainees were not legally employed, searching for work, or eligible for public assistance prior to their arrests.

Access to family members and friends should also be facilitated for pretrial detainees. Conjugal visitation should be the norm and steps ought to be taken to ensure the privacy and dignity of detainees and their spouses or partners during visitations. Similarly, access to educational or job training programs should be facilitated, especially for detainees who were enrolled in such programs prior to their arrests. Even things like supervised excursions to parks or entertainment venues ought to be considered if pretrial detainees' lives are to be made as normal as is consistent with the preventive function.

It might be objected that though losses and disabilities of various kinds are more or less inevitable side effects of pretrial detention, the government does not intend them and therefore should not be under any obligation to ameliorate these effects or compensate detainees for having to endure them. After all, those held in pretrial detention must have done something to merit being in the predicaments they are in. Further, imprisonment for crimes imposes numerous disabilities or losses on individuals that the government is not expected to make up for, even if the government does not specifically intend to impose them on individuals. Pretrial detention might be thought to be enough like imprisonment to merit being conceived of in a similar light.

Granted, many—though not all—of the individuals who are assigned pretrial detention will have "done something" to find themselves in the predicaments they are in.[17] This might be enough to show that they merit the deprivation of their liberty until the charges against them are adjudicated. But it does not show that they merit all of the other disabilities and losses that pretrial detention inflicts, not if the aim of such detention is solely preventive. It is a mistake to view the losses of liberty, comfort, paid labor, and access to family and friends as an indivisible package, whether our focus is on imprisonment proper or pretrial detention.[18] Even convicted prisoners retain legal rights in whole or in part, and the courts have held that, with respect to some of them, the government must take positive steps to facilitate their exercise or realization.[19] More to the point, there are persuasive moral arguments that convicted prisoners not only retain rights but should have the exercise of those rights facilitated by the government if prisoners are not to suffer degradation (especially in the form of eroded capacities for moral responsibility) or profound diminishment of their abilities to re-enter society and function effectively.[20] If these arguments are persuasive in relation to individuals actually convicted of crimes, then they are presumably much stronger in relation to individuals whose guilt has yet to be authoritatively established.

It also will be objected that the reforms in pretrial detention I advocate will not actually work to fully distinguish it from ordinary prison confinement. It is undeniable that individuals held in pretrial detention, even under the improved conditions I urge, will continue to be stigmatized to some extent. Their status as law-abiding members of the community will remain in doubt.[21] But it is implausible to hold that detainees themselves would see no difference between existing forms of pretrial detention and the form I propose. The differences would be stark, even if reformed pretrial detention would not remove all taint from the individuals held in it.[22] The improved amenities and opportunities would also, it seems, alter the way in which pretrial detention appeared to the public. It would be much harder for members of the public to lump together, in their minds, pretrial detainees with ordinary prisoners confined for their crimes. They would see the two being treated very differently even if both were confined. Also, the public would have to foot the bill for the improved amenities and opportunities afforded pretrial detainees. Though it is not part of my argument for substantially improved pretrial detention conditions, these costs might serve the useful purpose of stemming the public's enthusiasm for pretrial detention. Perhaps that lessened enthusiasm would eventually percolate down to prosecutors and judges.

Granted, it is partly the increased costs entailed by reforming pretrial detention that will make doing so politically and economically infeasible. My purpose in discussing such reforms is more theoretical than practical. We should not dismiss pretrial detention because current forms of it are execrable. We should imagine it at its best, or at least better than it is, and then ask whether and how it can be justified. Of course, it we do not reform it, then it remains perilously close to legal punishment, and the conditions under which it is justified should have to resemble those under which we believe the punishment of individuals is justified. Since most of the individuals charged with crimes are likely to be unwilling, at the stage at which bail hearings occur, to admit their guilt, or will not have not done so as part of a formal plea process, this means that the government should have to furnish proof of their guilt that comes close to the reasonable doubt standard to the judge who must make the decision whether to release them on bail or remand them without it. There is also the question whether the government's evidence should be subject to contestation by defense counsel. In the next section, I sidestep these questions, assuming that pretrial detention has been reformed so that its resemblance to legal punishment is less of an obstacle to its use.

The Qualifying Conditions for Pretrial Detention

In addition to the dismal conditions of much pretrial detention, part of what concerns many is the relative ease with which it is imposed by the courts. Far from being the exception for the (disproportionately poor) individuals charged with crimes, it is too often the rule, especially in countries such as the United States. Legal scholars trace the slackness in eligibility criteria for pretrial detention in the United States to the Federal Bail Reform Act of 1984 and to the Supreme Court's 1987 decision in *United States v. Salerno*.[23] The former authorized pretrial detention on a finding by a judge that a defendant was "dangerous" and declined to impose upon judges the responsibility of finding that the evidence against a charged defendant established a "substantial probability" of the defendant's guilt as a condition of pretrial detention. The act also did little to limit the length of pretrial detention. The *Salerno* decision held that pretrial detention was not punishment and that assigning it to those accused persons thought to be dangerous served a legitimate regulatory—that is nonpunitive—purpose.

The defects in *Salerno* and the Federal Bail Reform Act have been well documented by others.[24] Since I support some preventive pretrial detention, my aim in this section is the limited one of articulating and briefly defending the qualifying conditions for such detention. We are much too lax about imposing it and so should tighten up our criteria for its use.

The qualifying conditions that should be placed on pretrial detention are of various kinds. First, we should insist, at least generally speaking, that it be used only on defendants whose alleged crimes satisfy some minimal level of seriousness.[25] I would urge an "imprisonable offense" test, according to which the only individuals eligible for pretrial detention would be ones who, if found guilty, are apt to be assigned custodial sanctions. Even if we reform pretrial detention in the ways outlined in the previous section, it seems wrong to detain individuals on charges that are unlikely to result in their imprisonment. For in that case, the pretrial losses and deprivations inevitably imposed on individuals will exceed anything that can be defensibly imposed on them after they are convicted. Granted, many criminal offenses come with sentence ranges that include a term of custody at their top ends.[26] We could permit individuals to be eligible for pretrial detention so long as they were charged with offenses that have custody as a possible outcome. But I would go further and require the government to show that custody is a likely outcome, in a given defendant's case, if she is found or pleads guilty, rather than a possible one. Given that the majority of crimes processed by the criminal justice system are relatively minor, one implication of this first qualifying condition would be that many of the persons accused of crimes would not be eligible for pretrial detention.[27] This is, I believe, as it should be. Pretrial detention should be rare, not commonplace.

Second, we should require government officials to demonstrate that they have substantial evidence of the guilt of defendants whom they wish to detain for imprisonable offenses.[28] Pretrial detention is not justified if officials can demonstrate only that they have "probable cause" to proceed with charges against individuals. Satisfying that weaker test might be enough to justify their proceeding with the adjudication of charges against individuals, but it seems too weak to justify the burdens of pretrial detention, even under much-improved conditions. Unless government officials meet the stronger test, their attempts to detain those whom they suspect of crimes will be largely indistinguishable from efforts to detain individuals whom they deem to be dangerous but cannot show, based on recent charges, are likely to be convicted of offenses for which they are apt to be imprisoned.

Yet satisfaction of the first two conditions is not enough, in my view. For it is possible to imagine cases in which defendants (*a*) are charged with offenses for which they are likely to face prison terms, and (*b*) are likely to be convicted of them, but (*c*) pose no credible threat to others in the community. For instance, sometimes individuals charged with aggravated assault or homicide (allegedly, we should say) victimized others who harshly provoked them. Those charged might not have targeted strangers; they also might not have histories of unprovoked violence or predation. Whether such defendants should be detained, as opposed to being released on bond, perhaps while subject to a variety of conditions, might be a close call. But it does not seem inconceivable or irresponsible for them to be released if there is little reason to believe that they pose a threat to others in the community. Hence, I would require the government to satisfy a third requirement, one that we might term a "dangerousness" condition. The government should have to convince a judge that a defendant whom it wishes to detain is "reasonably likely" to commit further, imprisonable offenses pretrial. The government could satisfy this test in several ways. First, it could argue that, given a defendant's lengthy criminal history, the current alleged offense appears to be another incident in a life significantly marked by serious criminal conduct.[29] Second, the government could argue that, given certain specific features of the alleged current offense, there is good reason to believe that the defendant poses a significant threat to the community. For instance, if the alleged offense involved violence against persons unknown to the defendant or in the absence of provocation or other mitigating factors, then pretrial detention might be in order even in the absence of the defendant having a history of significant offending. Third, a defendant might be reasonably deemed dangerous if he has made dire threats against others, either before or after his arrest, that he has not fully and voluntarily renounced.

It might be objected that the dangerousness condition ought to suffice, all by itself, to justify pretrial detention, regardless of whether individuals have been charged with imprisonable offenses. After all, why should it matter what kind of offense with which an individual has been charged if there are credible grounds for believing that she poses an imminent threat to others in the community? However, as I subsequently argue, substantial evidence that one has committed a serious offense does matter, for it indicates the recent activation of one's dangerous dispositions or impulses. That combined with persuasive evidence that they might be activated again in the near future constitutes adequate grounds for detaining individuals. In the absence of evidence of recent serious offenses, we would be detaining people on rather flimsy evidence of their "mere dangerousness," as critics of pretrial detention for preventive purposes sometimes allege.

Even if the government can satisfy the first three conditions, it should also have to demonstrate that there are no alternative, less restrictive means to prevent the crimes that it fears defendants might commit before the current charges against them are fully adjudicated.[30] In some cases, the posting of a substantial bond, along with requiring defendants to satisfy other requirements, might be sufficient to protect the community. Defendants' established roots in a community, including the support and oversight of their families, ought to count for something toward keeping them out of pretrial detention. Also, defendants could be required to surrender their passports, report their whereabouts and activities on a regular (and perhaps daily) basis to the authorities, or wear electronic monitoring devices in lieu of pretrial detention. Some defendants, especially those with checkered pasts, histories of absconding, and few ties to the communities in which they have been charged with crimes, will and should have a hard time convincing a judge that there are less intrusive means than pretrial detention to provide assurance to the community that they will not quickly reoffend. But not all defendants will be like this, and the government should have to rebut their claims that alternative means will work to monitor and control them.

Finally, we should look for ways to keep pretrial detention brief. The prosecution might be periodically required to establish that it is making "reasonable progress" toward bringing the case against a detainee to trial, with the threat of release of the defendant from detention if the government fails to do so.[31] We could also require the government to give priority to the cases of pretrial detainees, in the sense that they would automatically move up in the queue of cases scheduled for trial adjudication. Further, we could require the government to periodically renew its request for the pretrial detention of accused persons. Even if nothing much had changed that would invalidate the government's case for continued detention, the burden of having to justify it on a recurring basis might give the government some incentive to speed up the trials of persons held in custody.

Pretrial Detention and the Presumption of Innocence

Suppose that we reform pretrial detention so that it is not like ordinary imprisonment and restrict its use in the ways detailed in the previous section. Is it still plausible to argue that pretrial detention is never justified solely on the grounds that the authorities fear that the accused poses a threat to others in the community? Consider the following case: Suppose that Jones has been arrested and charged with rape. Suppose also that Jones has previous convictions for rape involving persons unknown to him and that his assaults always involved a specific modus operandi that is again evident in the current case. Suppose also that the physical and other evidence strongly implicates Jones, though Jones denies his guilt. Does anyone seriously doubt that Jones might be reasonably detained prior to his trial? As a matter of fact, numerous scholars do doubt it.[32]

One common argument against pretrial detention is that it conflicts with the presumption of innocence.[33] Individuals who have merely been charged with crimes have not yet been authoritatively shown to be guilty of them and so something other than citizens in good standing in the community. Even if pretrial detention conditions are dramatically improved, they impose significant liberty deprivations on individuals in the absence of a demonstration, beyond a reasonable doubt, that they deserve them. Also, pretrial detention likely cannot be shorn of all of its stigmatizing effects. Individuals detained will be made by it to appear guilty and dangerous—at least that is what members of the community seem likely to infer from decisions by the courts to authorize their detention. Yet if one subscribes to the view that we should, as far as possible, regard and treat accused persons as if they are materially innocent, then the tension between doing so and pretrial detention appears undeniable.

In previous chapters, I have expressed skepticism about a pretrial presumption of innocence. Hence, it should come as no surprise that I am unpersuaded by arguments to the effect that pretrial detention is in conflict with the PI. Again, we should urge the authorities to exercise considerable caution as they move to arrest and charge individuals with crimes. They should avoid too easily or quickly presuming the material or probative guilt (which is not the same as presuming either their material or probative innocence) of suspects, because they should bear in mind their own susceptibility to error and the unpredictable nature of the adjudicative process. Even when the authorities have convincing evidence of the guilt of individuals, they should fully support and abide by the rules and expectations of due process, rather than seeking to thwart or sidestep them. Citizens generally should refrain from presuming the guilt of the arrested or accused and should insist that charge adjudication follow fair and strict procedures. On error distribution accounts of the adjudication process, the societal commitment to due process is grounded in the strong preference to avoid wrongful convictions of the innocent over wrongful acquittals of the guilty. On the moral assurance account defended in chapter 5, we observe rigorous standards of due process in order to ensure that when we punish individuals, we do so justifiably.

More than caution by criminal justice officials is needed. We also should insist that they bear successive burdens of justification as they move from suspicion to stopping and questioning individuals, to arresting and investigating them, to charging them with crimes. Yet such burdens of justification are not grounded in a preadjudication presumption of innocence, and indeed such a presumption struggles to account for them. Instead, they are grounded in basic rights to liberty and autonomy, which are progressively intruded upon as legal authorities proceed to develop cases against individuals for their suspected crimes. The greater such intrusions, the more demanding the burdens of justifying them should be, albeit they cannot, consistently with police and prosecutors doing their jobs, approach the burdens placed on the government to establish guilt in criminal trials. Importantly, none of the critics of pretrial detention suggest that individuals cannot be treated as suspects. Accordingly, there is a long list of things that individuals can be required to do or provide the authorities that they might strongly wish not to do or provide. Further, no one denies that individuals charged with crimes can be required to post bail in order to assure the community that they will appear and answer to the charges against them.[34] Indeed, the posting of bail is routinely cast as a mostly benign alternative to pretrial detention, one that does not conflict with the presumption of innocence. Yet we would never think to require citizens whose good standing in the community is not somewhat in doubt to offer us such assurance.[35]

If we can require criminal suspects and those charged with crimes to do a host of things that we would never require of citizens whose good standing in the community is undoubted, this raises the question why we cannot impose the further burden of pretrial detention on some individuals charged with crimes. As I have conceded, such detention ought to be difficult to justify, given the extent and duration of its intrusion upon individuals' basic rights. Also, the conditions under which individuals are detained ought to be reformed; such detention is not punishment and should not be like it. Further, we could require the authorities to keep pretrial detention brief and regularly justify its continuation. Given such precautions and safeguards, it seems implausible to suggest that no individuals charged with crimes can be preventively detained, no matter how grave the charges against them, powerful the evidence in support of those charges, or palpable the danger that they represent to others in the community.

As we have seen, supporters of a pretrial presumption of innocence might argue that the presumption is progressively defeasible in the pretrial context.[36] On such an account, the presumption operates to ground the kinds of progressively more stringent justifications for intrusions into the lives of citizens seemingly required by enforcement of the criminal law.[37] But first, there is the problem of explaining how the PI can be overcome at each stage of official intrusion into the lives of suspects or formally accused persons only to bounce back to ground further justificatory burdens. Once the PI is initially breached, as it were, why is it not altogether vanquished? Second, even if, somewhat mysteriously, it can be resurrected, how is it that its second, third, or fourth comings produce progressively stronger justificatory burdens on criminal justice officials? Third, it is not apparent how a defeasibility approach can yield a sharp line between some ways in which the PI is appropriately defeated and others in which it is not. Arrests, searches of their property and records, formal charges that hang over them, bail requirements and conditions, and court appearance requirements are far from trivial intrusions upon the lives of individuals, yet the PI must be understood to accommodate them. How, then, is pretrial detention in a wholly separate category, rather than existing along a continuum of official defeasement of the PI? Finally, how can an account according to which the PI is defeasible avoid the implication that some individuals are presumed less innocent than others? The defeasibility account would seem to entail that the PI can be partial or qualified. Yet I would have thought that individuals are either presumed innocent or they are not.

Detention for Some Purposes, Not Others?

Though there is considerable resistance to employing pretrial detention to prevent some kinds of pretrial crimes, because it is thought that doing so contravenes the PI, there is less resistance to employing it to prevent other kinds. In particular, pretrial detention for those who might abscond before the charges against them have been adjudicated, or who might interfere with the course of justice (e.g., by threatening witnesses against them), is believed by many scholars to be less problematic.[38] It would seem to matter whether potential pretrial detainees have been caught in the act of absconding or interfering with the course of justice, or whether it is only feared that they will do so based on, say, their past criminal records. Many who object to pretrial detention aimed at preventing robberies, rapes, or murders do so on the grounds that such criminal acts should not be presumed likely to occur or cannot with much accuracy be predicted. Yet similar objections should hold for absconding or interferences with the course of justice that are only surmised by the authorities. Moreover, even if defendants have been caught in the act of absconding or interfering with the course of justice, we might question why such (to this point) mere allegations that they have committed further crimes constitute grounds for pretrial detention, though reasonable fears that they will commit other, and perhaps much more serious crimes, purportedly do not.

In response to the concern that justifying pretrial detention for some purposes but not others creates an inconsistency, Duff argues that when we detain individuals who have absconded or interfered with the course of justice, we are not necessarily acting merely to prevent future crimes. Instead, we might be stopping crimes already in progress, as when individuals acting in self-defense, or authorities acting in the defense of others, use coercion to interfere with crimes in progress.[39] As a rationale for pretrial detention, Duff's has quite limited scope. It does not seem that his argument could be used to support the pretrial detention of individuals charged with crimes who the authorities merely have very good reason (based on their lengthy criminal histories) to believe will abscond or interfere with the course of justice. Their absconding or interfering is not yet underway. A further difficulty is that the police might not detect some interferences with the course of justice until after they are fully completed. Defendants might have already gotten to and intimated witnesses, or bribed them, or killed them. Pretrial detention of such defendants after they have already acted in these ways will not be easily defended on the grounds that it prevents the completion of crimes.[40]

Marc Miller and Martin Guggenheim likewise defend pretrial detention for those who abscond or interfere with the course of justice, but are uneasy about defending it for those who it is thought might commit other kinds of offenses. Miller and Guggenheim admit that deprivation of liberty is sometimes justified in the absence of a clear punitive purpose. The government can quarantine individuals who have contagious diseases and who cannot otherwise be kept from infecting others. It can also confine and treat the seriously mentally ill, or confine those who are in the country illegally until they can be deported.[41] Likewise, when the government detains individuals charged with crimes because it fears they might abscond or interfere with the course of justice, it has as its legitimate purpose ensuring complete and fair trials (or other adjudication of the charges against them). However, Miller and Guggenheim contend that when the purpose of pretrial detention is purely preventive, based on a concern to incapacitate individuals so that they do not commit further, pretrial crimes, then detention is illicit because it is indistinguishable from legal punishment. No nonpunitive purpose is served by such detention. Moreover, individuals so detained have not yet been authoritatively convicted of any crimes or shown to have been responsible agents at the time of their (alleged) crimes.[42]

However, even if detention in some cases is purely preventive, it does not follow that it is the equivalent of legal punishment. For one thing,

Miller and Guggenheim leave out of their account of legal punishment the requirement that it involves the authoritative censure of the conduct of individuals.[43] Whatever else we say or think about individuals held in pretrial detention for preventive purposes, it seems incorrect to say or think that their past conduct is already being authoritatively censured. It is not, at least not until they are convicted and sentenced by a judge. Of course, Miller and Guggenheim might argue that existing conditions of pretrial confinement are so similar to those endured by the officially censured (and punished) that pretrial detainees are, tacitly if not yet officially, condemned for their crimes. But as we have seen, the conditions of pretrial detention could be altered so that the appearance of prematurely imposed censure would be harder to infer from them. If pretrial detainees were kept in different, and much nicer, facilities, compensated for lost income, and guaranteed access to family members and friends, it would be harder to cast their losses of liberty as involving censure and thus legal punishment.

Also, Miller and Guggenheim seem prepared to accept the pretrial detention of individuals not yet convicted of absconding or interfering with the course of justice, including individuals who the authorities only reasonably fear will do such things.[44] But if individuals can be detained for some predicted crimes, why not for others, especially in cases in which the latter might turn out to be much more serious crimes? Further, if individuals are detained pretrial because the government fears that they will abscond or interfere with the course of justice, it is hard to see how, given Miller and Guggenheim's account, they are not *being* punished.[45] Miller and Guggenheim can claim that the government has another purpose in detaining them, but (*a*) that is a distinction likely to be lost on those detained, and (*b*) we might wonder why it is so important for the government to pursue that purpose to its completion in the absence of some concern about the criminal proclivities of the individuals in question. It is not clear whether Miller and Guggenheim accept the "imprisonable offense" constraint on eligibility for pretrial detention that I have urged. If they do not, then their position will support the pretrial detention of individuals charged with relatively minor offenses, to ensure the course of justice, but not individuals with lengthy criminal histories charged with very serious crimes if, for some reason, they appear unlikely to abscond or interfere with the course of justice. That seems an awkward position to defend.

Finally, Lawrence Tribe has argued that focusing pretrial detention narrowly on defendants who might abscond or interfere with the course of justice serves the larger deterrent aims of the criminal law by ensuring the integrity or completion of the adjudicative process.[46] The idea seems to be that if we do not take steps to see that process through, by detaining those who would escape or thwart its outcomes, then we will not appear serious about enforcing the criminal law, to our ultimate detriment. Yet this argument is unconvincing. We show our commitment to the deterrent purposes of the criminal law, in the main, by arresting, charging, and convicting individuals of having violated its strictures. We do so, further, by arresting (or rearresting) those who abscond or interfere with the course of justice, charging them with those crimes, and attempting to convict and sentence them. The idea that the deterrent function of the criminal law will be substantially weakened if we do not, additionally, detain pretrial those who abscond or interfere with the course of justice, or appear prepared to do so, stretches credulity. Moreover, if, pretrial, we return to the community individuals who we have good reason to believe will commit further, quite serious crimes, that might lead some citizens reasonably to question our seriousness about seeing to the enforcement of the criminal law.

Let me come at the contention that we can detain persons in order to ensure the course of justice, though not to prevent other crimes, in a different way. According to some legal scholars, until persons are duly convicted of crimes, they are to be presumed responsible citizens in good standing in their communities. Yet responsible citizens, if they are accused of criminal wrongdoing, will not be prone to absconding or interfering with the course of justice. It is not even clear why such citizens should be required to post bail to assure us that they will appear; that should be presumed. This then suggests that pretrial detention in order to ensure the course of justice implicitly communicates some distrust of persons. Precisely because they have been formally charged with crimes, we are less certain about their commitment to being responsible citizens. If we add to that a history of previous offenses, whether of interferences with the course of justice or other crimes, such doubts on our part about their commitment to responsible citizenship seem increasingly warranted. Yet it is not clear how to square such reasonable doubts with a presumption of innocence or why such doubts should be confined to their prospects for refraining from certain kinds of future lawbreaking but not others. It might be claimed that pretrial detention in order to ensure the course of justice does not involve us in taking a stance on the likely guilt or innocence of persons with respect to the current charges against them.[47] Thus, such detention is fully consistent with the PI. But I wonder whether this is correct, especially if we insist upon some level of evidence sufficiency in relation to the current charges before we authorize pretrial detention for any purpose. Also, pretrial detention premised on the need to prevent further serious crimes of other kinds is consistent with the possibility that the accused will not be convicted on the current charges. Such detention does not preclude due process with respect to the current charges or preordain its outcome.

It might be claimed that pretrial detention in order to prevent absconding has a distinctive justification: We need accused persons to participate in the adjudication process in order to fully and properly determine the accuracy of the charges against them. However, such an argument seems unconvincing for two reasons: First, accused persons can elect to remain silent during the pretrial process and during their trials. Indeed, during their trials, accused persons do not have to offer any kind of affirmative defense. Their attorneys might elect only to dispute the government's case, with the aim of creating reasonable doubts about it. Having the accused present but silent seems of scant value when it comes to determining the accuracy of the charges against them. Second, accused persons can be tried in absentia, especially if they are represented by competent attorneys who defend them (which, again, does not require active participation by the accused at their trials) against the charges. This seems less than ideal, of course, primarily because defense counsel might be hamstrung in their efforts by not having the accused available for consultation. But this assumes that the accused cannot communicate their wishes to defense counsel through back channels, as it were. Also, it is unclear why we should not see this disadvantage to the accused as freely incurred once they made the decision to abscond. So long as the government has made reasonable efforts to locate the accused and return them to the relevant jurisdiction, trials in absentia do not seem fatally flawed exercises in due process.

Detention, Dangerousness, and Prediction

Other arguments against preventive pretrial detention exist, though they are not usually couched in terms of its incompatibility with an alleged pretrial presumption of innocence. One of these arguments says that if we are justified in detaining suspects or defendants pretrial based on their alleged dangerousness, then the logic of such a policy requires us to detain anyone whom the authorities deem to be dangerous, whether or not they have recently been charged with offending.[48] If a person's past criminal history, or perhaps his actuarial characteristics (being young, unemployed, and a drug user) make him a viable candidate for pretrial detention, then why should such characteristics not lead us toward more worrisome forms of preventive detention, ones detached from evidence of recent offending? Lawrence Tribe offers a further wrinkle to this argument with the suggestion that if mere dangerousness is a sufficient condition of preventive pretrial detention, then why should individuals who have been acquitted of the most recent charges against them be released from detention if the authorities believe them to have been wrongly acquitted and still dangerous?[49]

However, it is misleading to characterize the selective use of pretrial detention as constituting detention for "mere dangerousness." In my view, we might justifiably employ it for individuals charged (or soon to be charged) with recent offenses for which imprisonment is a likely outcome of conviction, the government can offer strong proof of their guilt, there is substantial evidence that they pose a threat to others, and there are no other means, besides detention, to prevent further crimes. This is hardly detention for mere dangerousness based on something as nonspecific as an individual's actuarial characteristics. Instead, it is detention based on considerable evidence that an individual's dangerousness has recently manifested itself in one or more imprisonable offenses and is likely to do so again before the charges for those recent alleged acts are resolved.[50] Also, if a defendant is acquitted, then a crucial part of the grounds for detaining him—that his dangerousness has apparently manifested itself in one or more recent imprisonable offenses—disappears. His detention would no longer be pretrial but preventive detention proper, with all of its attendant hazards and difficulties, not the least of which is that there is no natural endpoint to it.[51] Granted, the authorities might believe that the individual is dangerous, perhaps because his acquittal turned on the exclusion of damning but improperly obtained evidence. They therefore might have good reasons to monitor his activities closely, but not to confine him.

Tribe also suggests that if we detain individuals for preventive purposes, in the absence of evidence that they are unable to control their actions, we treat them as if they are incapable of moral responsibility.[52] But this does not follow, for there is no contradiction in believing that an individual is capable of moral self-restraint but also (based on evidence of her criminal history or features of her alleged current crimes) that she is unlikely to exhibit it consistently. We can reasonably view some individuals as morally weak or feckless human beings without regarding them as psychopaths for whom moral considerations have no purchase. Moreover, in many legal jurisdictions, psychopaths are treated as responsible beings for the purposes of the criminal law.[53] Suppose that someone who has previously been determined to be a psychopath, one with a lengthy and violent criminal history, is arrested and charged with an imprisonable offense and the evidence is convincing that she committed it. Would opponents of pretrial detention for preventive purposes balk at remanding such an individual until the current charges against her are authoritatively resolved? That seems an unpromising position to defend.

Another objection to pretrial detention for preventive purposes is that we are very bad at predicting who will commit future crimes, even if it is clear that they have likely committed them in the past. Critics of pretrial detention routinely cite studies suggesting that for every true positive prediction, there are two false positives.[54] Also, they cite statistics suggesting that a very low percentage of defendants charged with crimes commit further crimes prior to the current charges against them being tried, plea-bargained, or otherwise resolved.[55] Yet as Albert Alschuler convincingly argues, the evidence relied on in making these arguments suffers from a near-fatal defect, namely, that the accused persons deemed most dangerous by the government rarely get released prior to their trials and so given the opportunity to offend pretrial.[56] Such individuals will not show up in the relevant studies, though they are surely the ones about whom we should be most concerned.[57] Also, studies of pretrial crime that include individuals remanded under current, lax standards for detention are bound to find that many of them pose little threat. After all, if the government has to show only that there is "probable cause" to believe that accused persons are dangerous, this will inevitably sweep in many individuals who could be safely released (after posting bond or without requiring them to do so). But from this we should be cautious about concluding that more rigorous pretrial detention criteria would fare no better in corralling those with worrisome criminal proclivities.

Further, it would be folly to insist that pretrial detention for preventive purposes can be justified only if we can predict with certainty that defendants will commit further offenses before the current charges against them are adjudicated. Some weight must be given to the gravity of the crimes they might commit in addition to the probability that they will commit them. A 30 percent risk that a defendant might, in the interim, murder or rape someone else, or even a 10 percent risk that he might do so, could arguably be reasonable grounds for pretrial detention.

Concluding Remarks

Much pretrial detention is scandalous. It is too much like the imprisonment of individuals actually convicted of crimes, is imposed using lax criteria, and often lasts far too long. Yet most of these defects in it are remediable, and the pointed and difficult question we then face is whether it is ever justifiably used to protect the community from individuals who have been charged with serious offenses and regarding whom there is good reason to fear that they will commit further serious crimes before the current charges against them have been fully resolved. I have argued that it is. The evidence against some individuals charged with serious crimes will be powerful and the character of their acts, or their past histories, will strongly suggest that they pose substantial threats to others if they are released before the current charges against them are fully resolved. Though briefly remanding them under conditions that are no more harsh than necessary to prevent such crimes is an imposition, so are many other things we routinely require of suspects and individuals charged with crimes. True, it is more of an imposition than most of these, but it does not follow that it is unjustified in a limited number of cases.

It is hard to see how pretrial detention premised on the prevention of serious crimes that might inflict grave harm on individuals is inconsistent with the PI, but requiring the accused to post bail or remain in detention because they pose flight risks or are deemed likely to interfere with the course of justice is not. Responsible citizens accused of crimes should be trusted to appear to answer to the charges against them and refrain from actions designed to taint or derail the legal proceedings that will determine their fates. If in spite of this we take steps to ensure that accused persons show up for their trials and refrain from corrupting them, this suggests some diminishment in their presumed good standing. It is possible, though far from unproblematic, to maintain that the PI is defeasible in the pretrial context. But if it can be, then it is not apparent why it cannot be reasonably interpreted to permit pretrial detention for crime prevention purposes.

CHAPTER 8 | Incomplete Prosecutions and the Presumption of Innocence

WHEN INDIVIDUALS ARE ARRESTED for or charged with crimes, their lives are often altered in ways from which they will unable to recover easily or fully, even if they are never convicted of criminal wrongdoing. Arrest, investigation, and formal accusation stigmatize individuals, besmirching their good names and reputations, at least on the assumption that they had them to begin with.[1] More than this, those charged with crimes, or merely suspected of them, may be suspended from their jobs, or lose them outright. If the formally accused are held in pretrial detention, then lost jobs, along with the much-needed income that goes with them, are almost assured, and relations with spouses and other family members will be strained. Further, pretrial detention makes the accused look guilty, as detainees are typically kept in facilities alongside individuals already convicted of crimes.[2] And such detention can last months or even years.[3] Individuals ultimately acquitted of all charges against them will struggle to reclaim their positions of honor and respect in their communities.

I shall refer to arrests that do not lead to charges, or charges that do not result in convictions, as "incomplete" prosecutions. Not all incomplete prosecutions are "failed" prosecutions. In some cases, police or prosecutors decide not to file or continue to press charges for very good reasons—namely, they determine that the individuals who have fallen under suspicion do not appear to be guilty of criminal wrongdoing. Indeed, when police or prosecutors discontinue prosecutions in such cases, their doing so should be viewed as "successes." We very much want the authorities to respond in these ways to the emerging evidence when doing so is appropriate. Also, some prosecutions are obviously more incomplete than others. In cases in which arrests occur but charges do not follow, it might be said that prosecutions have never actually commenced. Though I concede this point, I want a term that neutrally covers the diverse group of cases in which individuals become entangled in the criminal justice system to some extent or other, but are not convicted.

The grounds for incomplete prosecutions are often opaque. Police have considerable discretion in deciding not only whom to arrest but which arrests to refer to prosecutors.[4] Also, depending on the legal system in question, prosecutors might have enormous discretion in deciding whom to charge and with what to charge them.[5] In some legal systems, if prosecutors decide not to file charges, or to do so and drop them, they do not have to explain their reasons for doing so, at least not up to the point at which official indictments have been handed down. Further, juries in common-law countries issue general verdicts, which preclude them from having to explain why they acquitted defendants.

All of this means that many incomplete prosecutions will be ambiguous in their import concerning the conduct of the individuals who have fallen under official suspicion. Did police not refer an arrest to prosecutors because they decided that the individual arrested was likely innocent of the crime or crimes of which they suspected him, or did the police instead decide to enlist the individual as an undercover informant? Did prosecutors decline to file charges because they decided that the individuals whom the police arrested were not guilty of the crimes for which they were arrested? Or did prosecutors decide not to file charges, or subsequently drop them, because they could not muster enough convincing evidence against those whom they continue to suspect of having committed crimes (perhaps because crucial pieces of evidence were ruled inadmissible by a judge)? Jury acquittals are notoriously ambiguous, especially in countries with binary verdict systems. "Not guilty" verdicts are consistent with most jurors believing that the accused were likely guilty, just not guilty beyond a reasonable doubt. But acquittals might also signify that jurors believed the accused were probably innocent.

The ambiguities surrounding incomplete prosecutions are what hinder the abilities of those arrested for or accused of crimes to resume their former lives. Individuals not convicted of crimes can point to the incomplete prosecutions against them and claim exoneration. But arrest and charging records might dog them for years to come, and acquittals might be viewed by others in society as "injustices" or "escapes" more than "exonerations." It is thus natural to ask what, if anything, we owe the subjects of incomplete prosecutions. It is clear that the government must not impose legal sanctions on them, or encourage private citizens to engage in vigilante actions against them. Although important, seeing to it that neither of these occurs might do little to help the arrested or accused to regain the trust and esteem of their fellow citizens.

In this chapter, I approach the question whether we should do more to aid those whose prosecutions were incomplete by examining it through the lens of the presumption of innocence. As we saw in chapter 4, the PI can be interpreted in several different ways in the trial context. The trial context is a unique one, however. In it, we want the individuals charged with rendering verdicts to subject the government's evidence against accused persons to a stern test. Therefore, urging jurors or judges to begin trials with a framing perspective according to which the accused are regarded as materially innocent appears needed and appropriate. Yet I argued against the adoption of such a perspective in the pretrial, or preadjudication, context. There, insisting that legal officials, and members of the public, adopt and act according to nonpresumptions of material or probative guilt seem more sensible.

The contrast between a presumption of material innocence and a nonpresumption of guilt is central to the analysis of incomplete prosecutions in this chapter. Simply put, if individuals are to be regarded and treated as if they are materially innocent, as far as possible, until they are convicted of crimes, then it is initially unclear whether any steps are needed to help the subjects of incomplete prosecutions. Efforts to help such individuals repair their names and reputations seem at odds with the attitudes and treatment to which their presumed citizenship in good standing entitles them. Still, proponents of PI_m might acknowledge the ways in which official suspicion or accusation is damaging to individuals' future life-prospects and so support societal efforts to help them get on with their lives. Perhaps employers, licensing boards, credit agencies, and other parties with whom the subjects of incomplete prosecutions come into contact should be encouraged, or required, to regard and treat them as citizens in good standing, regardless of their past records of arrests and official accusation. One question that we will consider is whether such prescribed attitudes and conduct are reasonable given the very real risks that some of those arrested or charged might pose.

In line with my rejection of a pretrial PI, I urge a different approach to the subjects of incomplete prosecutions. If nonpresumptions of material or probative guilt are more defensible pretrial, then "caution" ought to be our guiding principle, along with a commitment to fair and accurate investigative and adjudicative procedures. Yet caution is not to be confused with naiveté. Arrest, charges, and trials convey important signals about individuals. Many of the individuals who become entangled in the criminal justice system are guilty of criminal misconduct, even if they are never convicted of it. Of course, some are entirely innocent, and some are guilty only of minor or highly infrequent forms of it. Thus, my account does not support a "one size fits all" approach to the subjects of incomplete prosecutions. Policies or procedures that require legal officials or citizens to treat and regard all subjects of incomplete prosecutions as responsible citizens, come what may, seem inadvisable. Though we should look for ways to help those with arrest and charging records to get on with their lives, I argue that we should balance the desirability of doing so against the value of preventing future crimes, some of which might turn out to be serious.

The chapter proceeds as follows: In the first section, I note the casual ways in which, outside of the criminal justice context, we typically go about gathering information about our fellow citizens and acting on that information. I then turn to the signals about our fellow citizens conveyed by incomplete prosecutions and examine the factors that determine how much significant information they convey. In the second section, I outline some of the remedies that might be provided to those arrested or charged, though never convicted, to enable them to more fully resume the exercise and enjoyment of their basic moral and legal rights. The third section then lays out, in a general way, various approaches we might take to the subjects of incomplete prosecutions. Although my primary focus will be on the PI_m and the non-PG accounts, I briefly discuss other approaches that lie somewhere between the two. The remainder of the chapter discusses the implications of all of these approaches for the remedies outlined in the second section.

Evaluating the Signals Sent by Incomplete Prosecutions

In everyday life, we have a variety of reasons for acquiring information about our neighbors, coworkers, those whom we might hire for their professional services, or those with whom we interact in more or less organized settings. In acquiring this information, we typically draw on our own or others' observations and experiences with the persons in question. Before we hire a contractor to work on our house, for instance, we might consult with organizations that keep records of complaints about contractors, or we might ask coworkers or neighbors what they thought about one or more of the contractors who did work for them. Depending on how trustworthy or knowledgeable we believe our coworkers or neighbors to be—something that is itself the product of observations of them, experiences with them, or advice from others who know them better—we arrive at provisional judgments about which contractor is likely to do the best job for us. We might, of course, encounter conflicting opinions about the contractors we are considering from those we consult, or their views might be contradicted by records of complaints compiled by organizations such as the Better Business Bureau. In such cases, we might not know what to conclude and so might continue to search for contractors whose reputations are more uniformly positive. How serious or conscientious about all of this we should be will typically depend on what is at stake—whether we need something relatively undemanding, such as having our lawn mowed, or more complex, such as having our house renovated. In some cases, when it is a matter simply of forming impressions about the people with whom we interact at work or in our neighborhoods, we rely heavily on clues from their behavior or demeanor—how they speak, treat other persons, their apparent honesty or willingness to reciprocate favors, and so on.

The opinions that we form about our fellow citizens often lead us to extend various kinds of benefits or opportunities to them or to withhold them. Extending such benefits or opportunities to them will often make their lives easier or better. Withholding such benefits or opportunities might not make their lives worse, but it might deprive them of the means to make their lives go better. Even if we are careful and conscientious in forming opinions about other persons and acting on them, as we surely should be, the evidence and clues that we rely on will rarely enable us to draw conclusions about them with anything approaching certainty. It would be inappropriate, it seems, to insist that in the course of forming and acting on opinions about others, we should employ the exacting "reasonable doubt" standard, such that we ought to never act on an opinion about others if there is room for reasonable doubt about whether our opinion is correct. Not only would insisting upon such a standard be a prescription for paralysis in our everyday interactions, our decisions to withhold benefits or opportunities from others is nothing like inflicting legal punishment—with its characteristic censure and hard treatment—upon them.[6] Granted, there are occasions on which we ought to act with considerable care in making and acting on decisions of these kinds. For instance, in making decisions about whom to hire for a job, employers should make careful assessments of the relevant kinds of evidence. But even hiring decisions will often, and defensibly it seems, come down to impressions or hunches about individuals that would never survive an epistemic standard of near certainty. And this will especially be true when there are a number of qualified candidates for a position among whom employers must choose.

Of what relevance are the preceding points to our thinking about a defensible approach to the subjects of incomplete prosecutions? It seems clear that arrest, charge, and trial records are relevant to our interactions with them, at least when we become aware of them. As I have already noted, much of what goes on in the criminal justice system is effectively anonymous. Lots of people are arrested for or charged with misdemeanors, and we might never learn about more than a few such incidents.[7] Yet if we are employers, members of licensing boards, or lenders, we might learn of such things rather more often. How should we respond if and when we do? It is easy to say that, short of their having terminated in criminal convictions, we should ignore or attempt to ignore records of incomplete prosecutions. But I believe that such an approach is untenable. Instead, a more evidence-based and balanced approach to such records makes more sense. What would such an approach have us take into account?

First, and most obviously, the character of the suspected or alleged misconduct seems relevant. Was the person arrested or charged with a misdemeanor or with a felony? The more serious the suspected misconduct, the more worrisome, though admittedly uncertain, the signals that the record sends. Alleged acts of violence or predation, in particular, will invariably—and I argue reasonably—give us more pause than alleged acts of public intoxication or disorderly conduct.

Second, how far along in the criminal justice process did the investigation and suspicions of the authorities proceed? Was there only an arrest without charges, or were there charges and perhaps a trial at which the accused person was acquitted? Did charges drag out for a time until they were ultimately dismissed? This might suggest that prosecutors had good reason to believe that the individual in question was guilty as charged. Also, trials might reveal considerable evidence of wrongdoing by accused persons, though not evidence that was convincing (to the jury or judge) of guilt beyond a reasonable doubt.

Third, how frequently has the person in question been arrested, charged, or tried, though without being convicted of any crimes? A single arrest without any charges being filed is one thing; numerous arrests or charges, though without any convictions, are another. Admittedly, the possibility of "usual suspects" policing must be borne in mind: Police will often investigate, arrest, or seek charges against individuals who already have past records, perhaps whether those records are of convictions or only of arrests and charges.[8] But it will, and I believe should, make a difference to our thinking about and interacting with a person if she has repeatedly been arrested for or charged with crimes, even if she has never been convicted.

Fourth, how recent was the incomplete prosecution? In some cases, individuals might have been arrested, charged, or acquitted many years ago, but since then their records are spotless. Especially if the incomplete prosecution occurred when an individual was young and since then he does not appear to have had any encounters with the authorities, it might be reasonably claimed that his "record" should be downplayed or ignored. By contrast, recent arrests, charges, or acquittals might be an indication of active or continuing criminal proclivities.

Fifth, is the person's record of incomplete prosecutions mixed with one or more actual convictions? Granted, criminal convictions are game-changers all by themselves, and it might be thought that we should not confound matters by examining them alongside records of incomplete prosecutions. But suppose that a person's conviction was well in the past, such that it might reasonably be dismissed or downplayed, yet recently she was arrested or charged or acquitted of one of more offenses. It might seem, in that case, that there is some real possibility that she has returned to her former ways, a possibility that would not arise if not for her previous convictions.

Individuals who are the subjects of incomplete prosecution might usefully be conceived along a continuum. At one end will be individuals who were, well in the past, arrested once but never charged on suspicion of relatively minor criminal misconduct. At the other end will be individuals with repeated arrests, charges, and trial acquittals for offenses that are relatively serious, some of whom might have one or more convictions in their distant pasts. In the middle will be individuals with one or more arrests or charges in the relatively recent past, some of which might have involved more than minor forms of wrongdoing. In my view, this continuum should be kept in mind as we think about the principles regulating our treatment of the subjects of incomplete prosecutions.

Remedies

In the event of incomplete prosecutions, it might seem obvious that one thing is owed to the individuals who have been temporarily caught up in the criminal justice system: We should not impose criminal sanctions on them. Unfortunately, the law in some jurisdictions does not fully accept this "obvious" proposition, as it permits judges to, in some cases, base sentences, in part, on criminal offenses of which individuals were suspected (or charged with) but never convicted.[9] Granted, those suspected of crimes with which they have not been charged, or charged with and acquitted of some crimes, will have been convicted of others, or else the possibility of their being sentenced based on unproven misconduct would not arise. So perhaps this is not really a case of legal sanctions being imposed on individuals in spite of their having been acquitted. Nonetheless, the practice comes closer to punishing persons for criminal misconduct that has not been proven in a court of law than many legal scholars would like it to be. In any event, let us set this dubious practice to one side and focus instead on the more positive remedies we might adopt to help the subjects of incomplete prosecutions. In this section, my aim is to identify and briefly describe such measures, while offering only limited comment about them. More thorough analyses of them will be provided in later sections.

To begin with, we could require law enforcement officials to insert into the public record some explanation of why, despite having arrested individuals or charged them, prosecutions were never commenced or were discontinued. In particular, if officials concluded that other individuals committed the crimes in question, they could be required to say so, on the record. This would give some subjects of incomplete prosecutions recourse in the event that employers, credit agencies, or licensing boards uncovered their records of arrests or charges and inquired about them. Of course, the explanations proffered by law enforcement officials might not work to clear the names and reputations of all of the subjects of incomplete prosecutions, since the explanations might say simply that prosecutions were discontinued for lack of evidence. Alternatively, such explanations might say that the individuals in question were granted immunity from further prosecution in exchange for their testimony against others. Explanations such as these will leave substantial doubts about the innocence of the formerly arrested or charged. There is also the question whether such explanations should be inserted into the public record by law enforcement officials as a matter of course, or whether they should be inserted only at the request of the subjects of incomplete prosecutions. Given the ambiguous and possibly damaging character of some of the explanations that might be provided by the authorities, it might be claimed that whether to require them ought to be up to the subjects of incomplete prosecutions.

Another remedy, one common in many jurisdictions, is to allow for records of arrests or charges to be officially expunged under certain conditions.[10] In theory, at least, expungement would leave individuals with clean slates. Prospective employers, credit agencies, or licensing boards would not, after it occurred, be able to access records of arrests or charges filed but dropped. There are questions about the feasibility of expungement in the digital age.[11] It might not be possible, any more, to fully purge records of arrests or dropped charges once they appear somewhere in the digital domain. More to the point, there are numerous questions about the defensibility of expunging arrest or charging records. Should they be completely expunged, such that police, prosecutors, and sentencing judges would not have access to them? Should the severity of the crimes in question matter, such that it should be harder to expunge records of arrest or charges when the crimes individuals were suspected of or charged with were grave? Should the possibility of expungement depend in any way on the number of times that individuals have previously been arrested or charged? Should expungement be immediate in the event of incomplete prosecutions, or should there have to be some time-lapse during which the individuals in question incurred no further arrests or charges? Further, would individuals whose arrest or charging records have been expunged be permitted to conceal such records (i.e., lie about, or at least omit mentioning them) when applying for jobs, licenses, or loans? Likewise, if legal officials retained access to such records, though the public did not, would such officials be obligated to conceal them if contacted by employers or credit agencies? And finally, should expungement be automatic, or should individuals with the relevant records have to request it?

A third remedy, one that would to some extent obviate the need for others, would involve attempting to preserve the anonymity of the subjects of incomplete prosecutions by prohibiting the public disclosure of the names of individuals caught up in the early stages of the criminal justice process.[12] It is useful to distinguish "prompted" from "unprompted" disclosures of the names of suspects. In many jurisdictions, police and prosecutors routinely make public the names of individuals arrested for or charged with crimes, especially if the individuals are adults.[13] This is "unprompted" disclosure, as it often occurs without anyone—prospective employers or the press, for instance—specifically inquiring about records of arrests or charges. Yet this public naming of suspects or formally accused persons is not only embarrassing to them, it likely damages their good names and reputations and might lead other citizens to believe that the individuals so identified are guilty of criminal wrongdoing. "Prompted" disclosure, by contrast, would occur if the authorities routinely withheld information about arrests or charges yet revealed it to specific agencies or prospective employers at their request. Prompted disclosure would have more limited effects on the good names and reputations of persons, though it might result in their being denied such things as jobs, housing, or licenses.

Nondisclosure as a remedy for the impact of incomplete prosecutions on individuals' lives could take various forms. Two pertinent questions that need to be addressed with regard to such a remedy are, first, at what point in the criminal justice process would disclosure become justified, and, second, would a ban on disclosure be appropriate regardless of the seriousness of the criminal misconduct of which persons were suspected? We could, for instance, prohibit the naming of persons arrested or suspected of crimes, whether prompted or unprompted, until a judge had found at least "probable cause" that they were guilty of having committed one or more crimes.[14] The probable cause threshold would shield some subjects of incomplete prosecutions from the glare of publicity. Yet since "probable cause" is a weak evidential standard, it would not afford much protection to many other subjects of incomplete prosecutions. Should we therefore extend the ban on public disclosure further into the criminal justice process, perhaps to the point at which they go to trial, assuming they ever do so, or further still, until persons are convicted of one or more charges (whether by pleading guilty or by trial verdict)? If our concern is to minimize the stigma arising from incomplete prosecutions, it might seem that the ban should be extended up to the point at which persons suffer actual convictions. Granted, it would be difficult to avoid public disclosure of the names of trial defendants, since trials are public events during which the accused must be present and might be recognized by some members of the public in the courtroom. Still, the aim of a disclosure ban could be to minimize the glare of publicity, recognizing that it might be impossible to eliminate it entirely. In any event, the more important objections to extending the ban so far into the criminal justice process have to do with legitimate government interests in gathering evidence against accused persons, which might be aided by publicly naming suspects, and the public interest in minimizing its exposure to risk.[15] And notice, these two objections seem more convincing when the crimes of which persons are suspected or charged are serious. Perhaps a ban on the public disclosure of the names of suspects or charged persons is more defensible, including more defensible further into the criminal justice process, when the criminal activities under investigation are relatively minor. Yet when the charges are more serious, the public interests in gathering evidence against suspects and limiting the risks of further victimization might weigh in favor of disclosure or earlier disclosure.

A fourth remedy would be to prohibit discrimination by employers, licensing boards, or credit agencies against individuals who have been arrested for or charged with crimes but not convicted of them. Some jurisdictions prohibit discrimination against individuals who have been convicted of crimes and served their sentences, though the ones that do prohibit it incorporate various qualifications and exceptions into the ban, thereby permitting discrimination in some cases.[16] If such policies are defensible, then it ought to be easier to justify antidiscrimination provisions concerning individuals who have not been convicted. The enforcement mechanism for such provisions would presumably consist of civil lawsuits against those who appear to have violated it. Whether civil lawsuits would be effective is debatable. Employers or credit agencies who got wind of an individual's arrest or charging record might be able to invoke other plausible grounds for refusing to hire or extend them credit. Still, the difficulties in enforcing antidiscrimination provisions need not lead us to reject them outright. The more pertinent questions concern their advisability. In particular, should we prohibit discrimination against those who have become entangled in the criminal justice system no matter how serious or recent the charges against them, or no matter how many arrests or charges they have accrued, though they have never been convicted? To do so might be to put employers, coworkers, and members of the public at some risk. Notice that we could adopt more narrowly crafted antidiscrimination provisions. For instance, we could prohibit discrimination against individuals arrested for or charged with crimes who can produce official explanations for their incomplete prosecutions that effectively exonerate them. Or we could prohibit discrimination against individuals whose arrest or charging records involved misdemeanors and who have avoided further entanglement with the criminal justice system for some determinate period of time.

Trial acquittals raise different kinds of issues. When a case has gone to trial, it seems unlikely that expungement will help individuals clear their names and reputations. Again, trials are public events, and records of them, and all of the hearings and legal maneuverings leading up to them, presumably must be maintained. Nor are police or prosecutors apt to go on the record after failed prosecutions and state that other individuals were likely guilty of the crime or crimes of which an individual has just been acquitted. Those acquitted might publicly proclaim their innocence. But legal officials and many in the public might refuse to believe them, and reasonably so given the evidence they have seen.

There are various ways in which acquittals could be disambiguated, so that they would more decisively distinguish defendants whom a jury (or judge) believed likely to be innocent from defendants whom fact-finders deemed to be likely, though not conclusively (that is, beyond a reasonable doubt) guilty. One possibility is to adopt the tripartite verdict structure of the Scottish legal system, in which juries have three options—"guilty," "not guilty," or "not proven."[17] The latter two options enable juries to distinguish between accused persons whom they believed innocent, or likely to be so, and ones against whom there was considerable, though not sufficiently compelling, evidence. Defendants who earned "not guilty" verdicts would be better positioned to claim some measure of official vindication, and this would presumably help them in putting their lives back together and gaining acceptance in the communities from whence they came and hope to return. Another possibility is to permit accused persons found "not guilty" to petition the jury for a further finding of "innocence," or perhaps "likely innocence."[18] Again, acquitted defendants armed with such further findings would be better equipped to gain back something approaching their former lives.

A third possibility would be to require juries (or judges) to give reasoned verdicts, ones in which they briefly explained the grounds for their decisions[19] Reasoned verdicts are the norm in many civil law countries in which judges, or mixed panels of professional and lay judges, render verdicts. But in common-law countries, general and therefore unexplained verdicts are typical. We can easily imagine reforms that would work to disambiguate jury verdicts, especially acquittals. There could be a standard verdict form in which jurors were required to indicate why they voted to acquit the accused person. In particular, jurors could be required to say whether the vote to acquit was due to the lack of compelling evidence against the defendant or because they believed the defendant not likely to be guilty of the charges against him. One option would be for jurors to reach a common explanation that would then be indicated on the form. One suspects that the explanation concurred upon would most often be one to the effect that the evidence was inconclusive, although a few defendants might earn unanimous votes of innocence or likely innocence. Another option would be to require each juror to (anonymously) indicate his or her reasons for voting to acquit. This option would yield more complex information about acquittals. Obviously, mixed explanations for acquittals would leave accused persons in a more ambiguous position socially (although not legally). But if a sizable majority of jurors stated that they believed the accused person in a given case to be innocent, or likely so, this could help the person to regain some footing in society.

Beyond disambiguation, two other remedies for individuals whose criminal prosecutions terminate in acquittals should be briefly mentioned, though I shall mostly ignore them in the remainder of this chapter. Some legal jurisdictions permit acquitted defendants to recover compensation from the government for the costs of their defenses, assuming that those costs were not already borne by the government.[20] Doing so enables the acquitted to recoup some of what might have been the heavy economic losses incurred in mounting trial defenses. Still, accused persons might have incurred other economic losses, in the form of lost jobs, ones for which such a remedy does them little good. More to the point, recouped legal expenses are unlikely, by themselves, to remove the taint of having been charged, put on trial, and having evidence of one's criminality put on display for all to see.

Many legal jurisdictions also permit malicious prosecution lawsuits. If successful, such suits enable accused persons to demonstrate, in a public setting, that they were wrongly targeted by police or prosecutors, and thus unjustifiably subjected to the ignominy of prosecution for crimes that it should have been clear to the authorities they did not commit. As a remedy for the negative consequences of incomplete prosecutions, such lawsuits suffer from two substantial defects. First, there is reason to believe that they are very unlikely to succeed, in part because the courts have sought to insulate prosecutors from liability except when their conduct is egregious.[21] This means that some, and perhaps most, of the individuals who might benefit from disambiguated verdicts will be unlikely to benefit from malicious prosecution lawsuits. Second, and more importantly, many failed prosecutions will not be malicious. Prosecutors will often act responsibly in filing charges against individuals and pursuing them through trial adjudication, even if acquittals of those individuals are the ultimate outcomes. Police and prosecutors should not be held liable for damages when they acted reasonably in arresting and charging individuals in response to clear, though perhaps not quite sufficiently convincing, evidence of criminal wrongdoing.

Conceptions of the Presumption of Innocence

Not surprisingly, how one approaches the remedies outlined in the previous section will depend, to a considerable extent, on one's views about the PI. In this section, I review several competing accounts of the PI, ones that can be found, sometimes in fragmentary and undeveloped form, in the growing literature on the subject. These accounts are not diametrically opposed to one another, in the sense that they invariably have different implications for our treatment of the subjects of incomplete prosecutions. However, where they overlap, they often provide different rationales for the prescribed forms of treatment.

Since we have already seen these competing accounts in previous chapters, I characterize them summarily. For the most part, my attention in this chapter will be on PI_m and non-PG, as I believe these to be the two most worthy candidates for consideration. Yet other accounts exist and will be referred to as the analysis proceeds.

PI_m

On this account, we are to strive, so far as possible, to regard and treat those suspected or accused of crimes *as if* they are responsible citizens, at least until such individuals are proven to be otherwise.[22] Responsible citizens, or citizens in good standing, are not necessarily exemplars of virtue, but they are individuals who are presumed to be law-abiding.[23] Their being suspected or formally accused of crimes does not establish anything (yet) regarding their guilt, and they certainly should not be subject to any censure or penal deprivations merely because they have fallen under suspicion.

As we have seen in previous chapters, if this account is to be plausible, the qualifying phrase "so far as possible" must be included so as to permit enforcement of the criminal law. Why is this? Because the individuals who come under the suspicion of the authorities reasonably can be required to do any number of things that citizens in good standing are not required to. The police must be able to stop, question, and detain individuals whom they suspect of crimes. If arrested, suspects can be searched, photographed, fingerprinted, and, in some jurisdictions, required to give DNA samples. The police might also be permitted to search the homes, businesses, or other property of suspects after obtaining warrants. Prosecutors might then follow up with charges, and the accused will be required to appear to answer to them. All of these official actions, even if adequately justified in a given case, are not ones that seem consistent with regarding or treating individuals *as if* they are materially innocent; hence the necessity of the "so far as possible" qualifying phrase.

Yet once prosecutions have come to an end without producing convictions, it would seem that PI_m requires us to regard and treat the subjects of incomplete prosecutions as fully citizens in good standing in their communities. If the presumption of material innocence has not been rebutted by the authorities at trial, or effectively waived by the accused as part of a defensible guilty plea process, then the status quo ante ought to be restored.[24] It might even seem that, on the PI_m account, efforts to help the arrested or accused to regain their good names and reputations should not be needed because they would imply some doubt about their material innocence.

I have already indicated that I do not believe that PI_m must be so interpreted. Its proponents can acknowledge the damage done to the names and reputations of individuals by arrest, official accusation, or trial. Employers, creditors, and licensing boards, not to mention neighbors, coworkers, and even friends, might not regard and treat those arrested for or charged with crimes as they regard and treat individuals who have never become entangled with the criminal justice system. Yet in the absence of convictions, the aim of incomplete prosecution remedies should be to help the subjects of incomplete prosecutions regain their positions of good standing in their communities. Remedies that repair the good names and reputations of the formerly suspected or accused should be adopted; remedies that leave their good standing in doubt should be eschewed. The promotion of a kind of official and unofficial amnesia about incomplete prosecutions would seem to be the most defensible aim.

Before proceeding further, I must once again call attention to the awkwardness of attempts to transport the PI out of the context of the criminal trial, where its scope, duration, and purpose are relatively clear and well defined. If the PI holds in the context of incomplete prosecutions, to whom does it apply, what is its scope, who has the burden of rebutting it, what rebuts it, and what are the consequences of its rebuttal? These are all questions the answers to which must be supplied. Notice that the PI, in such a context, must be prospective and continuing, in ways that it is not in the trial context.[25] If the subjects of incomplete prosecutions are to be presumed materially innocent, it is for purposes of our future treatment of them in a wide range of circumstances. Notice also that it is not clear on whom lies the burden of proof to rebut it or whether it can be rebutted. Finally, the consequences of its rebuttal will not be the conviction of individuals, but instead, denials of such things as jobs, credit, or licenses. These might all amount to significant setbacks in the lives of individuals, but they are not legal punishment and might not be government-imposed. Importantly, it is not only proponents of PI_m who must address these challenges to the coherence of extending it outside the trial, but so also must proponents of the other two conceptions of the PI to which I now turn.

PI_n

How one interprets this account of the PI depends, to some extent, on one's position regarding how we ought to regard and treat our fellow citizens generally. If, prearrest or preaccusation, we are to regard and treat them as materially innocent of criminal misconduct, PI_n instructs us to adopt the stance that we simply do not know whether those arrested, charged with, or acquitted of crimes were materially guilty of them. Accordingly, PI_n involves some diminishment of the presumed good standing of the subjects of incomplete prosecutions. Official and unofficial agnosticism toward their law-abidingness becomes the new norm. Hence, remedies for incomplete prosecutions consistent with such agnosticism are to be preferred to ones encouraging or requiring us to regard and treat the subjects of incomplete prosecutions as materially innocent or materially guilty.

However, it could be argued that since we are usually ignorant concerning the law-abidingness of the vast majority of our fellow citizens, neutrality on this score ought to be the prearrest or preaccusation norm. Oddly, in that case, their having been arrested, accused, or acquitted of charges should not make much difference in how we regard and treat persons. Yet since incomplete prosecutions inevitably do seem to alter the perceived standing of persons, I shall ignore this variation on PI_n in what follows. My sense is that anyone inclined to support PI_n will say that, prearrest or preaccusation, persons ought to be viewed more positively—as citizens in good standing.

PI_{ep}

On this account of the PI, arrest and formal accusation will typically cast some doubt on the material innocence of persons, at least assuming that, prior to entanglement with the criminal justice system, we were not to regard and treat our fellow citizens as equally likely to be (materially) guilty as innocent of criminal misconduct. Though PI_{ep} constitutes some diminishment in the good standing of the subjects of incomplete prosecutions, it is far from a presumption of their material guilt. Thus, remedies that are consistent with or promote an even-handed stance toward the guilt or innocence of the subjects of incomplete prosecutions will be supported by PI_{ep}. Remedies that tip the scales toward regarding and treating the formerly accused as either materially innocent or guilty should be avoided.

Non-PG

Non-PG requires that the subjects of incomplete prosecutions should be regarded and treated *as if* their material or probative guilt has not been authoritatively established.[26] Non-PG is not really a presumption of *innocence*, as we have already seen. It is fully consistent with substantial doubts about the material innocence of those arrested for, charged with, or acquitted of criminal offending. At the same time, it acknowledges that police and prosecutors make mistakes about arresting or charging persons with crimes. They also revise their views about whether individuals whom they at one point suspected of crimes actually committed them. Indeed, the fallibility of the early stages of the criminal justice process should lead all of us, whether we are public officials involved in the enforcement of the criminal law, or private citizens concerned with its enforcement, to be cautious about jumping to conclusions about the individuals caught up in it.[27]

Nonetheless, non-PG does not preclude employers, creditors, licensing agencies, and members of the public from seeking more information about the events that led to incomplete prosecutions. Neither does it preclude use of that information in making decisions about whether to extend the subjects of incomplete prosecutions various kinds of benefits or opportunities. As we have seen, in some cases that information might not tell us much of significance about individuals. Arrests on suspicion of minor forms of criminal misconduct long in the past and not followed up with official charges should not give a reasonable employer, creditor, or licensing board much pause. Subjects of incomplete prosecutions with records of these kinds will be the most deserving candidates of efforts to help them regain the full exercise and enjoyment of their moral and legal rights. However, other records of incomplete prosecutions will be more ominous, and non-PG might not forbid making decisions based on them that work to the disadvantage of individuals. Non-PG supports more selective efforts to restore the good names and reputations of the individuals who have been arrested or charged but not convicted than does PI_m. In particular, non-PG seems consistent with weighing the benefits of helping those whose citizenship in good standing has been called into question against the drawbacks to doing so.

Analysis of the Remedies

What do the accounts mapped out in the previous section imply about whether or to what extent we should adopt the remedies discussed earlier to help the subjects of incomplete prosecutions regain some semblance of their former lives? In addressing this question, my aim is not to provide comprehensive analyses of the available remedies. Doing so is beyond the scope of this chapter. Instead, my focus will be on the competing accounts and their implications for how we should approach and think about the remedies—in particular, whether they would have us adopt them in whole or in part, or eschew them altogether. In general, I contend that it will be harder for any of the PI accounts to support the adoption of such remedies, or to support the adoption of sensible versions of them, than it will be for the non-PG account.

Official Explanations

First, consider the remedy of requiring criminal justice officials or the courts to explain or at least clarify the decisions that led to incomplete prosecutions. As we have seen, there are two distinguishable ways in which we might provide the public with more information about these decisions. First, in cases that do not result in trials, police and prosecutors could be required to explain why arrests did not lead to charges or charges were dropped. Second, in cases that end in acquittals by the courts, juries or judges could be required to explain their verdicts, or defendants could be given the option of verdicts that distinguish between findings that the evidence against them was not convincing beyond a reasonable doubt and findings that they were materially innocent, or perhaps likely so.

To what extent would PI_m support efforts to clarify the considerations that led police, prosecutors, judges, or jurors to make their decisions? In some cases, disambiguation would help to clear the names and reputations of the formerly suspected or accused, thereby enabling criminal justice officials and the public to, once again, regard and treat them as citizens in good standing. The problem is that in other cases, perhaps many of them, disambiguation would point toward the likely (though unproven) guilt of individuals. Jurors in criminal trials might explain their verdicts by saying that they believed the accused were probably guilty, given the government's case, though not guilty beyond a reasonable doubt. Prosecutors might say that they dropped charges because crucial incriminating evidence against the accused was ruled inadmissible by the courts. And so on. It does not seem that PI_m would encourage the disclosure of explanations for incomplete prosecutions if doing so would make it more difficult for members of the public to regard the formerly arrested or accused as materially innocent. Also, with respect to police or prosecutorial decisions not to proceed further with cases, PI_m seems more consistent with making such explanations of official actions available at the discretion of the individuals formerly arrested or accused. In that way, individuals who would be made to appear less than materially innocent by such explanations could avoid their disclosure. Ambiguity in such cases might be more conducive to viewing the formerly arrested or accused as citizens in good standing. For similar reasons, the PI_m account might square better with acquittal disambiguation options that operated at the discretion of defendants. A blanket requirement of reasoned verdicts would cast some acquitted defendants in an unfavorable light.

PI_n and PI_{ep} would likewise offer limited support for official explanations of incomplete prosecutions. Police or prosecutorial explanations for why arrests did not proceed to charges, or charges were not pursued through to full adjudication, might cast considerable doubt on the material innocence of individuals. If, for instance, prosecutors explained their decisions to drop charges by referencing the fact that highly incriminating evidence against the accused was ruled inadmissible by the courts, doing so would not encourage members of the public to view the formerly accused neutrally, or as equally likely to be materially innocent as guilty. Similarly, if reasoned jury verdicts said that the government's case, while credible, did not amount to proof beyond a reasonable doubt, they would comport poorly with neutral or equal probability stances toward the material innocence of the accused. Worse than this, explanations that tended to fully exonerate the formerly suspected or accused would likewise comport poorly with neutrality or equal probability stances toward their material innocence. But how can it be a drawback to official explanations of incomplete prosecutions that they help the materially innocent, though wrongly suspected or accused, to more fully regain their reputations and therefore get on with their lives?

With non-PG, the emphasis is more on acknowledging the ways in which the criminal justice process can go awry than on, perhaps futilely, encouraging the public to regard criminal suspects or formally accused individuals neutrally or as materially innocent. Since individuals can be caught up in the criminal justice process despite no wrongdoing on their part, they should be provided the means to clear their names and reputations. One way in which they could be enabled to do so is by requiring police and prosecutors to explain their decisions to not continue with cases, especially when those officials have concluded that those initially suspected or charged were likely innocent. This would give innocent individuals something in the public record which they could reference when asked about previous arrests or charges by prospective employers, credit agencies, and licensing boards. Similarly, disambiguated acquittals would help some former defendants—those who fact-finders concluded were most likely innocent of the charges for which they stood trial. Of course, disambiguated acquittals would not help all defendants, and police or prosecutorial explanations of why they did not continue in their efforts to effect the legal punishment of the suspected or accused would not help many of them to clear their names and reputations. These possibilities, in turn, raise the question whether, according to the non-PG account, we should opt for forms of incomplete prosecution disambiguation that come only at the request of the individuals who were formerly suspected or accused.

The problem with "protecting" the formerly suspected or accused by allowing them to keep the grounds for incomplete prosecutions ambiguous is that it would deprive the public of potentially valuable information about such individuals, information that might be used in order to prevent or minimize victimization at the hands of such individuals. Though non-PG requires us to recognize and take seriously the ways in which the criminal justice process is fallible, the fact is that the process is not entirely untrustworthy. Though the wholly innocent should be provided the means to regain their status in their communities, non-PG does not require us to regard and treat those individuals whom we have some reason to believe are guilty of criminal misconduct *as if* they are materially innocent. Indeed, non-PG seems entirely consistent with mandatory disclosure of the reasons why police or prosecutors did not attempt to see prosecutions through to their completion. In general, the more information the public has about why police and prosecutors acted as they did, the better. Of course, those who have an interest in concealing their wrongdoing might object to mandatory disclosure of the grounds for official decisions that cite insufficient evidence as opposed to likely innocence. But it is not clear why non-PG would require us to take such objections seriously, though it would urge us to be cautious in using any information about arrests or charges in ways that are detrimental to the subjects of incomplete prosecutions.

To the preceding, it might be objected that there will be costs, in some cases, to having police, prosecutors, or the courts publicly explain their decisions by saying that individuals suspected or formally accused of crimes were, in their view, likely to be materially innocent. Some individuals who were actually guilty of the crimes in question will manage to thereby clear (either partially or wholly) their names and reputations. This might put other individuals with whom such "exonerated" individuals interact in the future at greater risk. Perhaps it is better to keep the grounds for incomplete prosecutions ambiguous so that members of the public remain unsure how to regard persons formerly suspected or accused of crimes. Further, official explanations of incomplete prosecutions might not help all of the formerly suspected or accused who were, in fact, wholly innocent of any criminal misconduct. Instead of police, prosecutors, or the courts saying that their investigations have concluded that such individuals were innocent or probably so, legal officials might explain their decisions by saying that the evidence against such individuals was inconclusive. Such explanations would lump the innocent with the likely guilty or at least suspect.

Though we must concede these potential costs to disambiguation, I do not believe that they show it to be undesirable, all things considered. First, one suspects that the number of cases in which police, prosecutors, or the courts exonerate the materially guilty will be few and far between. Police and prosecutors, in particular, are apt to err on the side of caution in their explanations for their decisions to not proceed further with charges against individuals. This means that such officials will tend to offer explanations that cite insufficient evidence for their decisions not to pursue prosecutions further. Similarly, it seems doubtful that many guilty defendants will get disambiguated jury verdicts that exonerate them. A few juries might be tricked by clever defendants or their attorneys into doing so, but not many of them will be, one suspects.

Second, there is, as we have seen, a "cost" to not providing incomplete prosecution disambiguation, especially to the materially innocent. In the absence of disambiguation remedies, the innocent will not be able to distinguish themselves from the other individuals who remain suspect because they have been arrested or charged with crimes. Worse than this, the absence of disambiguation remedies might make it easier for the actually guilty to claim that they have been exonerated by the police, prosecutors, or the courts. Though many members of the general public will not be fooled by such proclamations, some might be. Disambiguation remedies will make it harder for the guilty who benefit from incomplete prosecutions to claim that the criminal justice process has shown them to be citizens in good standing.

Third, though some actually innocent individuals might not receive explanations for their incomplete prosecutions that effectively vindicate them, they will not be worse off under disambiguation schemes than they are under current practices. Current practices that require little, if any, explanation of incomplete prosecutions do not afford the innocent the opportunity to distinguish themselves from the guilty who managed to escape conviction. Required explanations for incomplete prosecutions would help some subjects of incomplete prosecutions who were, in fact, innocent of criminal misconduct.

Expungement

Another way in which we might help the subjects of incomplete prosecutions to regain their standing in their communities is by expunging their records of arrests or charges. If we are to regard and treat those never convicted of crimes as if they are fully members in good standing in their communities, as PI_m insists, then it would seem that we ought to lean toward expunging most such records. Yet this would mean wiping clean the arrest and charging records of individuals no matter how serious the charges against them, how far along in the adjudication process they got before charges were dropped or dismissed, how often they have been arrested or charged, or how recently. It is not apparent how the PI_m approach could make distinctions among the subjects of incomplete prosecutions; none have been convicted, so why should any of them be dogged by their records of arrests and charges? This would mean that individuals arrested and charged numerous times with serious crimes, although never convicted, would be indistinguishable from individuals never arrested at all.

However, it could be argued that, consistent with the PI_m, expungement should not be complete. Instead, records of past arrests or charges not resulting in convictions could be kept available to law enforcement officials, or perhaps to employers of certain kinds (for instance, banks or security firms), if not to the general public. Recall that PI_m requires only that suspects and the formally accused should be regarded and treated as materially innocent, "so far as possible." If police or prosecutorial access to records of incomplete prosecutions is vital for enforcement of the criminal law, then PI_m might support it. And it might do so even if such access seems in some ways inconsistent with the requirement to treat or regard suspects and charged individuals as if they are materially innocent.

As we have seen, however, the "so far as possible" qualifying phrase must be interpreted narrowly, or else it will not serve to restrain the actions of criminal justice officials. Earlier, I suggested that we might permit actions by such officials that cast doubt on the material innocence of persons if those actions are *necessary* for enforcement of the criminal law. If they are not—if there are alternative means to enforcing the criminal law that do not cast the innocence of persons into doubt—then criminal justice officials should be required to employ them, even if they are more costly or somewhat less effective. Whether maintaining official access to records of arrests and charges is necessary to law enforcement seems a close call. Though it would aid enforcement in some cases, by enabling police to identify likely suspects when crimes were committed, or by confirming that individuals whom they already suspect were worth investigating further, police would still have other means of identifying suspects. Even if a case can be made for the necessity of access to such records by law enforcement officials, extending such access to private employers is another matter. Their interests are not so much in enforcing the criminal law as in protecting their businesses. Moreover, maintaining official access to past records of arrests and charges might result in more police monitoring or harassment of individuals formerly suspected or accused of crimes, or contribute to the problematic practice of "usual suspects" policing.[28] Neither of these possibilities would seem to sit well with the PI_m approach. It should also be noted that expungement might turn out to be a futile remedy in some cases, since law enforcement officials will remember that some individuals currently under suspicion or investigation were once caught up in the criminal justice system, though never convicted of any crimes.

With PI_n and PI_{ep}, I shall be brief. Complete expungement of the records of incomplete prosecutions would not seem to set well with either approach. Expungement would eliminate any grounds employers, creditors, or licensing boards have to regard and treat the subjects of incomplete prosecutions as anything other than citizens in good standing. Such an outcome seems inconsistent with a stance toward the formerly accused according to which they are to be regarded and treated neutrally or as equally likely to be materially guilty as innocent. Could these approaches support partial expungement, so that law enforcement officials retain access to records of incomplete prosecutions? Again, such access might help officials identify or confirm suspects in new cases. Yet to view persons as "likely suspects" hardly seems the same as viewing them neutrally or as equally likely to be materially innocent as guilty. This suggests that PI_n and PI_{ep} can offer limited support to partial expungement regimes. One possibility, however, would be to add the "as far as possible" qualifying phrase to the two approaches, so that they can be made to better accommodate enforcement of the criminal law. If it could then be shown that permitting law enforcement officials to retain access to records of incomplete prosecutions is necessary for enforcement of the criminal law, the two approaches might be rendered consistent with policies of partial expungement.

Under the non-PG approach, there is more to be said for expunging the arrest or charge records of some individuals than other individuals. In particular, those whom police or prosecutors have come to regard as innocent or likely innocent of the criminal conduct of which they were earlier suspected, would have strong cases for having their records expunged. For somewhat different reasons, it makes sense to expunge the arrest or charge records of those whose suspected criminal activities were relatively minor, especially after some period of time has elapsed in which the individuals in question have not fallen under further suspicion. Even if such individuals were, in fact, guilty of the crimes of which they were earlier suspected, the charges might not seem serious enough to allow them to hinder individuals indefinitely. It might also make sense to expunge the arrest or charge records of individuals suspected of more serious crimes if considerable time has passed with no further indications of their involvement in criminal misconduct. And this might especially be true if the records were accrued when the individuals were young and they are now mature adults.

Yet as the crimes for which individuals were arrested or charged become more serious, or as their incidents of arrest or charges become more numerous or were more recent, although never resulting in convictions, then the case for expunging their records, on the non-PG approach, seems more tenuous. Again, records of arrests or charges for more serious crimes should be expunged if police or prosecutors concluded that the individuals whom they formerly suspected were innocent of the crimes in question. But often, legal officials will conclude only that they cannot prove the guilt of the individuals whom they suspect. When the crimes of which individuals are suspected are serious, or not-so-serious but repeated, expungement will seem a dubious practice, at least until a substantial amount of time elapses during which individuals have not been arrested for or charged with further crimes.

Not only should legal officials have access to the arrest and charging records of individuals suspected of felonies or numerous misdemeanors, so, it seems, should prospective employers, credit agencies, and members of the public. Employers and credit agencies should be able to find out whether individuals seeking work or credit have been arrested for or charged with serious crimes, or numerous minor ones, of which they were never officially cleared. Members of the general public, though they might not be motivated to seek out public records of their fellow citizens' past encounters with legal authorities, should not be denied access to those records, especially when those encounters were frequent or involved suspicions of serious misconduct. Again, on the non-PG approach, official suspicions or accusations, when not authoritatively proven, should be treated with caution. Mistakes are made by the authorities and the appearance of serious criminal conduct by individuals might be misleading. But the Non-PG approach seems more consistent with selective expungement policies than does the PI_m approach. Maintaining public access to records of arrests and charges should be the norm in some cases even if the fallibility of the criminal justice system is fully acknowledged and kept in view.

One significant problem with any policy of record expungement is that it would put individuals formerly suspected or accused of crimes in an awkward position when they are asked by prospective employers, credit agencies, licensing boards, or their fellow citizens whether they have ever been arrested or charged with criminal offenses.[29] Should individuals conceal and therefore lie about arrests or charges in their pasts that are no longer matters of public record? If they tell the truth, then the benefits of expungement will be lost. Law enforcement officials would face a similar dilemma if expungement is only partial, such that officials retain access to records of arrest or charges, though members of the public do not (in some or all cases). We could limit the exposure of legal officials to questions that would force them to lie or prevaricate by prohibiting them from revealing what they know to those not directly involved in law enforcement.[30] In that case, most individuals or organizations would have access only to the public record, which might have been selectively expunged. In what follows, I assume that legal officials should be discouraged or prohibited from sharing what they know about individuals whose arrest or charging records have been expunged from public view. My focus will be on how PI_m and non-PG would have us think about the dilemma faced by individuals whose past records have been expunged.

On the PI_m account, there seems little that is problematic about the prospect of individuals concealing their past records, assuming that those records have been expunged. If individuals were never convicted of charges—perhaps not even charged—the presumption of material innocence was never rebutted or overcome. Thus, individuals should be regarded and treated as materially innocent. If concealing their past entanglements with the legal authorities aids them in being so regarded and treated, so much the better. True, if legal authorities are permitted to retain access to such records in perpetuity or for some limited period of time, they will be less likely to regard or treat the individuals in question as materially innocent. But the authorities probably did not do so to begin with and likely cannot be made to do so (though they might still be encouraged to do so).

The non-PG approach, as we have seen, is consistent with more selective and partial expungement. In some cases, the benefits of enabling individuals to escape the possibly detrimental effects of their past arrest or charging records outweigh the public interest in law enforcement or further crime prevention. Again, this most likely will be true when the crimes in question were not very serious to begin with, the evidence against individuals was not strong enough to sustain charges or continued prosecution, or the occurrence of the suspected criminal activity is far enough in the past that we should be reluctant to let it encumber individuals in the pursuit of jobs, credit, or respect and esteem in their communities. Yet this, in turn, suggests that when those whose records have been expunged are asked about past arrests or charges, their concealment of these incidents is justified because the balance of reasons supports it, rather than because they are entitled to be regarded and treated as if they are materially innocent. But concealment it is, even if justified.

This awkward feature of expungement, along with what might be its practical infeasibility in the digital age, could lead us to favor the alternative of full public disclosure of the reasons why prosecutions were never completed. Such disclosure would give at least some subjects of incomplete prosecutions the opportunity to openly and effectively dispute the truth of the official suspicions or allegations against them, rather than having to lie about them. Of course, the downside to such an approach is that other individuals, some of whom might be entirely innocent of criminal misconduct, will have a harder time exonerating themselves. They might have to rely on claims to the effect that the offenses of which they were suspected were minor, long in the past, or not such as to warrant charges or persistence in attempts to prosecute them. We could help such individuals by prohibiting unreasonable forms of discrimination against them. The issues raised by such a ban are examined in a later section.

Limits on the Public Disclosure of Names

If we limited the public disclosure of the names of criminal suspects and formally accused persons, then remedies such as expungement and official explanations for incomplete prosecutions would be, in some instances, unnecessary. It is, after all, public allegations against named persons by the authorities that do much of the damage to their reputations, independently of whether they are ever convicted of crimes. Before turning to an examination of how the different accounts of the PI might have us approach a ban on the public disclosure of suspects or formally accused persons' names, let me begin with some preliminary comments that will serve to set the issues to be addressed in better perspective.

First, it should be apparent that whatever the parameters of such a ban, it will not prevent some information about the persons suspected of or charged with crimes from leaking out. Obviously, the authorities will know the names of those whom they suspect or have charged, and we might reasonably expect that such knowledge will spread beyond the few persons directly involved in a given case. Also, the family members and friends of suspects will likely know that they have been arrested, are being investigated, or have been charged with crimes. So too will neighbors, coworkers, and employers, especially if the accused suddenly fail to show up at home or at work for extended periods of time, which they might do if they are held in pretrial detention. Also, required court appearances or the serving of search warrants will alert those beyond the immediate families of suspects that something is afoot. What all of this means is that a disclosure ban, whatever its character, will only shield suspects or accused persons from adverse reactions by members of the public with whom they are not all that likely to come into contact. This is not to suggest that such bans are therefore pointless. In particular, if future employers cannot, because of them, discover that job applicants were, at one point, arrested for or suspected of crimes, or charged with them, their inability to do so will aid the subjects of incomplete prosecutions. But we should not expect more from public disclosure bans than they are apt to deliver.

Second, as we have seen, the majority of the offenses processed by contemporary criminal justice systems are relatively minor. Again, about 80 percent of the cases processed by the US courts involve misdemeanors.[31] Further, some of the remaining 20 percent will involve minor felonies, and thus not crimes in which the public has much interest. It is serious crimes, or perhaps less serious but notorious ones, that capture the public's attention, usually because the media casts them in the glare of publicity. Much of what goes on in the criminal justice system is already anonymous, even when the process eventuates in convictions. It is apt to be more so in the case of incomplete prosecutions. But this suggests that many of the subjects of incomplete prosecutions will not derive much benefit from a ban on public disclosure of their names. No one is paying much attention to what happens with or to them. Those who are—members of their families, their neighbors, coworkers, and employers—will likely be paying attention despite the ban.

This brings us to a third point: The individuals who would most benefit from nondisclosure of their names—individuals charged with serious crimes—are ones who are arguably less entitled to it, for the reasons hinted at earlier. The public interest in investigating and prosecuting such crimes is presumably greater, as are the risks those suspected of or charged with them pose to others. Appeals to the public for help in resolving serious crimes will be more successful, in some cases, if the authorities can publicly identify the likely perpetrators and thus alert citizens that they might have information useful to the authorities.[32] Independently of that, when individuals are suspected of or charged with serious crimes, there seems a stronger case for notifying the public of such facts, so that they can take appropriate measures to guard against being victimized. Of course, some in the community will know of or suspect the risks that individuals arrested or charged with crimes pose to them even if there is a ban on public disclosure of their names. But others will be alerted to those risks earlier or more vividly in the absence of such a ban.

How, then, would those who subscribe to PI_m regard such a ban, and what limits, if any, on it would they endorse? Those who subscribe to PI_m confront a paradox if they cast such bans as part of an effort to encourage the public to regard and treat suspects and formally accused persons as if they are materially innocent until or unless charges against them eventuate in convictions. The point of such bans is to prevent persons from being regarded as suspects or accused persons in the first place, rather than as suspects or accused persons who are presumptively innocent. Hence, if supporters of PI_m are to make sense of nondisclosure, it must be in different terms. The idea must be that banning disclosure of the names of suspects will prevent at least some members of the public (not all, as we have seen) from regarding and treating some of their fellow citizens as something less than citizens in good standing with respect to the criminal law. Being a suspect, or being a formally accused person, calls a person's good standing into question; a disclosure ban would prevent members of the public who do not independently know of a person's entanglement with the criminal justice from discovering it. This account only makes sense, it would seem, given an understanding of the PI according to which it constrains our conduct and attitudes independently of official suspicion or accusation—if we are, in other words, to regard and treat our fellow citizens as if they are materially innocent just because they are our fellow citizens. I have already argued, in chapter 2, that the PI does not so constrain us. But set that point aside for the time being.

The next question concerns what, if any limits, PI_m supporters would accede to on such disclosure bans. Would they limit them to the early stages of the criminal justice process, perhaps up to the point at which the government is deemed by a judge to have crossed the "probable cause" threshold? Or would they insist that disclosure bans endure for longer, perhaps up to the point at which accused persons are formally convicted of one or more charges? Also, would PI_m supporters limit the disclosure ban to persons suspected of only minor forms of criminal misconduct, or would they extend it to all suspects, regardless of their alleged crimes?

On the first question, I believe that the most plausible answer is that those who subscribe to PI_m should seek to extend the ban as far as possible, up to the point at which the PI has been rebutted by trial or plea conviction. It is only at the point of conviction that the PI has been fully overcome, after all. A ban on public disclosure up to the point of "probable cause," by contrast, seems a halfhearted remedy if our aim is to protect the reputations of individuals who might never be convicted of anything. Why stop encouraging members of the public to view persons as less than citizens in good standing at such a relatively early point in the criminal justice process given that lots of prosecutions fizzle or fail well after it? On the second question, it is hard to see how supporters of PI_m could draw any sort of principled distinction based on the kinds of allegations against individuals in crafting a disclosure ban. More serious allegations are just that—allegations, until they are converted into convictions. Indeed, those suspected of or charged with more serious crimes are precisely the individuals more in need of having their reputations safeguarded until due process has taken its full course. To suggest that the public needs notice of the allegations against them so that citizens can take steps to avoid victimization sounds rather too close to a presumption that the accused are guilty just because the charges against them are grave.

Granted, supporters of PI_m could acknowledge that, in some cases, public disclosure of the names of suspects is vital to gathering further evidence against them. As we have seen, those who subscribe to PI_m claim that persons are to be treated as materially innocent, "so far as possible," where this qualifying phrase is to be interpreted as permitting enforcement of the criminal law. If public disclosure is necessary for enforcement of the criminal law, PI_m supporters might be willing to allow it. Still, it seems clear that this concession on their part ought to be interpreted in the narrowest way possible. In lots of cases, the authorities will not need to publicly disclose the names of suspects or charged individuals in order to build solid cases against them. In such cases, PI_m supporters should reject disclosure. They should also, it would seem, insist that the authorities demonstrate the need to disclose the names of suspects to the courts, rather than engage in disclosure solely at their discretion. The default position should be nondisclosure, unless the government can show the need for it.

Non-PG encourages all of us—whether criminal justice officials, victims, or members of the public—to refrain from jumping too quickly or firmly to the conclusion that suspects or charged persons are materially or provably guilty. Again, the earliest stages of the criminal justice process are especially fallible, and its outcomes are unpredictable. The information about crimes and suspects that police and prosecutors have at that point is often tenuous or incomplete. Early public disclosure of suspects' names might tarnish the reputations of individuals against whom police and prosecutors ultimately file no charges or do so and drop them because of lack of evidence. More importantly, early disclosure will harm those whom the authorities charge but subsequently deem unlikely to be guilty. There seems little need for early disclosure of names, and this seems especially true if the crimes involved are not serious. The public interest in responding decisively to such offenses is slight, and the risks posed by those alleged to have perpetrated them are unlikely to be significant. The few who might be at some risk from such individuals are apt to know of their entanglement with the criminal justice system.

Moreover, when the crimes under investigation are mostly minor in character, other considerations weigh against the public disclosure of the names of suspects or formally accused persons, and especially against their early public disclosure. First, public disclosure will blemish their reputations, perhaps needlessly if they are never convicted, and thus might diminish both the legitimate opportunities available to them and their motivations to pursue them. One of the reasons that we protect juvenile offenders from public disclosure of their names is that we do not want them to be labeled as "criminals," thereby reducing their incentives for reform, or worse, pushing them further in the direction of deviance.[33] Yet these reasons against disclosure in the case of juveniles ought to have some weight in determining our policies regarding the disclosure of the names of adults involved (or allegedly so) in criminal offending. Second, we might worry that the public will do more than regard named suspects as probably guilty, which is bad enough, but that it will go further and deem them to be entirely irresponsible or unreliable, if not hopelessly violent or predatory. The possible demonization of offenders, including alleged offenders, is something to be discouraged and more urgently so when the offending alleged is not all that serious. Many individuals commit one or more misdemeanors without becoming fully involved in violent or predatory lifestyles. However, the public might not be especially adept at or motivated to draw distinctions among offenders in ways that they should. Disclosure bans will shield accused persons from such irrational and potentially damaging reactions on the part of the public.

Nonetheless, when the criminal misconduct of which persons are suspected or charged is more serious, then the reasons for publicly identifying them, including identifying them earlier in the criminal justice process, will have greater weight. The public interest in punishing serious offenses is stronger, as is its interest in minimizing risks while the adjudication process runs its course. Both of these interests might auger in favor of disclosure well before the adjudication process has eventuated in convictions of the accused. Again, the non-PG approach does not require us to adopt a uniformly optimistic attitude toward accused persons.

In addition to permitting earlier disclosure of the names of suspects or accused persons when the offenses under investigation are serious, the non-PG approach might permit forms of prompted disclosure when individuals have been the subjects of numerous incomplete prosecutions in the recent past. Suppose that we lean toward nondisclosure of the names of suspects and accused persons when their crimes are relatively minor, at least up to the point at which they are on trial for or actually convicted of crimes. We still might permit prompted disclosures by the authorities of past incomplete prosecutions when contacted by private security agencies, banks, or other prospective employers who want to learn about any suspected involvement in criminal activities by job applicants. As we have seen, the non-PG approach does not require us to close our eyes to evidence that individuals are involved, on a continuing basis, in criminal activities. In this vein, a plausible case for disclosure by the authorities could be made if individuals have numerous incidents of entanglement in the recent past, though none resulting in convictions. Granted, we might want to accompany such disclosures with express cautions about inferring too much from them. But non-PG would not foreclose disclosure on the dubious grounds that we should be relentlessly encouraged to regard and treat our fellow citizens as law-abiding in the absence of their actually having been convicted of any crimes.

What would the PI_n and PI_{ep} approaches support by way of disclosure or nondisclosure policies? As we have seen, the most plausible way in which to interpret these two approaches is by taking them to operate in the postsuspicion context. Accordingly, we should either view suspects or formally accused persons neutrally, in terms of their likely material innocence or guilt, or as equally likely to be materially innocent as guilty. Yet if this is correct, then it will be difficult for either of these approaches to avoid the paradox noted earlier. Unless the names of suspects or accused persons are publicly disclosed, neither of the perspectives on persons that they recommended will become operative. Of course, they both might be interpreted as prescriptive approaches about how we should regard and treat our fellow citizens generally, independently of official suspicions or accusations against them. So interpreted, neither would yield true presumptions of innocence, at least not material innocence, though they do not constitute presumptions of guilt or even probable guilt. If they can be so interpreted, then what insights do they offer about the public disclosure of the names of suspects or accused persons?

The answer will depend on what we believe such disclosures will do by way of affecting the attitudes toward and treatment of the persons so identified by other members of the community. If disclosure would simply call the law-abidingness of persons into doubt, and little more, than PI_n and PI_{ep} would permit it. And this would appear to be true whenever disclosure occurs or regardless of the nature of the crimes alleged. If, on the other hand, we believe that disclosure would lead members of the community to believe that those so identified were probably materially guilty, then both approaches would be inconsistent with it. Moreover, it seems they would have to reject disclosure regardless of (*a*) the stage to which the investigation of crimes or the adjudication of charges against individuals had progressed, and (*b*) the seriousness of the alleged offenses. I say this because it would not seem to matter how far along a case had proceeded or how grave the charges if the likely effect of disclosure would be to tip public attitudes against accused persons. Neither approach can support that.

Which effect does it seem more reasonable to believe that public disclosure is likely to have? My sense is that the latter of the two scenarios is the more plausible one. It better accounts for why we are concerned about the subjects of incomplete prosecutions. Public disclosure of the names of suspects or accused persons sets back their interests and arguably more so than by mildly calling their law-abidingness into question. The more important point is this one, however: Regardless of what we believe the most likely effect of public disclosure to be, PI_n and PI_{ep} yield simplistic approaches to the complex issues raised by it. Neither approach encourages us to weigh the many considerations for and against disclosure.

Bans on Discrimination

A further remedy involves efforts to discourage discrimination by public or private employers, public agencies, creditors, or licensing boards against individuals with records of incomplete prosecutions. As noted earlier, numerous legal jurisdictions prohibit discrimination against individuals with actual criminal records, although all of them build in exceptions and qualifications to this ban.[34] Not surprisingly, in my view, these exceptions and qualifications make reference to such things as the seriousness of the charges of which individuals were convicted, the number and recency of their convictions, and the extent to which their convictions indicate that they might pose special risks to vulnerable populations. Such limits on a discrimination ban might be thought defensible in cases of individuals with past convictions, but are they defensible in cases of individuals who were never convicted?

On the PI_m approach, it would seem that antidiscrimination provisions not only ought to be adopted, they ought to be categorical. Again, individuals never convicted of crimes should continue to be regarded and treated as citizens in good standing. If they are denied jobs or credit for suspected or alleged, but unproven, crimes, then employers and credit agencies that discriminate against them do so unjustifiably. Such discrimination should be prohibited, and those who believe themselves to have suffered it should be permitted to sue and recover damages.

Supporters of PI_m could argue that discrimination against the subjects of incomplete prosecutions is sometimes justified, particularly when and to the extent that it is vital for enforcement of the criminal law. For instance, police agencies or private security firms might reasonably refuse to hire those who have been arrested and charged with crimes on numerous occasions in the past, albeit never convicted of them. Though such a line of argument makes sense in relation to individuals with records of convictions—individuals whose presumptions of citizenship in good standing have been rebutted on one or more occasions—it is hard to see how such a position can be squared with PI_m when the individuals involved have never been convicted. The wariness of some of the subjects of incomplete prosecutions that it embodies seems at odds with the prescribed optimism of PI_m. It is also worth noting that if employers or credit agencies are prohibited from discriminating against the subjects of incomplete prosecutions, and thus employ or extend credit to persons who subsequently commit crimes, nothing about the PI_m approach prevents law enforcement officials from pursuing them vigorously at that point. The question is whether it is consistent with the PI_m approach to guard against anticipated criminal conduct prospectively by refusing to hire or extend credit to individuals with records of incomplete prosecutions. It does not seem that it is.

With PI_n and PI_{ep}, nondiscrimination provisions, especially blanket ones, seem to go too far. If we are to regard and treat the subjects of incomplete prosecutions neutrally, meaning that we are to take the stance that we do not know whether they are guilty or innocent of the criminal activity of which they were at least suspected at some point, it is not obvious that discrimination against them by employers, creditors, or licensing boards is unreasonable. As between two job candidates, for instance, one of whom has one or more arrests or charges on his record, though no convictions, and the other of whom has an entirely clean record, it seems reasonable for employers to favor the latter, all else being equal. After all, uncertainty about a person's past conduct is not the same as positive belief in his good citizenship. Something similar seems true if our stance toward the subjects of incomplete prosecutions is to be that it is equally likely they are guilty as innocent of past crimes. All things considered, it seems justifiable for employers to prefer job candidates whose pasts exhibit no such ambiguity.

On the non-PG approach, there is no blanket prescription to regard and treat those arrested or charged *as if* they are materially innocent, and thus no prima facie case for the notion that refusing to hire or extend them credit is indefensible and so should be prohibited. As we have seen, non-PG is fully consistent with attempts to disambiguate the meaning of incomplete prosecutions and with some selective expungement of arrest or charging records. Yet these measures will inevitably mean that more rather than less information about the suspected criminal misconduct of some individuals will be available. It would then seem odd to try to discourage employers, credit agencies, or landlords from acting on it in efforts to protect their own interests.

Granted, there will be cases in which the non-PG approach should support a ban on discrimination against the subjects of incomplete prosecutions. Easy cases will be those involving individuals who can provide official explanations of their past arrests and charges that exonerate them, but who still suffer discrimination by employers or credit agencies who remain wary of them. We should prohibit discrimination against such subjects of incomplete prosecutions. We might also enforce a broader antidiscrimination ban to protect the subjects of incomplete prosecutions against "unreasonable" denials of jobs, credit, or licenses. We could model such broader bans on those that already exist with regard to individuals who have criminal records. For instance, some US states prohibit discrimination by private employers against ex-offenders unless the employer can demonstrate a direct connection between the activities they will have to perform if hired and their past crimes.[35] Yet such qualified bans suggest that some discrimination against individuals with records of incomplete prosecutions might be justified. Again, the records of some individuals will be worrisome, even if the authorities never have managed to convict them of offenses or their convictions were long in the past. At most, the non-PG approach would support reminding employers, credit agencies, and the public in such cases that the criminal justice system is fallible, especially in its earliest stages, and that the guilt of persons should not be presumed.

Concluding Remarks

It might be claimed that one of the virtues of the PI_m approach, in the context of incomplete prosecutions, is that encourages us to do more than alternative approaches to help those whose lives have been marred by entanglement with the criminal justice system. Indeed, it is understandable, given the heavy toll such entanglement exacts on individuals, and the hostility toward perceived criminal offenders exhibited in some quarters of contemporary societies, why some theorists might believe that the logical way forward is to encourage all of us to presume the best about the subjects of incomplete prosecutions, rather than the worst.

However, it is possible to support efforts to help the subjects of incomplete prosecutions without encouraging attitudes about them that effectively blind us to differences among them. Many subjects of incomplete prosecutions should be enabled to get on with their lives, not because they were materially innocent of the crimes for which they were arrested or charged, but because their criminal wrongdoing was minor, the product of youthful indiscretion, long in the past, or overshadowed by records of good citizenship since it occurred. The main problem with our attitudes toward the likely though unproven guilty (just as it is toward the proven guilty) is the tendency to view and treat them as all being alike, and especially to view and treat them as if they are all irredeemably dangerous or untrustworthy. But that problem requires a different solution, one premised on drawing sensible distinctions among the subjects of incomplete prosecutions. Encouraging a simplistic and somewhat naive view about the subjects of incomplete prosecutions, as PI_m seems to, is unlikely to change people's attitudes toward the formerly arrested or accused, or produce defensible policies for dealing with them.

CHAPTER 9 | The Presumption of Innocence Postpunishment

MOST OF THE INDIVIDUALS convicted of crimes and sentenced for them will eventually complete their sentences. Even in a comparatively punitive country like the United States, the vast majority of criminal convictions are, as we have seen, for misdemeanors, the sentences for which, when they involve imprisonment at all, are typically no more than a year in length.[1] Unlike the persons entangled in the criminal justice system who were the subjects of the preceding chapter, convicted offenders have a legally and socially much less ambiguous status. They have either pled guilty or, in what amounts to no more than a small percentage of cases, have been convicted by a court after a trial. A few might protest their innocence, but most will not. They will serve their sentences and emerge into what is a substantially altered social and legal landscape. Presumed citizens in good standing they most decidedly are not, although for more than a few of them, ones who had lengthy criminal histories already, not much is changed by their most recent convictions and sentences.[2]

As most who study the criminal justice system are vividly aware, the difficulties faced by ex-offenders are not solely the product of their convictions and thus the altered attitudes that many of their fellow citizens will have toward them. Especially in the United States, but in other countries as well, those who have fully served whatever sentences were officially assigned to them by a court are subject to a wide variety of further legal exclusions, restrictions, required forms of conduct, or lost privileges and protections. Collectively, these are often referred to as "collateral consequences" of criminal conviction.[3] Their forms are many and dauntingly diverse: loss of voting rights, restrictions on the kinds of jobs for which ex-offenders can be hired, loss of parental rights, restrictions on where they may live, loss of access to social welfare programs, requirements to register with the authorities and continually report their whereabouts, and the refusal of society to protect them from discrimination based on their criminal histories. By law and custom, these collateral consequences are not conceived as part of offenders' formal criminal sentences. They are what Jeremy Travis terms "invisible punishment."[4] They are added onto normal sentences for a variety of reasons, ranging from concerns about the risks posed by ex-offenders, to the need to deter them from further crimes, to the desirability of depriving them (as "undeserving") of things to which other citizens are entitled.

Few scholars who have examined such collateral consequences find many of them to be defensible.[5] The list of complaints against them is lengthy and convincing: they are rarely subject to standard forms of desert-proportionality analysis—indeed, the hardships they pose for ex-offenders might exceed the difficulties wrought by their official legal punishment; many of them are poorly designed to reduce whatever are perceived to be the relevant risks, imposing losses or restrictions on many ex-offenders who pose little threat to the public; unfairly, it is alleged, individuals usually have little advance notice that enduring such consequences is one of the costs of offending; worse than the preceding, collateral consequences can be adopted by legislatures and imposed retroactively on ex-offenders; last but not least, such consequences exacerbate inequality by making the lives of ex-offenders, many of whom were poor or socially marginalized members of society to begin with, profoundly more trying. To the lattermost is often added the plausible assertion that one likely effect of collateral consequences is that they will leave individuals so desperate that they will have to resort to more offending in order to eke out some kind of living.

I have relatively little to add to most of the trenchant critiques of collateral consequences already in the literature. Instead, my focus in this chapter is more abstract and concerns two primary questions: First, to what extent, if at all, does our treatment of ex-offenders implicate the presumption of innocence? Can it be convincingly shown that our evident distrust of ex-offenders, revealed by our eagerness to control and limit their lives, is contrary to a proper understanding of the PI? My sense is that some scholars will maintain that it is, that our attitudes toward and treatment of ex-offenders ought to be governed, much more than it is, by a commitment to the restoration of their status as members in good standing in society. Not surprisingly, I attempt to show that such an approach is neither coherent nor plausible as a diagnosis of what is worrisome about our treatment of ex-offenders. Instead, I urge a different approach, one founded on the notion that what we should do for individuals who have fully served the sentences for their crimes is to restore them to full and equal status in society, a status that bestows upon them a range of undiminished legal rights and privileges.

Before turning to the debate about the PI in the context of our treatment of ex-offenders, I raise a different question: Should we conceive of the many losses and deprivations that we impose on ex-offenders as "external" to their legal punishment? I contend that we should not, that there is no sharp line between the kinds of censuring losses imposed on offenders as integral to their official sentences and those imposed on them as postpunishment consequences of their convictions. Stigmatizing losses imposed on individuals in response to their criminal convictions are, I argue, all of a piece. Collectively, they should be constrained by a commitment to both cardinal and ordinal proportionality, and should be imposed at sentencing by a judge. They should also all be made clear, in advance of any guilty pleas, to those accused of crimes, so that they will know what they face if they admit their guilt and accept their punishment. There should be no surprises when it comes to the punitive deprivations offenders will endure, and especially not retroactive ones.

What this reconceptualization of collateral consequences means is that once offenders have served their full sentences, including any of what are now regarded and treated as merely collateral consequences of conviction, their legal rights should be restored. They are not to be subject to risk-based infringements upon their legal rights, at least not ones to which other citizens are immune. Thus, offenders who have fully served their criminal sentences must be permitted to vote and to participate in social welfare programs. They should not be legally barred from occupations, deprived of their parental rights, or discriminated against solely on the grounds that they have past convictions. Importantly, my position is consistent with assigning some offenders sentences that impose lifelong legal losses or disabilities upon them. But these must be assigned up front, as it were, and made to comport with proportionality limits on legal punishment.

The view that offenders who have fully served their sentences should, once again, be treated as equals before the law must be distinguished from a view according to which ex-offenders are entitled to a substantive right to be presumed innocent. If other citizens regard ex-offenders with some, and perhaps considerable, distrust, and decline to associate with or offer them some of the many informal benefits of community life, such "natural penalties" of their perceived past wrongs do not, in my view, violate any substantive right of ex-offenders to be presumed innocent. Of course, if distrust of ex-offenders, or animus toward them, verges over into active violations of their legal rights, then ex-offenders must be protected and their rights vindicated. Similarly, if the police are wary or watchful of some ex-offenders, regarding their commitments to abide by the law as weak or tentative, this also, in my view, does not violate any substantive right of such individuals to be presumed innocent. But we must distinguish such beliefs and attitudes on the part of the police from active harassment of ex-offenders or the trumping up of charges against them to put them in their places. Such actions are wrong because they interfere unjustifiably with the rights of ex-offenders to get on with their lives.

The Case for Reconceptualizing Collateral Consequences

The dominant conceptual and normative approach to collateral consequences involves casting them as adjuncts to legal punishment, not as inherent aspects of it. Broadly speaking, this is in line with rulings by the US Supreme Court, which has held that collateral consequences are "merely regulatory" in character, and thus not part of the sentences meted out to offenders.[6] This has led the Court to impose only weak upper limits on the magnitude of postsentence civil restrictions and disabilities, to eschew "fair warning" requirements in relation to them, and even to accept their retroactive imposition.[7] Legal and social science scholars are harshly critical of the Court's passive acceptance of collateral consequences and have raised telling objections to many of the specific forms they take. However, there seems some reluctance among scholars to fully abandon the Court's basic conceptual and normative framework for thinking about collateral consequences, according to which they are add-ons to legal punishment, not integral to it. Indeed, some scholars have argued against construing collateral consequences as penal sanctions.[8] My aim in this section is to urge a reconsideration of these issues. There are clear advantages to regarding collateral consequences as criminal sanctions, even if doing so stretches our understanding of the character of such sanctions.

First, it is worth noting the considerable array of criminal sanctions that the courts employ in sentencing offenders. Though it might be natural to think of imprisonment as the paradigmatic sanction, in fact, many offenders receive noncustodial sentences for their crimes.[9] Again, most of the crimes that criminal justice systems are called upon to address are mildly to moderately serious in character. They involve drug possession and sales, thefts of modest amounts of property, public order offenses, simple assaults, and the like. As a result, many offenders are fined, assigned suspended custodial sentences, required to perform community service, required to provide restitution to victims, assigned to home detention, or given probation. Though considerably less harsh than custodial sanctions, these noncustodial sanctions appear to satisfy Andrew von Hirsch's "censure" and "hard treatment" requirements of legal punishment.[10] They are imposed in response to authoritative findings of criminal misconduct, convey reprobation for such misconduct, and impose losses or burdens on offenders that are typically somewhat onerous. They also set offenders apart from law-abiding members of society who are not made to endure them. Even imprisonment, as a criminal sanction, exists along a continuum of authoritatively imposed losses and deprivations. Not all prisons are alike, a point that becomes clear if one considers the range of penal regimes that exist across the world—some of them hopelessly barbaric and cruel, others considerably less so, and some explicitly designed to inflict as little harm on offenders as possible, or to resocialize them.[11]

Second, it seems a dubious enterprise to attempt to draw a sharp line, or indeed any discernible line, between what are undisputed criminal sanctions and most of what are regarded and treated as collateral consequences of conviction. The latter, as we have seen, impose various kinds of restrictions, disabilities, or losses of the benefits of full citizenship on offenders. There seems little doubt that these are meant to convey censure and so are stigmatizing, or that they are experienced by offenders as such.[12] Full and equal citizens are not usually told by the state where they can and cannot live, what occupations they can pursue, whether they can care for or have access to their children, whether they can vote (if they satisfy the normal age requirements), or whether they can receive social welfare services that they desperately need. All of these, when imposed on offenders in response to their crimes, constitute diminishments of their full and equal status as citizens. Many of them will make the lives of offenders difficult, sometimes (especially in the aggregate) considerably more so than the "official" legal sanctions that they have been made to endure.[13]

Third, one signal advantage of incorporating what are now treated as adjuncts to legal punishment into legal punishment proper is that they can thereby be made to better satisfy some of the basic requirements of just punishment: proportionality, fair warning, and nonretroactivity.[14] Suppose, for instance, that officially imposed losses and deprivations that are now treated as "merely collateral" had to be factored by sentencing judges, or the sentencing commissions that issue sentencing guidelines, into any sentences handed down to offenders. Instead of assigning offenders some (hopefully proportional) criminal sentence, and then letting collateral consequences accrue to them automatically, haphazardly (as these are subtracted to or added to by legislators), and without regard to their overall impact on offenders, sentencing commissions and judges were tasked with factoring them into sentences. This might induce judges or sentencing commissions to more carefully consider whether and to what extent any of what are now treated as adjuncts to legal punishment are appropriate in relation to given types of offenders, or in relation to particular offenders. As we have seen, one of the standard complaints about collateral consequences is that they are inflicted upon all offenders, or perhaps all offenders of certain types, without regard to their appropriateness given the diversity of offenses and offenders. This might change if those responsible for sentencing were required to treat all officially imposed losses and deprivations as aspects of the official punishment of offenders.

Just as importantly, folding collateral consequences into sentencing might encourage those responsible for sentencing to consider the character of the entire package of stigmatizing losses and deprivations being meted out to offenders. If we assume a commitment to both overall and comparative proportionality in sentencing, the result would likely have to be some adjustment in the elements of the overall punishment "packages" assigned to offenders.[15] No more would offenders be assigned a (hopefully proportional) sentence only to then experience further disabilities and losses tacked on automatically and without consideration given to whether their impact comparatively or absolutely overpunishes offenders. Also, we might hope that required official attention to the diverse elements of overall sentencing packages would spark more thoughtful consideration of the duration of what are now treated as adjuncts to legal punishment. Where collateral consequences are conceived as outside of legal punishment, it is easier to ignore important questions about how long offenders should be made to endure them. Again, one of the problems with collateral consequences as they are currently conceived is that there seems no inherent need to suspend or discontinue them at some point. They are not part of an offender's punishment, and so not seen as subject to proportionality constraints on sentencing.

Further, folding collateral consequences into legal punishment would enable us to reduce their surprising and retroactive features. If sentencing commissions had to factor all of the potential losses and disabilities attending criminal conviction into their sentencing guidelines, then there would be at least some advance warning to citizens that suffering such losses and disabilities might be the cost of criminal conviction. Or, if all of the stigmatizing losses or disabilities attending their guilty pleas had to be made clear to accused persons in advance of their pleas, accused persons would have fair warning of the sanctions they face if they admit their guilt. We should not exaggerate the likely impact of these changes. Many would-be offenders pay little attention to official sentencing guidelines; crafting such guidelines to incorporate all of the losses or disabilities that might be meted out to offenders in response to their crimes would not change that. And many accused persons prepared to admit their guilt might still be surprised by one or more of the elements in the sentencing package on offer to them in exchange for their pleas. But at least those tempted to plead guilty would know better what officially imposed losses and disabilities awaited them. More importantly, once a sentence was issued, there would be no further, retroactive add-ons to it, of the kinds now adopted by legislative bodies and tolerated by the courts.[16] A stigmatizing loss or disability in response to a conviction would have to be made part of an offender's official sentence; tacking them on later would not be allowed.

Fourth, the requirement that all losses and disabilities officially imposed in response to criminal convictions be incorporated into offenders' sentences would, to a considerable extent, simplify their postpunishment legal status. Once all parts of an offender's assigned sentence were served, the offender would be entitled to full and equal legal status, just like any nonoffender. Postpunishment, offenders could not be denied any of the legal rights and privileges accorded to other citizens, or suffer their abridgement or infringement. Ex-offenders would not, as a result, find themselves with the kinds of compromised legal statuses that many of them have when collateral consequences are treated as mere adjuncts to legal punishment. They would not be subject to regulations and restrictions regarding where they lived, what occupations they could pursue, whether they could vote or have automobile licenses, or whether they would have access to social welfare programs. Postpunishment, they would be full and equal citizens again and treated by the state as such.

If this seems alarming, then it is important to add that my position is fully consistent with some offenders being assigned sentences that impose lifelong stigmatizing losses or disabilities on them. Lifetime prison sentences might be justified, given my account. So might lifelong bans on driving, or having interactions with (one's own or others') children, or obtaining employment in certain occupations. My view is not that criminal sentences should never have permanent or lifelong elements, only that those elements must be prospectively incorporated into the sentences imposed on offenders and therefore subject to standard proportionality constraints. Some offenders might commit such serious offenses, or repeatedly commit so many of them, that more or less permanent stigmatizing losses or restrictions should be imposed on them. These would constitute elements of their sentences that they would presumptively (absent an official pardon, perhaps) never escape, although they might fully serve other elements of their sentences. However, many offenders would not be appropriately subject to such enduring stigmatizing losses, only to ones lesser in magnitude and shorter in duration. This means that some, and perhaps most, criminal offenders would, at some point, complete their sentences. At that point, on my view, they would be entitled to full and equal status as legal citizens, subject to no further stigmatizing losses or disabilities unless they were convicted of subsequent offenses.

Objections to a Ban on Collateral Consequences

In effect, what I am proposing is a ban on collateral consequences, insofar as these are understood as stigmatizing losses officially imposed on offenders as mere adjuncts to their criminal sentences. In this section, I consider objections to such a ban, though it is important to add, these objections rarely stem from a hearty embrace of the ways in which collateral consequences are currently imposed on ex-offenders.

It might be claimed that we can continue to treat collateral consequences as adjuncts to legal punishment and say that offenders who have fully served their official sentences ought to be, presumptively at least, treated as full and equal citizens. Zachary Hoskins has recently offered a cogent argument to this effect; his discussion also has the virtue of making clear that the range of justifiable collateral consequences is much smaller than is found in many legal systems.[17] On Hoskins's account, defensible collateral consequences aim primarily at reducing risks. If they are to be imposed justifiably, we must have clear evidence that they will reduce risks of significant kinds. Also, we must demonstrate that there are no other ways to reduce such risks without imposing restrictions on the conduct or privileges of ex-offenders, and the burdens of the restrictions must not exceed the benefits expected from them.[18] If these criteria were adhered to, Hoskins argues, that many fewer collateral consequences would be imposed than is now the norm. Simply stated, too many of the restrictions and disabilities imposed on ex-offenders have been adopted without proper regard to the risks they reduce, the alternative ways of reducing them, or the costs to ex-offenders.

There is much to be said for Hoskins's analysis. However, it implicitly reveals what I believe is the fatal flaw of continuing to conceive of collateral consequences as adjuncts to legal punishment proper. Hoskins argues that ex-offenders should be "presumptively" treated as equals once they have completed their sentences.[19] This sounds close to my own position, until we ask what kinds of considerations are to be permitted to rebut or overcome this presumption. It then becomes clear that ex-offenders' rights are, on Hoskins's account, appropriately subject to a risk-reduction calculus in ways in which the rights of nonoffenders are not. On Hoskins's account, ex-offenders' rights can be restricted if there are grounds of the appropriate kinds, independently of further criminal conduct, to believe that ex-offenders pose risks to others.[20] But normal citizens' rights are not usually restricted based on such risk assessments, even more reliable ones than are currently the norm in imposing many collateral consequences. Normal citizens must violate others' legal rights, or attempt to, or be on the verge of doing so before we think it appropriate for the authorities to interfere with their rights. It is not usually enough for them to be deemed as imposing unreasonable risks to others, and so subject to liberty restrictions, independently of specific harmful or harm-threatening actions on their part. But this is precisely what collateral consequences do; they diminish the legal rights and privileges of individuals because of their status as ex-offenders. Hoskins thus implicitly treats ex-offenders, individuals who have fully served their sentences, differently from other citizens. He makes their legal rights more fragile and thus susceptible to infringement by the government. In this way, he does not escape the pitfalls of conceiving of collateral consequences as distinct from legal punishment.

In their perceptive and thorough analysis of collateral consequences (or what they term "civil disabilities attending punishment"), Andrew von Hirsch and Martin Wasik recognize that if we justify such consequences on risk-reduction grounds, we are implicitly treating ex-offenders as less than fully equal citizens.[21] Again, we do not deprive citizens of a right as fundamental as liberty on grounds of risk except in unusual circumstances—quarantine or pretrial detention being two of the plausible exceptions. If collateral consequences infringed fundamental rights based solely on risk calculations, then von Hirsch and Wasik agree that they would be problematic.[22] Hence, von Hirsch and Wasik argue that such activities as driving a car or having a specific occupation—typical kinds of activities targeted by collateral consequences—are not fundamental rights. Since this is so, imposing such losses or restrictions does not, in their view, diminish the equal status of ex-offenders.[23]

Though intriguing, I do not believe that this argument is convincing. The right to liberty arguably consists of the right to have a wide range of choices about how one is to conduct one's life. It consists of the right to travel where and when one wishes, to live where one wishes, work in the occupation of one's choice, along with myriad other choices, subject, of course, to limits derived from others' basic rights. Granted, if we focus on any one of these choices, it might seem a stretch to denominate it a "basic" or "fundamental" right. Yet if enough of them are taken away from us, then at some point, the right to liberty becomes meaningless. Even if only one or two of them is taken away from us, then we are being treated differently than other citizens.[24] And if they are taken away from us in response to our having been convicted of one or more crimes, there seems little doubt that this sets us apart in a stigmatizing way. Besides, to disqualify someone from working in her chosen field, one for which she might have spent years acquiring the qualifications and experience, seems a pretty fundamental infringement of her liberty. It will not do for von Hirsch and Wasik to argue that legal punishment in the form of imprisonment is qualitatively different, and, as such, a much more drastic curtailment of a person's rights and so a strike against her equal status as a citizen. For though this seems correct, there is, as we have seen, a wide variety of noncustodial criminal sanctions that do not strike so hard or deeply against the basic rights of offenders. It seems unlikely that von Hirsch and Wasik would categorize these considerably less intrusive sanctions as something other than forms of legal punishment.

Von Hirsch and Wasik also contend that collateral consequences are distinct from legal punishment in not effectively censuring offenders for their crimes.[25] However, their argument for this claim is somewhat obscure. It is clear that they see the imposition of collateral consequences, when it is justified, to be based on the logic of risk reduction.[26] Risk reduction looks to the future; legal punishment censures, based on the gravity of past criminal choices.[27] Yet it seems doubtful that all collateral consequences have risk reduction as their goal. To some extent, at least, denials of access to social welfare programs such as low-interest educational loans and public housing appear to be premised on the notion that offenders are undeserving of such benefits, quite independently of the risks posed by permitting them to enjoy them. In a similar vein, the loss of voting rights has often been defended on grounds having to do with offenders having violated the social contract and so forfeited the right to participate in electing the officials who will determine the laws and enforce them.[28] Von Hirsch and Wasik might reject these arguments, as have others, but they suggest that collateral consequences are not as simply and straightforwardly aimed at risk reduction, as von Hirsch and Wasik allege. In fact, the rationales for them are strikingly similar, for the most part, to those offered for criminal sanctions such as imprisonment.

Setting the preceding point to one side, legal punishment, at least on von Hirsch's well-known account, is both expressive (in censuring the misconduct of offenders) and aimed at offering "supplemental prudential incentives" to would-be offenders, in the form of hard treatment, to convince them to refrain from offending.[29] Given the element of hard treatment in his account, it would be difficult for von Hirsch to deny that risk reduction is part of why we punish offenders.[30]

Fortunately, von Hirsch and Wasik provide other reasons to distinguish criminal sanctions and collateral consequences. They argue that it will be difficult to calibrate the impact of collateral consequences, thus thwarting applicability of the proportionality constraint to their imposition.[31] For how long, for instance, should we deny someone with a history of drunk driving a driver's license? For a month, a year, five years, or permanently? Similarly, for how long should we bar someone who has preyed upon those to whom she had occupational responsibilities from employment in the field for which she is otherwise well qualified? These are questions that seem to admit of few precise answers, and so such measures might seem ill-suited for use as criminal sanctions.

The problem with this argument is that parallel questions exist with regard to many commonly used criminal sanctions. For how long do we put a drug dealer on probation or sentence him to home detention, if that seems advisable? Three months, six months, a year, two years? Or what is the appropriate term of community service for someone who has illegally poached game from a park or animal preserve? The answers to these questions in relation to undoubted criminal sanctions seem as elusive and imprecise as they seem in relation to collateral consequences, so-called. Even with regard to imprisonment, a sanction that can be more precisely metered into weeks, months, or years, it has long been understood that determining sentence lengths for the various kinds of serious criminal offenses is far from an exact science; it seems more a matter of intuition or, perhaps, convention.[32] I really do not see how having to factor collateral consequences into offenders' sentences presents sentencing judges, or the sentencing commissions that provide the guidelines for sentencing decisions, with challenges that are unique if our aim is to preserve proportionality in sentencing.

Von Hirsch and Wasik further argue that collateral consequences are different from typical criminal sanctions in that the former will have highly variable effects on their recipients.[33] This too will make it difficult to ensure their proportional imposition on offenders. The problem with this argument is that critics of proportionality in sentencing have long argued that commonly used criminal sanctions have widely varying effects on their recipients.[34] How imprisonment will affect individuals depends on their previous experiences with it, their age, the kinds of offenses for which they are serving time, and the peculiarities of their psychological makeup. All of these factors present challenges for sentencing schemes that aim at proportionality. Likewise, the impact of fines on individuals depends significantly on the resources at their disposal. It has often been deemed a drawback to fines that the rich can pay them easily, whereas the poor might struggle to do so. Where is the proportionality in that, it might be asked.

The most persuasive argument that von Hirsch and Wasik offer concerns the difficulties with enforcing many of the kinds of losses and deprivations that are currently imposed postpunishment.[35] Though it should be possible to ensure that offenders are not issued driving licenses, it will be much harder to ensure that they are not actually driving. Similarly, it will be challenging to ensure that offenders are not living in areas from which they are barred or in public housing. No such challenges exist when it comes to assigned prison terms or fines; offenders either serve or pay them or not and enforcement seems relatively straightforward. Of course, the difficulties with enforcing certain kinds of officially imposed losses and disabilities might constitute a reason for eschewing them, whether they are conceived as mere adjuncts to legal punishment or aspects of it. But set that point to one side. Other considerations blunt the impact of von Hirsch and Wasik's argument. First, there are similar enforcement difficulties with some typical criminal sanctions. For instance, whether offenders are living up to the terms of their probation or suspended sentences is, one would imagine, a matter that eludes precise enforcement. Second, the difficulties with enforcing what are now treated as adjuncts to punishment will vary, depending on the loss, disability, or restriction involved. Felon disenfranchisement provisions should be relatively easy to enforce, not that this is a good reason to have them. Lists of felons could be maintained and voter registration agencies could be provided them and required to check them before issuing voting credentials. Likewise, official lists of individuals banned from certain types of occupations could be compiled, and employers could be required, by law, to consult them when making hiring decisions. Indeed, as our means of keeping records about people and tracking their whereabouts improve, as they surely will in the digital age, our abilities to enforce the losses, disabilities, and restrictions that most scholars believe are defensible as collateral consequences will be enhanced. Granted, some (e.g., driving license bans) will continue to present challenges. Yet they do so whether they are treated as part of an offender's legal punishment or adjuncts to it.

This brings me to a hard case for my own position. Up to this point, we have been considering losses, disabilities, or restrictions imposed by the government on ex-offenders. But one thing that many individuals who have served their sentences face is discrimination by private employers who are unwilling to employ them because of their criminal records.[36] So long as public agencies are not themselves involved in such discrimination, which they might be, of course, it will seem that the state is not responsible for depriving ex-offenders of decent opportunities to work and earn income. The decisions are being made by private employers, though it must be conceded that it is the state's courts that often enable such discrimination, by declining to treat it as an actionable ground for civil lawsuits. Discrimination against ex-offenders is tolerated by the courts, as being both rational and distinct from discrimination based on race, ethnicity, or gender.[37] Yet supposing that, at some point, ex-offenders should receive government protection against such discrimination, it might seem unclear how we would go about protecting them from it.

In the first place, it is important to note that not all such discrimination seems unjustified. As we saw in the previous chapter, a wide variety of factors seem relevant to decisions about how to treat those who have become entangled in the criminal justice system: their ages, the character of their offenses, the recency of their offenses, and the length of their criminal histories. Discrimination by private employers against individuals with lengthy and serious criminal records is one thing; discrimination by them against individuals with one or two minor convictions long in the past, when they were teens, and with clean records since then, is another.[38] I would have sentencing judges take such factors into account in determining whether and for how long offenders would be effectively unable to call upon the courts to protect them from discrimination by private employers. Offenders with longer or more serious records might reasonably be denied legal protection against discrimination for more extended periods of time. This would have the effect of consigning them to the secondary and part-time labor market.[39] Other offenders might not lose such protection at all or for brief periods of time.

The catch here is that, as a practical matter, it will be difficult for the courts to protect ex-offenders from such discrimination. Employers who get wind of individuals' criminal records, no matter how minor or long in the past the offenses involved were, might find legally unobjectionable ways to avoid hiring them. Also, the burdens of mounting lawsuits might effectively deprive ex-offenders of legal protection against discrimination. As a practical matter, the way around these problems could be for sentencing judges to order the expungement of offenders' records after some appropriate period of time. Minor offenses by youthful offenders might be expunged immediately upon completion of their sentences. The records of more serious or repeat offenders might be expunged after some number of years has passed with no further marks upon them.[40] Granted, devising and enforcing the terms of these varied provisions will present challenges to judges. But they are not challenges with which sentencing judges are wholly unfamiliar, for they already have to make complex judgments about such things as the length and conditions of probation, for how long an offender's driver's license should be suspended, and the amount and terms of required restitution payments.

I conclude that there is much to gain, both in terms of conceptual and normative coherence, and in terms of achieving fair and proportionate criminal sanctions, by folding whatever collateral consequences of conviction are defensible into the sentences assigned to offenders. If and when offenders fully serve their sentences, then they should be entitled to full and equal status as citizens. No longer would they be treated as individuals whose freedom and autonomy can be diminished on the grounds of risk imposition, grounds that mark them off as having lesser status.

Postpunishment and the Presumption of Innocence

Of what relevance, if any, is the preceding analysis to the debate about the nature and extent of the presumption of innocence? If one subscribes, as I do, to a narrow procedural account of the PI, according to which it makes sense only in the context of a criminal trial, then the answer will be "none at all." Obviously, if ex-offenders are arrested, charged with further crimes, and elect trial adjudication of the charges, then they are entitled to a presumption of innocence at the outset of their trials. But on my account, the PI has little to do with the ways in which we regard and treat offenders postpunishment.

What about more robust procedural accounts of the PI, according to which individuals are entitled to it once they are suspected of or charged with crimes? As we have seen, numerous scholars hold that individuals who have become entangled in the criminal justice system are entitled to a presumption of material innocence, so far as possible, while the charges against them are being investigated and authoritatively adjudicated.[41] On these more ambitious procedural accounts of the PI, conviction marks the point at which the PI has been fully rebutted, and something like a presumption of guilt, whether probative or material or both, takes its place. But what about offenders who have fully served their sentences? Are they, once again, entitled to a PI, understood as PI_m? It would seem not, at least not unless or until they are suspected of or charged with criminal offenses once again. In the absence of further entanglement with the criminal justice system, the more ambitious procedural accounts of the PI cannot make much sense of ex-offenders being entitled to some sort of presumption of their innocence. It is further charges, or at least investigations into their conduct by the police, that activate the PI.

This brings us to accounts of the PI according to which it is a substantive human right that individuals have regardless of whether they have fallen under suspicion or been charged with crimes by duly constituted legal authorities.[42] On these accounts, the entitlement of individuals to a presumption of innocence is not bounded at the front end of the criminal justice process by official suspicion or charges. But is it bounded at the back end, by official findings of guilt by a court of law or guilty pleas voluntarily entered before a court? Here, the answer seems a bit unclear. The most sensible way for proponents of such a view to proceed would appear to be this: Upon conviction, individuals are no longer to be presumed materially innocent of the specific kinds of criminal conduct with which they have been charged. Instead, a presumption of material guilt has taken the place of the PI, though only in relation to the proven (or acceded to) charges.[43] With respect to charges of which individuals have not been convicted, and indeed with respect to other forms of criminal misconduct, they are still presumed innocent and deserve to be treated as such. That much seems relatively clear and straightforward. Yet what does this account suggest about the imposition of collateral consequences of conviction? And does it have any implications for the debate about whether to include defensible forms of such consequences directly into the sentences assigned offenders?

With regard to the first question, if one subscribes to the view that there is a substantive right to be presumed innocent, then it would seem that one should regard the imposition of postpunishment collateral consequences with considerable skepticism. The losses, restrictions, and disabilities they involve, if conceived and treated as adjuncts to legal punishment, seem to convey profound distrust of ex-offenders.[44] The imposition of collateral consequences does not make sense except on the view that ex-offenders are dangerous or unreliable or unworthy. We do not monitor the whereabouts of citizens in good standing, tell them where they can live, what kinds of occupations they can have, or deny them access to public welfare benefits regardless of their need for them. If ex-offenders are, once again, citizens in good standing, then why should we permit the state to diminish their rights and privileges in these ways?

One possible response to this question would be to argue that the presumption of innocence is, after all, only a presumption. Perhaps what it means to be entitled to that presumption varies, depending on the context. As we have seen, Antony Duff has suggested that there might be numerous presumptions of innocence.[45] The kinds of considerations that appropriately rebut or overcome the PI in one context might be different from the kinds that rebut or overcome it in another. Along these lines, then, ex-offenders might be entitled to a substantive presumption of innocence but one that permits considerations of risk reduction to rebut it. Appropriately narrow and empirically validated collateral consequences therefore could be imposed on them in ways that are consistent with the PI.

Whatever the merits of Duff's suggestion in other contexts, in this one it seems unattractive. If ex-offenders' rights to be presumed innocent can be rebutted by considerations of risk reduction, so that collateral consequences can be legitimately imposed on them, then it is apparent that they are in a different legal position than their fellow citizens who are not ex-offenders. Typically, the PI of ordinary citizens can be rebutted, such that they can then have criminal sanctions justifiably inflicted upon them, only if they are found guilty of offending (or admit to it) in a court of law. The kinds of considerations thought capable of rebutting the PI in that context are of a different and stronger kind—proof beyond a reasonable doubt of legally proscribed conduct. If, by contrast, ex-offenders can have their legal rights and privileges denied or restricted by considerations of risk reduction, then the PI of ex-offenders is qualitatively different from the PI of their fellow nonoffending citizens. Ex-offenders, on this account, as on Hoskins's account, are officially treated as somewhat suspect. This seems an awkward position for proponents of a substantive right to be presumed innocent to defend.

Would proponents of a substantive right to be presumed innocent fare better if they endorsed the approach to collateral consequences of conviction that I have urged? The advantage to doing so, as I see it, would be that once offenders had fully served their sentences, their rights and privileges as citizens would neither be conceived nor treated differently from those of nonoffenders. The abilities of ex-offenders to live their lives as they see fit would not be subject to any further, officially imposed restrictions or depredations, at least not in the absence of subsequent arrests, charges, and convictions. In particular, ex-offenders would not be subject to limits or exclusions based on considerations of risk reduction. If we add to this the features of my approach according to which losses and disabilities could neither be imposed surreptitiously—without prior notice to offenders of their existence—nor retroactively, then we would come closer to the kind of legal regime that proponents of a substantive right to be presumed innocent standardly see as necessary if we are to respect and secure the PI. Such a regime inflicts punitive losses and deprivations on persons only after their presumptive innocence has been rebutted, in a court of law, by convincing evidence of their guilt on one or more charges.[46] Collateral consequences casually imposed as adjuncts to official sentences come a little too close to the sneaky punishment of citizens based on unproven concerns about what they will do, rather than on rigorous proofs of what they have done.

By this logic, the position that we come to is this: Proponents of a substantive right to be presumed innocent should insist that any and all officially imposed depredations of citizens' legal rights and privileges must be treated as aspects of their sentences for their proven crimes. Once offenders complete their sentences (subject to the proviso that some aspects of some offenders' sentences might be lifelong and so not subject to completion), they are once again entitled to a substantive presumption of innocence and with it, full and equal status as citizens. The question we now face is whether this is a coherent and illuminating position.

I contend that it is neither. First, with respect to its coherence, it is useful to gain some clarity about what a criminal conviction means if one subscribes to a substantive PI. Conviction on one or more charges means that an individual's presumed material innocence, at least with respect to those charges, has been rebutted. The government has succeeded in establishing, in a court of law and to an exacting standard of proof, that the individual acted in a legally proscribed manner and so is appropriately subject to legal punishment. However, nothing follows from this about the individual's lack of innocence in relation to other, unproven charges or the individual's conduct more generally. He or she is still to be presumed innocent, or so it would seem, in all other respects. Further, once the appropriate sentence for the crimes of which an individual has been convicted has been fully served, this does not magically wipe clean the government's having rebutted the individual's presumed innocence with respect to the proven charges. The individual's proven guilt on such charges remains intact, as it were. And since the individual should never have been presumed anything less than innocent of further criminal misconduct, there is no innocence, in other respects, to be restored by the individual's having fully served his or her sentence. To suggest otherwise seems muddled.

Second, it is not apparent how introducing a substantive right to be presumed innocent into the debate about the treatment of ex-offenders helps to illuminate the issues; indeed, it arguably obscures them. What matters, postpunishment, is whether offenders are restored to their full status as legal citizens, with all of the attendant rights and privileges this involves. This is a matter of their being treated by the state as equals, rather than of their presumed innocence. One can try to insist otherwise, by claiming that their presumed innocence is or ought to be the ground of their restored equality. But again, in certain respects their presumed innocence has been lost, whereas in most other respects it was never in need of being restored.

More to the point, it is not clear exactly who is supposed to be "presuming the innocence" of ex-offenders. Legal officials, in particular police and prosecutors, are apt to view some convicted offenders, even ones who have fully served their sentences, as likely suspects when subsequent crimes occur. This will especially be true when individuals have multiple convictions in the recent past and are known to the police, as they might well be, to still be involved in criminal activity. There are well-known dangers to such "usual suspects" policing, and it should be uncontroversial that police suspicions must not be permitted to verge over into active harassment of ex-offenders.[47] Such harassment constitutes a clear interference with the abilities of ex-offenders to get on with their lives and so a diminution in their status as equal citizens. But official suspicions, when they are used to narrow the field of possible criminal actors to be investigated, seem different. Proponents of a substantive right to be presumed innocent might argue that police and prosecutors should adopt a kind of "official amnesia" with respect to ex-offenders and their crimes, thereby presuming them innocent of any further crimes that have recently been reported or discovered. This would require such officials to begin the investigation of each new case de novo, as it were, without any working hypotheses about possible suspects. Yet not only would advocacy of such an approach likely fall on deaf ears, it hardly seems sensible. Again, there is a fine line between following hunches about likely suspects and actively harassing ex-offenders. There are dangers in the former, but I doubt that we want the police to altogether desist from having suspicions about certain people. Yet this would seem to be what a substantive right to be presumed innocent requires.

Perhaps it is members of the public who are to presume the innocence of ex-offenders who have fully served their sentences for their past crimes. What would doing so entail, exactly? We might agree that members of the public must refrain from actions that effectively deprive ex-offenders of their legal rights and privileges. Ex-offenders should not be harassed by members of the public or worse, attacked by them. Yet requirements that members of the public refrain from such actions can be grounded in the duties to respect the equal legal status of ex-offenders. Would proponents of a substantive right to be presumed innocent insist on more from members of the public? In particular, would they urge a more positive or generous stance toward ex-offenders, one that involved welcoming them back into their communities and extending all of the benefits of social inclusion to them? Should we invite ex-offenders into our homes, offering them our friendship or neighborliness, or go out of our way to meet and greet them?

The problem with such an account, it seems to me, is that it is unrealistic in what it requires of us as citizens of a liberal polity. The fact is, we make decisions all the time about to whom to extend our neighborliness or friendship, where these decisions are based on evaluations of the reliability of persons, their inclinations toward reciprocity or goodwill, their generosity, or simply their affability. Obviously, these evaluations can be made crudely or insensitively, but they need not be. Many of these kinds of decisions not only seem to be well within our legal and moral remit, they do not evidence any lack of moral (or civic) virtue, so long as they are made reasonably, as they might be.[48] In particular, it does not seem unreasonable for individuals to be cautious or wary of ex-offenders in some instances. A lot depends on the character of the crimes of which they were convicted, the length of their criminal records, the recency of their offenses, or whether the offenses can be plausibly viewed as indiscretions of youth. Would proponents of a substantive right to be presumed innocent have us ignore these things and thereby regard and treat all ex-offenders the same and as we regard and treat those whose criminal records are clean? This seems an untenable position to defend. Yet if neither legal authorities nor members of the public can be justifiably required to do more than act in accordance with the legal rights of ex-offenders, then who exactly is presuming the innocence of ex-offenders and to what effect? The answers to these questions remain elusive.

Concluding Remarks

Nothing in the preceding section should be taken to deny that we should respond more hopefully and generously to ex-offenders than we often do. The demonization of ex-offenders ought to be avoided. It neither speaks well of us nor helps them avoid future offending. Many ex-offenders will have committed relatively minor offenses. Some will have committed more serious ones long in the past, having lived respectable lives since then. Others will have committed crimes under the stresses and strains of social deprivation, substance addiction, or mental illness. We should be prepared to make these kinds of distinctions among ex-offenders and offer many of them second and even third or fourth chances. Yet in my view, little conceptual or normative clarity is gained by way of encouraging more constructive attitudes and conduct toward ex-offenders by invoking a substantive right to be presumed innocent on their behalf. Doing so obscures the variety of ex-offenders and the kind of equality to which, on my account, they are entitled. Once they have completed their criminal sentences, they should be treated by the law as equal citizens. They need not be treated as if their pasts do not matter, even if many of them should be enabled to transcend them.

| Epilogue

THROUGHOUT THE PRECEDING CHAPTERS, I have defended a limited role for the presumption of innocence, arguing against efforts by scholars to extend it beyond the criminal trial. In the course of elaborating these claims, I have noted that entanglement with the criminal justice system conveys useful signals about our fellow citizens, ones that it might be vital for us to heed. Yet the signals are, I have emphasized, often tentative, partial, or misleading. Thus, we ought to be careful in drawing conclusions from them about the character and conduct of our fellow citizens. In some cases, we should be hesitant to infer anything about the individuals arrested for or charged with criminal offenses, at least until the criminal justice process has progressed quite a ways. Even when the process produces convictions, what we should conclude about the character of offenders depends on a host of factors, not the least of which are the crimes of which they have been convicted and their histories of previous convictions. As we have seen, many of the offenses of which persons are routinely convicted are misdemeanors and so relatively minor. One or two such convictions should not lead us to conclude that a person is irredeemable and therefore never to be trusted. Numerous such convictions should not lead us to doubt their character if their offenses are long in the past and persons have made concerted efforts to change their ways.

Importantly, the claim that we should be prepared to receive and evaluate the signals about individuals sent by the criminal justice system presupposes that the officials who are authorized to arrest, investigate, charge, and process cases are, for the most part, conscientious and trustworthy. If they are not—if police and prosecutors are usually incompetent, corrupt, or malevolent—then the signals conveyed by the system will tell us little about those caught up in the process, except, perhaps, that they are hapless victims. That such essentially lawless regimes do or have existed at various times and places in the world is beyond dispute. But they have mostly been ignored in my analysis, which is not to say that the possibility of some incompetence, corruption, or malevolence on the part of the authorities has been. Indeed, it is partly because of the awareness that such things occur that I have urged considerable caution in drawing conclusions about the material and probative guilt of those charged with criminal offending. What I have resisted is the notion that, until the individuals caught up in the criminal justice system are duly convicted, we ought to regard and treat them as if their law-abidingness is nowise in doubt.

It might be argued that my narrow account of the PI, with its accommodation of some official and unofficial suspicion about the individuals who have been arrested for or charged with crimes, hews too closely to existing attitudes and practices toward the suspected or accused. Although I counsel against presuming the material or probative guilt of such individuals, it might be thought that more ought to be done to implore criminal justice officials, and the public, to reorient their attitudes toward those who have become ensnared in the criminal justice system. Maybe the whole point of employing the stirring rhetoric of the PI is to move police and prosecutors, and all of us, to do more than simply not presume the material or probative guilt of persons who have fallen under official suspicion. In an age in which criminal offenders are routinely demonized in the mass media, with some cast as moral monsters who will stop at nothing to gratify their incomprehensible (at least to the generally law-abiding) needs and desires, it might seem that stronger medicine is needed than urging restraint in drawing conclusions about the propensities of our fellow citizens. Only if we strive to regard and treat the suspected or accused as if they are innocent will we be able to prevent the mistaken convictions apt to eventuate when the public is moved to near-hysteria about crime and those believed to have engaged in it.

Again, however, I remain unconvinced that belaboring the PI will actually prove all that useful in tempering the public's insistence upon swift and harsh punishment of criminal offenders. We would do better, first and foremost, to inform the public about the less-than-serious nature of much of the offending dealt with by the criminal justice system. Most offenders are not murderers, rapists, or vicious maulers. Many are engaged in forms of criminal misconduct that harm mostly themselves or others who are, to some degree, participants in bringing about that harm. Others commit minor thefts or frauds that pose few life-threatening, or even significantly life-altering, risks. Next, the public also might be better informed about the costs and negative consequences of the severe punishment of minor offenders, along with the crippling effects of the many collateral forms of sanctions routinely visited upon them. Finally, the public might be usefully reminded that many of them participate in minor forms of criminal misconduct for which they have the luxury, often born of class or race, of being mostly immune from official detection and prosecution.[1]

Is it criminal justice officials, specifically police and prosecutors, who need the additional guidance and encouragement in carrying out their tasks provided by a prescribed PI with respect to the individuals who come under their purview? Perhaps, although more detailed instructions about how they should go about their tasks with a bit less zeal and a bit more willingness to admit their susceptibilities to error might do more to shield citizens from unjust arrests, charges, and convictions. For instance, there is evidence that a significant percentage of unjust convictions are the products of mistaken eyewitness identifications.[2] Yet such identifications are too often encouraged by police officers, using questionable methods. The dangers of relying on such identifications, let alone of manipulating them, ought to be part of the official training of police officers; they also should be frequently reminded of those dangers in subsequent training by their overseers. Similarly, police officers should be pointedly reminded of the patent risks posed by coercive interrogation techniques; better still, steps should be taken to eliminate the use of such techniques.[3] These and numerous other specific reforms in police and prosecutorial conduct in relation to suspects and formally accused persons should be our focus, rather than hectoring such officials to "presume the innocence" of persons whom they will often have reason to suspect of having committed crimes.

It might be objected that part of the point of urging a pretrial PI is to ensure that suspects and formally charged persons are treated with dignity by the authorities. We prescribe the PI not only to avoid errors, but to discourage police and prosecutors from treating the accused as if their guilt has already been determined or, worse, as if they are deserving of contempt or abuse. Again, however, it is one thing to insist that legal officials fully respect and adhere to due process and thereby refrain from punishing individuals until their guilt has been determined by a court of law. It is not the role of police or prosecutors to, all by themselves, determine the guilt of accused persons or commence their punishment. It is another thing to insist that police and prosecutors presume the material or probative innocence of the accused, in spite of the abundant evidence they might have seen against them, and in spite of their roles that require them to see to it that the guilty are investigated, arrested, charged, and convicted.

As for the notion that police and prosecutors should be strongly encouraged to respect the dignity of the accused, I fully concur. But the danger that they will not do so seems unlikely to stem from the belief that the accused are guilty and apt to be convicted. It seems more likely to stem from beliefs or attitudes about suspects or accused persons according to which reasonable suspicion of criminal misconduct somehow voids all moral limits on their treatment. As we have seen, entanglement with the criminal justice system does and likely has to entail some diminishment of the moral rights of individuals. The authorities have to be able to undertake measures that intrude upon the basic rights of suspects if they are to investigate crimes. But I have insisted that progressively stronger justificatory barriers must be mounted by the authorities as, and to the extent that, they infringe suspects' rights. At no point are all such barriers surmounted, such that legal officials are morally free to act with impunity toward the accused. Even convicted persons retain some basic rights in their entirety, though others are justifiably curtailed by legal punishment.[4] Suspects and accused persons presumably retain more of them and to a greater extent.

Finally, the authorities should be urged to retain some perspective on the persons whom they arrest, charge, and attempt to convict of crimes, and some humility as they go about their important tasks. Perspective is needed because few of those caught up in the criminal justice system are moral monsters; most are ordinary human beings who have made bad choices, ones that all too often stem from poverty, addiction, mental illness, or immaturity. Humility is needed because all of us are susceptible to making such choices. Police and prosecutors, no less than the rest of us, should acknowledge their human frailty and thus strive to treat those under their purview with sympathy and decency.

NOTES

Introduction

1. See Thomas Weigend, "There is Only One Presumption of Innocence," *Netherlands Journal of Legal Philosophy* 42 (2013): 196; Stefan Trechsel, "The Right to Be Presumed Innocent," in S. Trechsel and S. Summers, *Human Rights in Criminal Proceedings* (Oxford: Oxford University Press, 2006), 153–91; Hock Lai Ho, "The Presumption of Innocence as a Human Right," in *Criminal Evidence and Human Rights*, in P. Roberts and J. Hunter (eds.) (Oxford: Hart Publishing, 2012), 259–81; and R. A. Duff, "Pre-trial Detention and the Presumption of Innocence," in A. Ashworth, L. Zedner, and P. Tomlin (eds.), *Prevention and the Limits of the Criminal Law* (Oxford: Oxford University Press, 2013), 115–32.

2. Victor Tadros and Stephen Tierney, "The Presumption of Innocence and the Human Rights Act," *The Modern Law Review 67* (2004*)*: 402–34; Victor Tadros, "Rethinking the Presumption of Innocence," *Criminal Law and Philosophy* 1 (2007): 193–213; and Victor Tadros, "The Ideal of the Presumption of Innocence," *Criminal Law and Philosophy* 8 (2014): 449–67; and Patrick Tomlin, "Extending the Golden Thread? Criminalisation and the Presumption of Innocence," *Journal of Political Philosophy* 21 (2013): 431–47.

3. Trechsel, "Right to Be Presumed," 153–54; Ho, "Presumption of Innocence," 259; and Hamish Stewart, "The Right to Be Presumed Innocent," *Criminal Law & Philosophy* 8 (2014): 407–20.

4. Antony Duff, "Who Must Presume Whom to Be Innocent of What?" *Netherlands Journal of Legal Philosophy* 42 (2013): 185.

5. Here, I paraphrase Duff, "Who Must Presume?" 170.

6. See Larry Laudan, *Truth, Error, and Criminal Law: An Essay in Legal Epistemology* (Cambridge: Cambridge University Press, 2006), 95.

7. One theme to which I will continually recur throughout the book is the mostly anonymous character of much of what goes on in the criminal justice system. This anonymity is largely a function of the fact that the overwhelming majority of the cases processed by the system involve misdemeanors. See Jenny Roberts, "Why Misdemeanors Matter: Defining Effective Advocacy in the Lower Criminal Courts," *University*

of California-Davis Law Review 45 (2011): 277–372, and Alexandra Natapoff, "Misdemeanors," *Southern California Law Review* 85 (2012): 1313–75.

8. This is Andrew Ashworth's formulation of the presumption in "Four Threats to the Presumption of Innocence," *International Journal of Evidence & Proof* 10 (2006): 243, though Ashworth qualifies this statement with the phrase "so far as possible," in recognition of the necessity of permitting legal officials to investigate crimes and prosecute them.

9. For a useful primer on the kinds of police and prosecutorial tactics that produce errors, see Keith A. Findley and Michael S. Scott, "The Multiple Dimensions of Tunnel Vision in Criminal Cases," *Wisconsin Law Review* 2006 (2006): 291–397.

10. See Marc Mauer and Meda Chesney-Lind, *Invisible Punishment: The Collateral Consequences of Mass Imprisonment* (New York: The New Press, 2002).

11. For a cogent theory of criminalization, see A. P. Simester and Andrew von Hirsch, *Crimes, Harms, and Wrongs: On the Principles of Criminalisation* (Oxford: Hart Publishing, 2011).

12. I elaborate such an approach to legal punishment's justification in my "Some Surprising Implications of Negative Retributivism," *Journal of Applied Philosophy* 31 (2014): 49–62.

13. See Angela J. Davis, *Arbitrary Justice: The Power of the American Prosecutor* (Oxford: Oxford University Press, 2007).

14. For discussion, see Richard L. Lippke, *The Ethics of Plea Bargaining* (Oxford: Oxford University Press, 2011).

Chapter 1

1. Such a possibility is hinted at by Carl-Friedrich Stuckenberg, "Who Is Presumed Innocent of What by Whom?" *Criminal Law and Philosophy* 8 (2014): 303.

2. R. A. Duff, "Presuming Innocence," in L. Zedner and J. V. Roberts (eds.), *Principles and Values in Criminal Law and Criminal Justice: Essays in Honour of Andrew Ashworth* (Oxford: Oxford University Press, 2012), 51. See also Duff's "Who Must Presume Whom to Be Innocent of What?" *Netherlands Journal of Legal Philosophy* 42 (2013): 170–92.

3. Thomas Weigend, "There Is Only One Presumption of Innocence," *Netherlands Journal of Legal Philosophy* 42 (2013): 193–204; R. A. Duff, "Strict Liability, Legal Presumptions, and the Presumption of Innocence," in A. Simester (ed.), *Appraising Strict Liability* (Oxford: Oxford University Press, 2010), 130; Daniel Mendonca, "Presumptions," *Ratio Juris* 11 (1998): 399–412.

4. Duff, "Strict Liability," 130.

5. Nicholas Rescher, *Presumption and the Practices of Tentative Cognition* (Cambridge: Cambridge University Press, 2006), 29.

6. Larry Laudan, *Truth, Error, and Criminal Law: An Essay in Legal Epistemology* (Cambridge: Cambridge University Press, 2006), 104.

7. Laudan, *Truth, Error, and Criminal Law*, 101; Mendonca, "Presumptions," 401.

8. Of course, the proper limits of the criminal law are matters of significant and enduring controversy.

9. Larry Laudan, "The Presumption of Innocence: Material or Probatory?" *Legal Theory* 11 (2005): 339. See also Laudan's *Truth, Error and Criminal Law*, 96–97. For an

earlier statement of roughly the same distinction, albeit one that invokes the difference between "factual" and "legal" guilt, see Herbert L. Packer, *The Limits of the Criminal Law* (Stanford, Calif.: Stanford University Press, 1968), 166.

10. As Packer points out, numerous other conditions must be satisfied if the legal guilt of individuals is to be established (e.g., they must not have previously been tried for the same charges). See *Limits of the Criminal Law*, 165.

11. The "without reproach" formulation comes from Hamish Stewart, "The Human Right to Be Presumed Innocent," *Criminal Law and Philosophy* 8 (2014): 409, who attributes it to Immanuel Kant. The "citizen in good standing" formulation comes from Antony Duff, Lindsay Farmer, Sandra Marshall, and Victor Tadros, *The Trial on Trial*, vol. 3: *Towards a Normative Theory of the Criminal Trial* (Oxford: Hart Publishing, 2007), 113.

12. See Richard Posner, "An Economic Approach to the Law of Evidence," *Stanford Law Review* 51 (1999): 1514.

13. In Scotland, jurors in criminal trials have three verdict options: guilty, not guilty, and not proven. It might be thought that the second of these options at least comes somewhat closer to establishing the probative innocence of defendants than do "not guilty" verdicts in two-option jurisdictions. For discussion of the Scottish system, see Peter Duff, "The Scottish Criminal Jury: A Very Peculiar Institution," *Law and Contemporary Problems* 62 (1999): 173–201.

14. Laudan, "Presumption of Innocence," 342, although Laudan says this about the role of material innocence in the criminal justice process.

15. Laudan, "Presumption of Innocence," 349.

16. *Bell v. Wolfish*, 441 U.S. 520, 533 (U.S. 1979).

17. For discussion, see Andrew Ashworth, "Four Threats to the Presumption of Innocence," *International Journal of Evidence and Proof* 10 (2006): 241–79.

18. Ashworth, "Four Threats," 243. See also Stewart, "Human Right," 407, and Weigend, "There Is Only One," 198.

19. Ashworth, "Four Threats," 243.

20. Stewart, "Human Right," 409.

21. Victor Tadros and Stephen Tierney, "The Presumption of Innocence and the Human Rights Act," *Modern Law Review* 67 (2004): 402–34; Tadros, "Rethinking the Presumption of Innocence," *Criminal Law and Philosophy* 1 (2007): 193–213; Tadros, "The Ideal of the Presumption of Innocence," *Criminal Law and Philosophy* 8 (2014): 449–67; and Patrick Tomlin, "Extending the Golden Thread: Criminalisation and the Presumption of Innocence," *Journal of Political Philosophy* 21 (2013): 431–47.

22. Kevin R. Reitz, "Sentencing Facts: Travesties of Real-Offense Sentencing," *Stanford Law Review* 45 (1993): 523.

23. Thomas Weigend, "Assuming That the Defendant Is Not Guilty: The Presumption of Innocence in the German System of Criminal Justice," *Criminal Law and Philosophy* 8 (2014): 295.

24. Stefan Trechsel, "The Human Right to Be Presumed Innocent," in S. Trechsel and S. Summers, *Human Rights in Criminal Proceedings* (Oxford: Oxford University Press, 2006), 91; Hock Lai Ho, "The Presumption of Innocence as a Human Right," in P. Roberts and J. Hunter (eds.), *Criminal Evidence and Human Rights* (Oxford: Hart Publishing, 2012), 263; Liz Campbell, "Criminal Labels, the European Convention

on Human Rights and the Presumption of Innocence," *Modern Law Review* 76 (2013): 681–707.

25. Andrew von Hirsch and Martin Wasik, "Civil Disqualifications Attending Conviction: A Suggested Conceptual Framework," *Cambridge Law Journal* 56 (1997): 599–626, and Zachary Hoskins, "Ex-Offender Restrictions," *Journal of Applied Philosophy* 31 (2014): 33–48.

26. Laudan, *Truth, Error, and Criminal Law*, 66–76; Erik Lillquist, "Recasting Reasonable Doubt: Decision Theory and the Virtues of Variability," *University of California–Davis Law Review* 36 (2002): 85–197; Michael L. DeKay, "The Difference between Blackstone-Like Error Ratios and Probabilistic Standards of Proof," *Law and Social Inquiry* 21 (1996): 95–132.

27. Stewart, "Human Right," 413; see also Ashworth, "Four Threats," 249.

28. Trechsel, "Human Right," 164. Similar concerns have been expressed by Campbell, "Criminal Labels," 697.

29. Duff, "Who Must Presume?" (at 173) has suggested that there might have to be different presumptions of innocence that protect us in different contexts. For a pointed response, see Weigend, "There Is Only One."

30. R. A. Duff, "Pre-trial Detention and the Presumption of Innocence," in A. Ashworth, L. Zedner, and P. Tomlin (eds.), *Prevention and the Limits of the Criminal Law* (Oxford: Oxford University Press, 2013), 115–32. See also Laurence H. Tribe, "Preventive Justice in the World of John Mitchell," *Virginia Law Review* 56 (1970): 371–407.

31. In many continental legal systems, the standard of proof is characterized in terms of the principle of "in dubio pro reo," which is translated as "in doubt you must decide for the defendant." See John D. Jackson and Sarah J. Summers, *The Internationalisation of Criminal Evidence: Beyond the Common Law and Civil Law Traditions* (Cambridge: Cambridge University Press, 2012), 201.

32. On the psychological effects of imprisonment, see Craig Haney, *Reforming Punishment: Psychological Limits to the Pains of Imprisonment* (Washington, D.C.: American Psychological Association, 2006); for the economic effects of imprisonment, see Bruce Western, *Punishment and Inequality in America* (New York: Russell Sage, 2006).

33. On the difficulties in gaining reversals of convictions in the United States, see Keith A. Findley and Michael S. Scott, "The Multiple Dimension of Tunnel Vision in Criminal Cases," *Wisconsin Law Review* 2006 (2006): 348. In England and Wales, appellate courts are more inclined to examine the sufficiency of the evidence against those convicted of crimes, but they also discourage appeals with the threat of longer sentences in cases in which convictions are upheld. See Andrew Ashworth and Mike Redmayne, *The Criminal Process*, 4th ed. (Oxford: Oxford University Press, 2010), 372.

34. See Stephen A. Saltzberg, "Pleas of Guilty and the Loss of Constitutional Rights: The Current Price of Pleading Guilty," *Michigan Law Review* 76 (1978): 1265–307.

35. But see Julie R. O'Sullivan, "In Defense of the U. S. Sentencing Guidelines Modified Real-Offense System," *Northwestern University Law Review* 91 (1997): 1342–433.

36. See von Hirsch and Wasik, "Civil Disqualifications," 621, and Hoskins, "Ex-Offender Restrictions," 42.

37. Stewart, "Human Right," 415, concedes that what the authorities believe about suspects and the accused does not matter so long as they abide by relevant rules and procedures.

38. Stewart, "Human Right," 410, though Stewart adds that this is true only if members of the public have grounds for believing their fellow citizens guilty of wrongdoing.

39. *Bell v. Wolfish,* 441 U.S. 520, 533 (U.S. 1979).

40. William S. Laufer, "The Rhetoric of Innocence," *Washington Law Review* 70 (1995): 329–421.

41. Laudan, *Truth, Error, and Criminal Law*, 104.

42. See also Hock Lai Ho, *A Philosophy of Evidence Law: Justice in the Search for Truth* (Oxford: Oxford University Press, 2008), 227. Ho endorses the adoption by jurors of a "protective attitude" at the outset of trials toward the accused. This attitude should lead them to view the government's case with "a deliberate posture of skepticism."

43. R. A. Duff, "Dangerousness and Citizenship," in A. Ashworth and Martin Wasik (eds.), *Fundamentals of Sentencing Theory: Essays in Honor of Andrea von Hirsch* (Oxford: Clarendon Press, 1998), 152.

44. This would not preclude victims from filing civil suits to recover damages from those whom they believe have wronged them.

45. Ho, "Presumption of Innocence," 266; Duff, "Strict Liability," 134.

46. See Weigend, "Assuming the Defendant," 291, and Stuckenberg, "Who Is Presumed?" 308.

47. On the former, error distribution approach, see the references, *supra* note 26. On the moral assurance approach, see Duff et al., *The Trial on Trial,* 90; see also James Q. Whitman, *The Origins of Reasonable Doubt: Theological Roots of the Criminal Trial* (New Haven, Conn: Yale University Press, 2008), 211.

48. Thomas Weigend has questioned whether the PI and fair trial rights are related at all. He points out that those convicted of crimes who appeal their convictions have rights to fair hearings but they typically are no longer presumed innocent. Appellate review of verdicts often focuses on the fairness or adequacy of the procedures used to convict the accused, rather than the sufficiency of the evidence against them. Even if appellate review extends to the sufficiency of the evidence, the question the courts might focus on is whether one or more aspects of the evidence are in doubt, such that a verdict now appears to be "unsafe." Nothing about this requires the court to begin from the presumption that the convicted person is innocent. See Weigend, "Assuming the Defendant," 288.

49. Stefan Trechsel, "The Privilege against Self-Incrimination," in Stefan Trechsel and Sarah Summers, *Human Rights in Criminal Proceedings* (Oxford: Oxford University Press, 2006), 348.

50. Albert W. Alschler, "A Peculiar Privilege in Historical Perspective," in R. H. Helmholz, Charles M. Gray, John H. Langbein, Eben Moglen, Henry E. Smith, and Albert W. Alschuler (eds.), *The Privilege against Self-Incrimination: Its Origins and Development* (Chicago: University of Chicago Press, 1997), 181–204.

51. R. Kent Greenawalt, "Silence as a Moral and Constitutional Right," *William & Mary Law Review* 23 (1981): 15–71.

Chapter 2

1. Stefan Trechsel, "The Right to Be Presumed Innocent," in S. Trechsel and S. Summers, *Human Rights in Criminal Proceedings* (Oxford: Oxford University Press, 2006), 153.

2. Trechsel, "Right to Be Presumed Innocent," 155; Hock Lai Ho, "The Presumption of Innocence as a Human Right," in P. Roberts and J. Hunter (eds.), *Criminal Evidence and Human Rights: Reimagining Common Law Procedural Traditions* (Oxford: Hart Publishing, 2012), 259–81; Hamish Stewart, "The Right to Be Presumed Innocent," *Criminal Law and Philosophy* 8 (2014): 407–20; Liz Campbell, "Criminal Labels, the European Convention on Human Rights and the Presumption of Innocence," *Modern Law Review* 76 (2013): 681–707.

3. Stewart, "Right to Be Presumed," 409.

4. Stewart, "Right to Be Presumed," 413–14.

5. Trechsel, "Right to Be Presumed Innocent," 178.

6. Campbell, "Criminal Labels," 699.

7. Ho, "Presumption of Innocence," 266.

8. Alan Gewirth, *Reason and Morality* (Chicago: University of Chicago Press, 1978); Martha Nussbaum, "Capabilities and Human Rights," *Fordham Law Review* 66 (1997): 273–300; James Griffin, "Discrepancies between the Best Philosophical Account of Human Rights and the International Law of Human Rights," *Proceedings of the Aristotelian Society* 101 (2001): 1–28; and Jeremy Waldron, "Rights," in R. E. Goodin and P. Pettit (eds.), *A Companion to Contemporary Political Philosophy* (Oxford: Blackwell, 1993), 575–85.

9. Waldron, "Rights," 583.

10. Griffin, "Discrepancies," 14.

11. Cf. Griffin, "Discrepancies," 13.

12. Stewart, "Right to Be Presumed," 409.

13. Stewart, "Right to Be Presumed," 409.

14. Antony Duff has recently argued that "civic trust" requires us to presume innocence of our fellow citizens in the sense that we should not assume, in advance, as it were, that they are enemies who might attack us. Though Duff's account seems similar to Stewart's, Duff does not claim that it grounds a human right to be presumed innocent. For Duff's account, see "Who Must Presume Whom to Be Innocent of What?" *Netherland Journal of Legal Philosophy* 42 (2013): 170–92. I discuss his civic trust approach in the next chapter.

15. Stewart, "Right to Be Presumed," 413–14. See also Duff, "Who Must Presume," 174, and Andrew Ashworth, "Four Threats to the Presumption of Innocence," *International Journal of Evidence and Proof* 10 (2006): 249.

16. Cf. Thomas Weigend, "There Is Only One Presumption of Innocence," *Netherlands Journal of Legal Philosophy* 42 (2013): 202.

17. See John Braithwaite and Philip Pettit, *Not Just Deserts: Towards a Republican Theory of Criminal Justice* (Oxford: Clarendon Press, 1990), 63.

18. Marc Miller and Martin Guggenheim, "Pretrial Detention and Punishment," *Minnesota Law Review* 75 (1990): 335–426.

19. Douglas Husak, *Overcriminalization: The Limits of the Criminal Law* (Oxford: Oxford University Press, 2008); William J. Stuntz, *The Collapse of American Criminal Justice* (Cambridge, Mass.: Harvard University Press, 2011); and Michelle

Alexander, *The New Jim Crow: Mass Incarceration in the Age of Colorblindness* (New York: New Press, 2010).

20. Campbell, "Criminal Labels," 700.

21. Campbell, "Criminal Labels," 701–2.

22. Trechsel, "Right to Be Presumed Innocent," 178.

23. Trechsel, "Right to Be Presumed Innocent," 164.

24. Interestingly, Stewart, "Right to Be Presumed," at 410 and 415, admits both of these points.

25. Judges also should avoid publicly pronouncements concerning the "guilt" of accused persons who have been acquitted by juries.

26. Campbell, "Criminal Labels," 683–84.

27. Campbell, "Criminal Labels," 690–91.

28. Campbell, "Criminal Labels," 690.

29. Campbell, "Criminal Labels," 700.

30. Campbell, "Criminal Labels," 694.

31. See Campbell, "Criminal Labels," 703, where she claims that ASBOs "induce a certain community view of the person."

32. Campbell, "Criminal Labels," 700.

33. Ho, "Presumption of Innocence," 264.

34. Ho, "Presumption of Innocence," 266.

35. Ho, "Presumption of Innocence," 268.

36. Ho, "Presumption of Innocence," 271ff.

37. Ho, "Presumption of Innocence," 274.

38. Ho, "Presumption of Innocence," 272.

39. Hock Lai Ho, *A Philosophy of Evidence Law: Justice in the Search for Truth* (Oxford: Oxford University Press, 2008), 226.

40. For two illuminating accounts of the lingering effects of legal punishment, especially when it takes the form of imprisonment, see Craig Haney, *Reforming Punishment: Psychological Limits to the Pains of Imprisonment* (Washington, D.C.: American Psychological Association, 2006) and Bruce Western, *Punishment and Inequality in America* (New York: Russell Sage, 2006).

41. See Susan R. Klein, "Monitoring the Plea Process," *Duquesne Law Review* 51 (2013): 561.

42. See Andrew Ashworth and Mike Redmayne, *The Criminal Process*, 4th ed. (Oxford: Oxford University Press, 2010), 293–94.

43. See M. Langer, "From Legal Transplants to Legal Translations: The Globalization of Plea Bargaining and the Americanization Thesis in Criminal Procedure," *Harvard International Law Journal* 45 (2004): 1–64.

44. Ho, "Presumption of Innocence," 275.

45. See Josh Bowers, "Punishing the Innocent," *University of Pennsylvania Law Review* 156 (2007): 1134ff.

46. See Richard L. Lippke, *The Ethics of Plea Bargaining* (Oxford: Oxford University Press, 2011), 19.

47. Bowers, "Punishing the Innocent," 1134ff. See also Milton Heumann, *Plea Bargaining: The Experiences of Prosecutors, Judges, and Defense Attorneys* (Chicago: University of Chicago Press, 1977).

Chapter 3

1. Victor Tadros and Stephen Tierney, "The Presumption of Innocence and the Human Rights Act," *Modern Law Review* 67 (2004): 402–34; Victor Tadros, "Rethinking the Presumption of Innocence," *Criminal Law and Philosophy* 1 (2007): 193–213; Victor Tadros, "The Ideal of the Presumption of Innocence," *Criminal Law and Philosophy* 8 (2014): 449–67; and Patrick Tomlin, "Extending the Golden Thread? Criminalisation and the Presumption of Innocence," *Journal of Political Philosophy* 21 (2013): 44–66.

2. Tomlin, "Golden Thread," 46.

3. Antony Duff, "Who Must Presume Whom to Be Innocent of What?" *Netherlands Journal of Legal Philosophy* 42 (2013): 180–82.

4. Dale A. Nance, "Civility and the Burden of Proof," *Harvard Journal of Law and Public Policy* 17 (1994): 647–90.

5. Duff, "Who Must Presume?" 172.

6. Tadros, "Rethinking," 196.

7. Tadros, "The Ideal," 5; Tadros, "Rethinking," 199–200.

8. See Tadros, "Rethinking," 195, where he claims that a "proper understanding of the presumption of innocence requires a more nuanced understanding of the procedure-substance divide."

9. Tadros, "Rethinking," 197–98. See also Paul Roberts, "The Presumption of Innocence Brought Home? *Kebilene* Deconstructed," *Law Quarterly Review* 118 (2002): 49–50.

10. Tadros, "The Ideal," 1.

11. Tadros, "Rethinking," 196.

12. See Tadros's discussion in "The Ideal," 7.

13. Tadros, "Rethinking," 200.

14. Tadros, "The Ideal," 16–17.

15. Tadros, "The Ideal," 13.

16. Tadros, "The Ideal," 12.

17. Tadros, "Rethinking," 203.

18. Tadros claims that the legislature might interfere with the PI by stipulating a lower standard of proof for some offenses. See "Rethinking," 200.

19. Tadros and Tierney, "The Presumption of Innocence," 416. See also Andrew Ashworth, "Four Threats to the Presumption of Innocence," *International Journal of Evidence and Proof* 10 (2006): 268.

20. Again, see Tadros, "Rethinking," 198.

21. Tomlin, "Golden Thread," 53, 62.

22. Tomlin, "Golden Thread," 48.

23. Tomlin, "Golden Thread," 52.

24. Tomlin acknowledges some of the differences between the tasks of juries and lawmakers. See "Golden Thread," 56.

25. Tomlin, "Golden Thread," 63.

26. Tomlin, "Golden Thread," 58.

27. H. L. A. Hart, *The Concept of Law* (Oxford: Clarendon Press, 1961), 91–92.

28. Tomlin, "Golden Thread," 61–62.

29. Douglas N. Husak, "The Criminal Law as a Last Resort," *Oxford Journal of Legal Studies* 24 (2004): 207–35; and A. P. Simester and Andrew von Hirsch, *Crimes, Harms, and Wrongs: On the Principles of Criminalisation* (Oxford: Hart Publishing, 2011).

30. John Rawls, *A Theory of Justice* (Cambridge, Mass.: Harvard University Press, 1971), 48–50.

31. Patrick Tomlin, "Could the Presumption of Innocence Protect the Guilty?" *Criminal Law and Philosophy* 8 (2014): 431–47. Tomlin invokes a somewhat different "equivalency thesis" in this article (at 436), one citing the lack of inherent difference between errors of mistaken conviction and errors of excessive punishment. Yet I do not find the thesis any more plausible in this instance than in the previous one, where the focus was on errors of mistaken conviction and errors of mistaken criminalization. If we punish armed robber Smith excessively, by a six-year prison term rather than a (let us suppose more just) five-year term, then Smith has grounds for complaint. But Smith's grounds pale in comparison with Jones's, who, let us suppose, receives a six-year prison term for an armed robbery she did not commit. Indeed, it is not even obvious to me that Smith has as much to complain about if Jones receives only a mistaken one-year prison term. Jones's censure and hard treatment are entirely unjust, while Smith's is only excessive. And again, Jones could not have avoided her censure and hard treatment, while Smith presumably could have.

32. The skeptics, in addition to me, include Thomas Weigend, "Assuming that the Defendant Is Not Guilty: The Presumption of Innocence in the German System of Criminal Justice," *Criminal Law and Philosophy* 8 (2014): 291; and Carl-Friedrich Stuckenberg, "Who Is Presumed Innocent of What by Whom?" *Criminal Law and Philosophy* 8 (2014): 308.

33. R. A. Duff, "Strict Liability, Legal Presumptions, and the Presumption of Innocence," in A. Simester (ed.), *Appraising Strict Liability* (Oxford: Oxford University Press, 2010), 133–34.

34. The "presumption" against punishment of the innocent is not what Duff terms an "irrebuttable presumption of law," in "Strict Liability," 131. For such irrebuttable presumptions require courts to presume q given proof that p (e.g., to presume that if an accused person deceived a complainant about the purpose of a sexual act, then the act was not consented to). The societal presumption against punishment of the innocent cannot be plausibly interpreted as an instruction to a court; neither does it license an inference from proven facts to the drawing of some further conclusion.

35. Hence, it might be claimed that in certain narrow circumstances, to protect the innocent, we should preventively detain offenders beyond the point where they have served their sentences for their previous crimes. For discussion of this possibility, see R. A. Duff, "Dangerousness and Citizenship," in A. Ashworth and M. Wasik (eds.), *Fundamentals of Sentencing Theory: Essays in Honor of Andrew von Hirsch* (Oxford: Clarendon Press, 1998), 141–63; and Richard L. Lippke, "No Easy Way Out: Dangerous Offenders and Preventive Detention," *Law and Philosophy* 27 (2008): 383–414.

36. Duff, "Strict Liability," 137–39.

37. Of course, whether such businesses should be subject to civil liability is a separate question.

38. Duff, "Who Must Presume?" 180.

39. Duff, "Who Must Presume?" 181.

40. Nance, "Civility," 650–51.

41. Duff, "Who Must Presume?" 180.

42. Nance, "Civility," 652.

43. Duff, "Who Must Presume?" 180.

44. Nance, "Civility," 655.

45. Duff, "Who Must Presume?" 181.

46. Duff, "Who Must Presume?" 181.

47. Duff does say that we should be presumed civilly innocent until there is "evidence of guilt strong enough to warrant a trial." See "Who Must Presume?" 180.

48. Duff, "Who Must Presume?" 180.

49. Nance, "Civility," 648.

50. Jenny Roberts, "Why Misdemeanors Matter: Defining Effective Advocacy in the Lower Criminal Courts," *University of California–Davis Law Review* 45 (2011): 281; and Alexandra Natapoff, "Misdemeanors," *Southern California Law Review* 95 (2012): 1313–75.

51. The statistics on sexual assault in the United States should give proponents of civic trust some pause. It is estimated that a sexual assault occurs every two minutes in the United States, producing nearly 300,000 victims per year. See "How Often Does Sexual Assault Occur?" *Rape, Abuse & Incest National Network*, at https://www.rainn.org/get-information/statistics/frequency-of-sexual-assault (accessed January 12, 2015).

Chapter 4

1. Larry Laudan, *Truth, Error, and Criminal Law: An Essay in Legal Epistemology* (Cambridge: Cambridge University Press, 2006); Antony Duff, Lindsay Farmer, Sandra Marshall, and Victor Tadros, *The Trial on Trial*, vol. 3: *Towards a Normative Theory of the Criminal Trial* (Oxford: Hart Publishing, 2007); and John D. Jackson and Sarah J. Summers, *The Internationalisation of Criminal Evidence: Beyond the Common Law and Civil Law Traditions* (Cambridge: Cambridge University Press, 2012).

2. On the psychological effects of imprisonment, see Craig Haney, *Reforming Punishment: Psychological Limits to the Pains of Imprisonment* (Washington, D.C.: American Psychological Association, 2006); for the economic effects of imprisonment, see Bruce Western, *Punishment and Inequality in America* (New York: Russell Sage, 2006). See also Marc Mauer and Meda Chesney-Lind (eds.), *Invisible Punishment: The Collateral Consequences of Mass Imprisonment* (New York: New Press, 2002).

3. Laudan, *Truth, Error, and Criminal Law*, 95. See also Rinat Kitai, "Presuming Innocence," *Oklahoma Law Review* 55 (2002): 269.

4. See Milton Heumann, *Plea Bargaining: The Experiences of Prosecutors, Judges, and Defense Attorneys* (Chicago: University of Chicago Press, 1977), 137–39.

5. William J. Stuntz, notes that over 80 percent of those charged with felonies who go to trial are convicted. See "The Pathological Politics of Criminal Law," *Michigan Law Review* 100 (2001): 570.

6. Kitai, "Presuming," 272. See also Andrew Ashworth, "Four Threats to the Presumption of Innocence," *International Journal of Evidence and Proof* 10 (2006): 243.

7. William S. Laufer, "The Rhetoric of Innocence," *Washington Law Review* 70 (1995): 329–421; Richard D. Friedman, "A Presumption of Innocence, Not of Even Odds," *Stanford Law Review* 52 (2000): 873–87; and Duff et al., *Trial on Trial*, 113.

8. But see Antony Duff, "Strict Liability, Legal Presumptions, and the Presumption of Innocence," in A. P. Simester (ed.), *Appraising Strict Liability* (Oxford: Oxford University Press, 2005), 133. Duff argues that the standard of proof can be generated from the values underlying the presumption of innocence. Hock Lai Ho, in "The Presumption of Innocence as a Human Right," in P. Roberts and J. Hunter (eds.), *Criminal Evidence and Human Rights* (Oxford: Hart Publishing, 2012), 266, similarly contends that the high standard of proof follows from the substantive human right to be presumed innocent.

9. This interpretation of the presumption is suggested, though not defended as such, by Dale Nance in "Civility and the Burden of Proof," *Harvard Journal of Law and Public Policy* 17 (1994): 650.

10. Cf. Richard A. Posner, "An Economic Approach to the Law of Evidence," *Stanford Law Review* 51 (1999): 1477–546.

11. Friedman, "Presumption of Innocence," 880.

12. Laudan, *Truth, Error, and Criminal Law*, 104.

13. Laudan, *Truth, Error, and Criminal Law*, 106.

14. See Keith A. Findley and Michael S. Scott, "The Multiple Dimensions of Tunnel Vision in Criminal Cases," *Wisconsin Law Review* 2006 (2006): 340. On the worrisome effects of pretrial or extratrial information on jurors, see Dan Simon, "The Limited Diagnosticity of Criminal Trials," *Vanderbilt Law Review* 54 (2011): 189.

15. Hock Lai Ho, *A Philosophy of Evidence Law: Justice in the Search for Truth* (Oxford: Oxford University Press, 2008), 226.

16. Laufer, "Rhetoric," 409.

17. Laufer, "Rhetoric," 409. See also Findley and Scott, "Multiple Dimensions," 309.

18. For a sampling of the controversy, see Kent Greenawalt, "Silence as a Moral and Constitutional Right," *William & Mary Law Review* 23 (1981): 15–71; David Dolinko, "Is There a Rationale for the Privilege against Self-Incrimination?" *UCLA Law Review* 33 (1986): 1063–148; Stephen J. Schulhofer, "Some Kind Words for the Privilege against Self-Incrimination," *Valparaiso University Law Review* 33 (1991): 311–36; and R. H. Helmholz, Charles M. Gray, John H. Langbein, Eben Moglen, Henry E. Smith, and Albert W. Altschuler, *The Privilege against Self-Incrimination* (Chicago: University of Chicago Press, 1997).

19. Dolinko, "Rationale," 1075.

20. The idea that criminal trials should be structured to give us moral assurance that when we punish individuals we do so justifiably coheres surprisingly well with the historical reasons for adoption of the reasonable doubt standard. As legal scholars have shown, that standard was initially adopted not so much to protect innocent defendants as to convince reluctant jurors to convict defendants when jurors feared adverse divine judgment for mistaken convictions. Jurors feared for their mortal souls in reaching guilty verdicts. Perhaps they do not do so these days, but the gravity of the responsibility they have might be impressed upon them by reminding them that they are the innocent defendant's last, best hope to avoid legal punishment's potentially devastating erosion of their basic rights. On the history of the reasonable doubt standard, see

James Q. Whitman, *The Origins of Reasonable Doubt: Theological Roots of the Criminal Trial* (New Haven, Conn.: Yale University Press, 2008); and Anthony A. Morano, "A Reexamination of the Development of the Reasonable Doubt Rule," *Boston University Law Review* 55 (1975): 507–28.

21. Plea-bargaining practices in the United States appear cavalier about separating the guilty from the innocent and punishing the former according to their crimes. See, for instance, Oren Gazal-Ayal, "Partial Ban on Plea Bargains," *Cardozo Law Review* 27 (2006): 2295–348.

22. Findley and Scott, "Multiple Dimensions," 323–27. See also Brandon L. Garrett, *Convicting the Innocent: Where Criminal Prosecutions Go Wrong* (Cambridge, Mass.: Harvard University Press, 2012).

23. Findley and Scott, "Multiple Dimensions," 348. In England and Wales, appellate courts are more likely to review the sufficiency of the evidence used to convict individuals than in the United States. However, appeals there are discouraged to some extent by the possibility that longer sentences might be imposed by the appellate courts than were originally imposed by trial courts. On this, see Andrew Ashworth and Mike Redmayne, *The Criminal Process*, 4th ed. (Oxford: Oxford University Press, 2010), 372.

24. Norman Lefstein contrasts the indigent defense systems in the United States and in England and Wales in "In Search of Gideon's Promise: Lessons from England and the Need for Federal Help," *Hastings Law Review* 55 (2004): 835–929.

25. Lefstein, "Gideon's Promise," 838–39. See also Stephen B. Bright and Sia M. Sanneh, "Fifty Years of Defiance and Resistance after *Gideon v. Wainwright*," *Yale Law Journal* 122 (2013): 2150–74.

26. Albert W. Alschuler, "The Prosecutor's Role in Plea Bargaining," *University of Chicago Law Review* 36 (1968): 64.

27. Of course, life too can be taken in jurisdictions that have capital punishment. However, it does not make sense to characterize punishment as, in this case, "curtailing" or even "infringing a right," since life is all or nothing.

28. Jeremy Waldron, "Introduction," in J. Waldron (ed.). *Theories of Rights* (Oxford: Oxford University Press, 1984), 14; and Douglas Husak, *Overcriminalization: The Limits of the Criminal Law* (Oxford: Oxford University Press, 2008), 92.

29. Martha Nussbaum, "Capabilities and Human Rights," *Fordham Law Review* 66 (1997): 273–300.

30. Trials might not be the only way in which proof of criminal guilt is appropriately established. Properly structured plea systems might also do so.

31. See Larry Laudan, "The Rules of Trial, Political Morality, and the Costs of Error: Or, Is Proof beyond a Reasonable Doubt Doing More Harm Than Good?" in L. Green and B. Leiter (eds.), *Oxford Studies in Philosophy of Law*, vol. 1 (New York: Oxford University Press, 2011), 195–227.

32. Laudan, *Truth, Error, and Criminal Law*, 103.

33. Laudan, *Truth, Error, and Criminal Law*, 102, also argues that PI_m would require jurors to believe in the material innocence of defendants up to a point and then, all of a sudden, change their minds and come to believe in their material guilt. But it seems much more natural to believe that jurors will gradually be persuaded by the evidence as it is presented by the government if that evidence is powerful and the defense does not effectively counter it. Of course, we will want them to start with PI_m and evaluate

the evidence carefully, initially giving the benefit of the doubt to defendants. Yet as the evidence against defendants mounts up, assuming it does, the presumption might be gradually eroded.

34. Laudan, *Truth, Error, and Criminal Law*, 101. See also Daniel Mendonca, "Presumptions," *Ratio Juris* 11 (1998): 399–412.

35. Laudan, *Truth, Error, and Criminal Law*, chapter 3. See also Erik Lillquist, "Recasting Reasonable Doubt: Decision Theory and the Virtues of Variability," *University of California–Davis Law Review* 36 (2002): 85–197; and Michael L. DeKay, "The Difference between Blackstone-Like Error Ratios and Probabilistic Standards of Proof," *Law and Social Inquiry* 21 (1996): 95–132.

Chapter 5

1. These familiar elements of criminal trials are found, with slight variations, in most modern legal systems. Further, Article 6(1) of the European Convention on Human Rights and Article 14(1) of the International Covenant on Civil and Political Rights guarantee the right to fair, public, and impartial hearings on criminal charges. See John D. Jackson and Sarah J. Summers, *The Internationalisation of Criminal Evidence: Beyond the Common and Law and Civil Law Traditions* (Cambridge: Cambridge University Press, 2012), 96.

2. The classical source for this preference is William Blackstone's *Commentaries on the Laws of England* (Boston, Mass.: Beacon Press, 1962), 420. As Alexander Volokh has amusingly shown, there is little agreement among historical writers about the proper ratio by which we should prefer acquittals of the guilty to convictions of the guilty in his "n Guilty Men," *University of Pennsylvania Law Review* 146 (1997): 173–216. For a clear, contemporary statement of the preference, see Paul Roberts, "Double Jeopardy Reform: A Criminal Justice Commentary," *Modern Law Review* 65 (2002): 393–424.

3. See Larry Laudan, "The Rules of Trial, Political Morality, and the Costs of Error: Or, Is Proof beyond a Reasonable Doubt Doing More Harm Than Good?" in L, Green and B. Leiter (eds.), *Oxford Studies in Philosophy of Law*, vol. 1 (New York: Oxford University Press, 2011), 195–227.

4. See Erik Lillquist, "Recasting Reasonable Doubt: Decision Theory and the Virtues of Variability," *University of California–Davis Law Review* 36 (2002): 85–197; Michael L. DeKay, The Difference between Blackstone-Like Error Ratios and Probabilistic Standards of Proof," *Law and Social Inquiry* 21 (1996): 95–132; and Larry Laudan and Harry Saunders, "Re-thinking the Criminal Standard of Proof: Seeking Consensus about the Utilities of Trial Outcomes," available at *SSRN*: http://ssrn.com/abstract = 1369996, especially 15–16 (accessed June 23, 2015).

5. See Laudan's critique of such a notion, "Rules of Trial," beginning at 208.

6. In addition to the references cited in note 4, see Lawrence H. Tribe, "Trial by Mathematics: Precision and Ritual in the Legal Process," *Harvard Law Review* 84 (1971): 1329–93 and John Kaplan, "Decision Theory and the Fact-Finding Process," *Stanford Law Review* 20 (1968): 1065–92.

7. See Laudan, "Rules of Trial," 202–8.

8. See Lillquist, "Recasting Reasonable Doubt," 96–103.

9. See Lillquist, "Recasting Reasonable Doubt," 110; Tribe, "Trial by Mathematics," 1379–80.

10. See DeKay, "Difference Between," 106, and Laudan and Saunders, "Re-thinking," 10.

11. This formulation of the presumption of innocence is Larry Laudan's in *Truth, Error, and Criminal Law: An Essay in Legal Epistemology* (Cambridge: Cambridge University Press, 2006), 104.

12. It is commonplace to distinguish a full burden of proof, beyond a reasonable doubt, placed on defendants to support any affirmative defense made, and an evidential burden, according to which defendants must present enough evidence of a defense to make it a live issue at trial and thus one that the government must then rebut beyond a reasonable doubt. See Andrew Ashworth, "Four Threats to the Presumption of Innocence," *International Journal of Evidence and Proof* 10 2006): 269.

13. There is smallish literature discussing the theoretical problem of how to reconcile human rights with legal punishment, especially since the latter infringes upon basic rights in fairly obvious ways. Some argue that criminal offenders forfeit their rights and so legal punishment, inflicted by state authorities, does not conflict with offenders' rights. See A. John Simmons, *The Lockean Theory of Rights* (Princeton, N.J.: Princeton University Press, 1992); and Christopher W. Morris, "Punishment and Loss of Moral Standing," *Canadian Journal of Philosophy* 21 (1991): 53–79. I have argued against the right forfeiture view and in favor of the view that legal punishment should be understood as justifiably curtailing rights. See my "Criminal Offenders and Right Forfeiture," *Journal of Social Philosophy* 32 (2001): 78–89, and *Rethinking Imprisonment* (Oxford: Oxford University Press, 2007), chapter 6.

14. Jeremy Waldron, "Introduction," in J. Waldron (ed.), *Theories of Rights* (Oxford: Oxford University Press, 1984), 14–15.

15. See Amartya Sen, "Rights as Goals," in Stephen Guest and Alan Milne (eds.), *Equality and Discrimination: Essays in Freedom and Justice* (London: Association for Legal and Social Philosophy, 1984), 12–26; and Martha Nussbaum, "Capabilities and Human Rights," *Fordham Law Review* 66 (1997): 273–300.

16. For discussion of rights as having lexical priority over other interests, see Jeremy Waldron, "Rights in Conflict," *Ethics* 99 (1989): 503–19.

17. Waldron, "Introduction," 15.

18. The view that legal punishment consists of censure and hard treatment is Andrew von Hirsch's. See his *Censure and Sanctions* (Oxford: Clarendon Press, 1993).

19. For evidence about the ways in which imprisonment damages individuals psychologically, see Craig Haney, *Reforming Punishment: Psychological Limits to the Pain of Imprisonment* (Washington, D.C.: American Psychological Association, 2006). For the economic impact of imprisonment on offenders' lives, see Bruce Western, *Punishment and Inequality in America* (New York: Russell Sage, 2006).

20. For a useful summary of the ways in which criminal investigations (and subsequent trials and appellate review) can go awry, see Keith A. Findley and Michael S. Scott, "The Multiple Dimensions of Tunnel Vision in Criminal Cases," *Wisconsin Law Review* 2006 (2006): 291–397.

21. It might be objected that there are circumstances in which government officials, or private citizens, intrude upon the basic rights of citizens without first having to gain approval for doing so from a court or other body that makes an official finding the citizens in question have committed crimes or are likely to have done so. Police

officers can temporarily restrain individuals who attempt or commit crimes, as can private citizens. In some circumstances, police officers and private citizens justifiably kill those who threaten or do violence without first having to gain permission to do so from independent tribunals. True enough, but interrupting crimes or restraining individuals in the act of committing them, though such actions curtail rights, do so only temporarily and therefore must be distinguished from legal punishment, which censures individuals for their illegal conduct and imposes potentially much more devastating losses upon them. Killings by police officers or private citizens in defense of themselves or others are likewise distinguishable from the legal punishment of offenders. If justified, killings in self- or other-defense are matters of necessity in ways that legal punishment, coming well after crimes have been committed, is not. Also, killings in self- or other-defense are officially reviewed after the fact and, in cases in which they do not appear justified, the perpetrators can be charged with crimes. We do not take such infringements of the rights of others lightly. Nor should we do so.

22. Milton Heumann, *Plea Bargaining: The Experiences of Prosecutors, Judges, and Defense Attorneys* (Chicago: University of Chicago Press, 1977), 57–61.

23. I discuss in more detail the contours of a properly structured plea system in Richard L. Lippke, *The Ethics of Plea Bargaining* (Oxford: Oxford University Press, 2011).

24. Malcolm M. Feeley, *The Process Is the Punishment: Handling Cases in a Lower Criminal Court* (New York: Russell Sage, 1979).

25. See Josh Bowers, "Punishing the Innocent," *University of Pennsylvania Law Review* 156 (2007): 1132.

26. In the United States, before ratifying plea agreements, judges are supposed to verify that there is a "factual basis" for any guilty plea. There are doubts that, in reality, judges take this responsibility very seriously. See Jenia I. Turner, "Judicial Participation in Plea Negotiations: A Comparative View," *American Journal Comparative Law* 54 (2006): 212–23; and Albert W. Alschuler, "The Trial Judge's Role in Plea Bargaining, Part 1," *Columbia Law Review* 76 (1976): 1059–154.

27. On charge bargaining, see Albert W. Alschuler, "The Prosecutor's Role in Plea Bargaining," *University of Chicago Law Review* 36 (1968): 85. On fact bargaining, see Nancy J. King, "Judicial Oversight of Negotiated Sentences in a World of Bargained Punishment," *Stanford Law Review* 58 (2005): 293–308.

28. See Yue Ma, "Prosecutorial Discretion and Plea Bargaining in the United States, France, Germany, and Italy," *International Criminal Justice Review* 12 (2002): 38.

29. See Sarah J. Summers, *Fair Trials: The European Criminal Procedural Tradition and the European Court of Human Rights* (Oxford: Hart Publishing, 2007), 171; and J. Jaconelli, "Rights Theories and Public Trial," *Journal of Applied Philosophy* 14 (1997): 168–75.

30. Heumann, *Plea Bargaining*, 137–39.

31. Jaconelli, "Rights Theories," 172.

32. On police culture and the emphasis on solidarity, see John Kleinig, *The Ethics of Policing* (Cambridge: Cambridge University Press, 1996), 68–71. Heumann, in *Plea Bargaining*, is especially insightful on the pressure on all participants in the US criminal justice system to "cooperate" to keep the system functioning efficiently. Of course, the

members of British and European-style prosecutorial and judicial bureaucracies might behave quite differently than US officials, who are more often answerable to the public through direct elections.

33. Plea bargaining disposes of upwards of 95 percent of cases in the United States. In England and Wales, Andrew Ashworth and Mike Redmayne report, over 90 percent of cases in the magistrates' courts produce guilty pleas, while over 70 percent do so in the Crown Courts. See Ashworth and Redmayne, *The Criminal Process*, 4th ed. (Oxford: Oxford University Press, 2010), 295–96.

34. Andrew Stumer argues that public trials at which the government's evidence is available for all to see and evaluate are crucial to the promotion of the rule of law. See *The Presumption of Innocence: Evidential and Human Rights Perspectives* (Oxford: Hart Publishing, 2010), 38.

35. For recent examinations of criminal procedure in common-law and civil-law systems, see Jackson and Summers, *Internationalisation of Criminal Evidence*, and Summers, *Fair Trials*. See also Franklin Strier, "Making Trials More Truthful," *University of California–Davis Law Review* 30 (1996): 95–182.

36. Here I draw on Laudan, *Truth, Error, and Criminal Law*, 82–83; and Alex Stein, *Foundations of Evidence Law* (Oxford: Oxford University Press, 2005), 178–79.

37. See Ronald J. Allen and Brian Leiter, "Naturalized Epistemology and the Law of Evidence," *Virginia Law Review* 87 (2001): 1491–550.

38. Lillquist, "Recasting Reasonable Doubt," 146.

39. The literature on so-called recidivist premiums is substantial. For a useful summary and discussion of the main lines of argument, see Richard S. Frase, *Just Sentencing: Principles and Procedures for a Workable System* (New York: Oxford University Press, 2013), chapter 4.

40. See, for instance, Peter Cane, *Responsibility in Law and Morality* (Oxford: Hart Publishing, 2002).

41. The view that legal punishment vindicates the victims by annulling the false messages conveyed by crimes about their moral worth has been defended by Jean Hampton, in "A New Theory of Retribution," in R. G. Frey and C. W. Morris (eds.), *Liability and Responsibility: Essays in Law and Morals* (Cambridge: Cambridge University Press, 1991): 377–414.

42. Laudan, "Rules of Trial," 203–4.

43. See Robert Nozick, *Anarchy, State, and Utopia* (New York: Basic Books, 1974), 28.

44. Nozick, *Anarchy, State, and Utopia,* 29. See also Ronald Dworkin, *Taking Rights Seriously* (Cambridge, Mass.: Harvard University Press, 1977), 92

45. This is what is done in New Zealand. See John Miller, "Compensating Crime Victims within New Zealand's No Fault Compensation Scheme," at http://aic.gov.au/media_library/publications/proceedings/27/miller.pdf (accessed June 23, 2015).

46. Also, imprisonment, as an incapacitation device, is less effective than Laudan seems to think. There are certain kinds of crimes that imprisonment does little to reduce in communities. On this, see Franklin E. Zimring and Gordon Hawkins, *Incapacitation: Penal Confinement and the Restraint of Crime* (New York: Oxford

University Press, 1995), 54–58. On the crime-producing effects of harsh imprisonment, see Haney, *Reforming Punishment*, and Western, *Punishment and Inequality*.

47. See, for instance, Richard O. Lempert, Samuel R. Gross, and James S. Leibman, *A Modern Approach to Evidence*, 3rd ed. (St. Paul, Minn.: West, 2000), 327–28, and Bowers "Punishing," 1124.

48. See Findley and Scott, "Multiple Dimensions," 324–27.

49. See Bowers, "Punishing," 1127.

50. Many of those who plead guilty will be recidivists. As Bowers notes, they will find themselves in a terrific bind, even if innocent of the current charges against them. If they elect trial adjudication and testify as to their innocence, prosecutors will attempt to introduce their past records. Yet failure to testify might also prove hazardous. There are also the process costs of going to trial, which if the charges are minor to moderate, may exceed those of the legal sanctions imposed. See Bowers, "Punishing," 1130.

51. See William J. Stuntz, "The Pathological Politics of Criminal Law," *Michigan Law Review* 100 (2001): 520.

52. As vividly shown in *Bordenkircher v. Hayes*, 434 U.S. 357 (1978).

53. See William J. Stuntz, *The Collapse of American Criminal Justice* (Cambridge, Mass.: Harvard University Press, 2011), 58–59.

54. Stuntz, "Pathological Politics," 570.

55. Moreover, as Daniel S. Nagin argues, high-rate offenders are very likely to be apprehended by the authorities. See his "Deterrence and Incapacitation," in Michael Tonry (ed.), *The Handbook of Crime and Punishment* (New York: Oxford University Press, 1998), 364.

56. Laudan, "Rules of Trial," 216.

57. The notion that rights generate duties is elaborated by Waldron in "Rights in Conflict," 509.

58. See Stephen B. Bright and Sia M. Sanneh, "Fifty Years of Defiance and Resistance after *Gideon v. Wainwright*," *Yale Law Journal* 122 (2013): 2150–74, and Norman Lefstein, "In Search of Gideon's Promise: Lessons from England and the Need for Federal Help," *Hastings Law Journal* 55 (2004): 835–929.

Chapter 6

1. See Stefan Trechsel, "The Right to Be Presumed Innocent," in S. Trechsel and S. Summers, *Human Rights in Criminal Proceedings* (Oxford: Oxford University Press, 2006), 153–54.

2. Thomas Weigend, "There Is Only One Presumption of Innocence," *Netherlands Journal of Legal Philosophy* 42 (2013): 196, and "Assuming That the Defendant Is Not Guilty: The Presumption of Innocence in the German System of Criminal Justice," *Criminal Law and Philosophy* 8 (2013): 294.

3. Trechsel, "Right to Be Presumed," 174–78. See also Carl-Friedrich Stuckenberg, "Who Is Presumed Innocent of What by Whom?" *Criminal Law and Philosophy* 8 (2014): 301–16.

4. Trechsel, "Right to Be Presumed," 178; and Hock Lai Ho, "The Presumption of Innocence as a Human Right," in P. Roberts and J. Hunter (eds.), *Criminal Evidence and Human Rights* (Oxford: Hart Publishing, 2012), 264.

5. Hamish Stewart, "The Right to Be Presumed Innocent," *Criminal Law and Philosophy* 8 (2014): 414; and Andrew Ashworth, "Four Threats to the Presumption of Innocence," *International Journal of Evidence and Proof* 10 (2006): 249.

6. R. A. Duff, "Pre-trial Detention and the Presumption of Innocence," in A. Ashworth, L. Zedner, and P. Tomlin (eds.), *Prevention and the Limits of the Criminal Law* (Oxford: Oxford University Press, 2013), 115–32; and Lawrence H. Tribe, "An Ounce of Prevention: Preventive Justice in the World of John Mitchell," *Virginia Law Review* 56 (1970): 371–407.

7. Trechsel, "Right to Be Presumed," 166. For useful discussion, see John D. Jackson and Sarah J. Summers, *The Internationalisation of Criminal Evidence: Beyond the Common Law and Civil Law Traditions* (Cambridge: Cambridge University Press, 2012), 241–84.

8. *Bell v. Wolfish*, 441 U.S. 520, at 533 (1979).

9. Larry Laudan, "The Presumption of Innocence: Material or Probatory?" *Legal Theory* 11 (2005): 337, and *Truth, Error, and Criminal Law: An Essay in Legal Epistemology* (Cambridge: Cambridge University Press, 2006), chapter 4. See also Albert W. Alschuler, "Preventive Pretrial Detention and the Failure of Interest-Balancing Approaches to Due Process," *Michigan Law Review* 85 (1986): 550.

10. Laudan, "Presumption of Innocence," 337.

11. Laudan, "Presumption of Innocence," 348.

12. See *Missouri v. Frye*, 132 S.Ct. 1399, 1407 (2012), where the US Supreme Court cites statistics according to which over 97 percent of defendants in federal cases plead guilty and 94 percent of defendants in state courts do so. Andrew Ashworth and Mike Redmayne cite statistics from England and Wales according to which the guilty plea rates in magistrates' courts is over 90 percent, while in Crown Courts it is over 70 percent. See Ashworth and Redmayne, *The Criminal Process*, 4th ed. (Oxford: Oxford University Press, 2010), 293–94.

13. I have more to say about plea bargaining and appropriate charge adjudication in Richard L. Lippke, *The Ethics of Plea Bargaining* (Oxford: Oxford University Press, 2011).

14. Laudan, *Truth, Error, and Criminal Law*, 96–97; Herbert L. Packer employs a similar distinction, between what he terms "legal" and "factual" guilt and innocence. See Packer's *The Limits of the Criminal Sanction* (Stanford, Calif.: Stanford University Press, 1968), 167.

15. See Antony Duff, "Who Must Presume Whom to Be Innocent of What?" *Netherlands Journal of Legal Philosophy* 42 (2013): 170–92.

16. Stewart, "Right to Be Presumed," 415.

17. For notable exceptions to this claim, see Duff, "Who Must Presume?" and Stuckenberg, "Who Is Presumed?"

18. Again, a point made forcefully by Laudan, *Truth, Error, and Criminal Law*, 95.

19. As both Stewart, "Right to Be Presumed," 415, and Duff, "Who Must Presume?" 174 concede.

20. Ashworth, "Four Threats," 243.

21. See Josh Bowers, "Punishing the Innocent," *University of Pennsylvania Law Review* 156 (2008): 1125.

22. Stanley Z. Fisher, "In Search of the Virtuous Prosecutor: A Conceptual Framework," *American Journal of Criminal Law* 15 (1988): 197–261, and Fred C.

Zacharias, "Structuring the Ethics of Prosecutorial Trial Practice: Can Prosecutors Do Justice?" *Vanderbilt Law Review* 44 (1991): 45–114.

23. For discussion of the standard, see Craig S. Lerner, "The Reasonableness of Probable Cause," *Texas Law Review* 81 (2003): 951–1029. Lerner suggests that, as commonly interpreted by the courts, it requires more than "mere suspicion" but not "proof sufficient to establish guilt" (at 996).

24. For discussion of the effects on criminal trials of police and prosecutorial disclosure of information about cases pretrial, see Dan Simon, "The Limited Diagnosticity of Criminal Trials," *Vanderbilt Law Review* 64 (2011): 143–223.

25. But see the discussion of the need to protect the reputations of the accused in the next section.

26. As Duff, for one admits, in "Who Must Presume?" 179. See also Duff, "Pre-trial Detention," 125.

27. Indeed, in the United States, of those individuals charged with crimes whose charges are not dismissed by prosecutors or judges, about 99 per cent will be convicted, with the vast majority pleading guilty.

28. See Duff's discussion of the presumption of innocence and "civic trust," in "Who Must Presume?" 180. See also Dale A. Nance, "Civility and the Burden of Proof," *Harvard Journal of Law and Public Policy* 17 (1994): 647–90.

29. For a useful catalog of the ways in which criminal investigations can go awry, see Keith A. Findley and Michael S. Scott, "The Multiple Dimensions of Tunnel Vision in Criminal Cases," *Wisconsin Law Review* 2006 (2006): 291–397. See also Brandon L. Garrett, *Convicting the Innocent: When Criminal Prosecutions Go Wrong* (Cambridge, Mass.: Harvard University Press, 2011).

30. See the Innocence Project website at www.innocenceproject.org (accessed December 28, 2014).

31. One can easily imagine some exceptions to this claim, as when those charged with crimes indicate that they are prepared to offer some justification or excuse for their apparently criminal conduct. Assuming some of these defenses are valid, then it might be reasonable, though perhaps pointless, to insist that "victims" adopt a pretrial non-presumption of material innocence. Most of those who believe themselves to have been victimized will struggle to regard the accused as materially innocent.

32. Again, the vast majority of crimes (close to 80 percent) processed by the US criminal justice system are misdemeanors. See Jenny Roberts, "Why Misdemeanors Matter: Defining Effective Advocacy in the Lower Criminal Courts," *University of California–Davis Law Review* 45 (2011): 281.

33. As Weigend, "There Is Only One," 196, and Stuckenberg, "Who Is Presumed?" 313, seem to suggest.

34. Stewart, "Right to Be Presumed," 414; Ashworth, "Four Threats," 249; and Duff, "Who Must Presume?" 180.

35. The "probable cause" standard is used in the United States; the "reasonable prospect of conviction" standard is employed in England and Wales.

36. Weigend, "There Is Only One," 202, hints at a similar line of argument.

37. Trechsel, "Right to Be Presumed," 178; and Ho, "Presumption of Innocence," 264.

38. See Bowers, "Punishing," 1125.

39. Roberts, "Why Misdemeanors Matter," 281.

40. In Scotland, juries have three verdict options: "guilty," "not guilty," and "not proven." See Peter Duff, "The Scottish Criminal Jury: A Very Peculiar Institution," *Law and Contemporary Problems* 62 (1999): 173–201.

41. See Daniel S. Medwed, "The Zeal Deal: Prosecutorial Resistance to Post-conviction Claims of Innocence," *Boston University Law Review* 84 (2004): 125–83.

42. Duff, "Pre-trial Detention"; and Tribe, "An Ounce of Prevention." See also Marc Miller and Martin Guggenheim, "Pretrial Detention and Punishment," *Minnesota* Law Review 75 (1990): 335–426; and Una Ni Raifeartaigh, "Reconciling Bail Law with the Presumption of Innocence," *Oxford Journal of Legal Studies* 17 (1997): 1–21.

43. See Tribe, "An Ounce of Prevention," 406; and Duff, "Pre-trial Detention," 132.

44. See Duff, "Pre-trial Detention," 127–28.

45. Some of these conditions are stipulated by Miller and Guggenheim, "Pre-trial Detention," 407. See also Alschuler, "Preventive Pre-trial Detention," 566.

46. Miller and Guggenheim, "Pre-trial Detention," 421. See also Marian R. Williams, "The Effect of Pre-trial Detention on Imprisonment Decisions," *Criminal Justice Review* 28 (2003): 299–316.

47. Bowers, "Punishing," 1136. See also Malcolm M. Feeley, *The Process Is the Punishment: Handling Cases in a Lower Criminal Court* (New York: Russell Sage, 1979), especially chapter 7.

48. Weigend, "There Is Only One," 196.

49. Weigend, "There Is Only One," 196.

50. Trechsel, "Right to Be Presumed," 166.

51. Findley and Scott, "Multiple Dimensions," 334.

52. For useful critical discussion, see David Dolinko, "Is There a Rationale for the Privilege against Self-Incrimination?" *UCLA Law Review* 33 (1986): 1063–148.

53. Pat McAfee, quoted in "Colts Place Linebacker on Commissioner's Exempt List," at http://www.utsandiego.com/news/2015/jan/15/colts-place-linebacker-mcnary-on-commissioners (accessed February 1, 2015).

Chapter 7

1. Marc Miller and Martin Guggenheim, "Pretrial Detention and Punishment," *Minnesota Law Review* 75 (1990): 369; and Albert W. Alschuler, "Preventive Pretrial Detention and the Failure of Interest-Balancing Approaches to Due Process," *Michigan Law Review* 85 (1986): 517.

2. Miller and Guggenheim, "Pretrial Detention," 368; and Alschuler, "Preventive Pretrial Detention," 514. See also Shima Baradaran, "Restoring the Presumption of Innocence," *Ohio State Law Journal* 72 (2011): 724–76.

3. Miller and Guggenheim, "Pretrial Detention," 377–88; and Lawrence H. Tribe, "An Ounce of Prevention: Preventive Justice in the World of John Mitchell," *Virginia Law Review* 56 (1970): 382. However, Alschuler, "Preventive Pretrial Detention," 537–48, argues that legal scholars have been too willing to adopt skepticism with regard to our predictive abilities. For more recent evidence on our ability to predict pretrial offending, see Shima Baradaran and Frank L. McIntyre, "Predicting Violence," *Texas Law Review* 90 (2012): 497–570.

4. Miller and Guggenheim, "Pretrial Detention," 421. See also Marian R. Williams, "The Effect of Pre-trial Detention on Imprisonment Decisions," *Criminal Justice Review* 28 (2003): 299–316.

5. See Una Ni Raifeartaigh, "Reconciling Bail Law with the Presumption of Innocence," *Oxford Journal of Legal Studies* 17 (1997): 1–21; R. A. Duff, "Pre-trial Detention and the Presumption of Innocence," in A. Ashworth, L. Zedner, and P. Tomlin (eds.), *Prevention and the Limits of the Criminal Law* (Oxford: Oxford University Press, 2013), 115–32; and Baradaran, "Restoring."

6. See Miller and Guggenheim, "Pretrial Detention," 392; Duff, "Pre-trial Detention," 127; Tribe, "Ounce of Prevention," 396–402; and Baradaran, "Restoring," 768.

7. On this last point, see Tribe, "Ounce of Prevention," 405.

8. For a critical examination of current forms of imprisonment, see Richard L. Lippke, *Rethinking Imprisonment* (Oxford: Oxford University Press, 2007).

9. *United States v. Salerno* 481 U.S. 739, 747 (1987); see also Miller and Guggenheim, "Pretrial Detention," 353.

10. In fact, as Baradaran and McIntyre, "Predicting," point out (502), the majority of individuals held in local jails are ones awaiting final disposition of the charges against them.

11. Tribe, "Ounce of Prevention," 374–75, likens pretrial detention to the predicament of the king's messenger in Lewis Carroll's *Through the Looking Glass*, who is "in prison now, being punished; and the trial doesn't even begin until next Wednesday."

12. The claim that legal punishment's two main elements are censure and hard treatment comes from Andrew von Hirsch. See, for instance, his *Censure and Sanctions* (Oxford: Clarendon Press, 1993), 9–13.

13. See Josh Bowers, "Punishing the Innocent," *University of Pennsylvania Law Review* 156 (2008): 1136.

14. Miller and Guggenheim, "Pretrial Detention," 369.

15. A point made by Duff, "Pre-trial Detention," 132.

16. See John Kleinig, "The Hardness of Hard Treatment," in A. Ashworth and M. Wasik (eds.), *Fundamentals in Sentencing Theory* (Oxford: Clarendon Press, 1998), 295. Also, as Catherine T. Struve has noted, the Supreme Court is clear that imprisonment following criminal conviction appropriately involves hardship. See Struve's "The Conditions of Pretrial Detention," *University of Pennsylvania Law Review* 161 (2013): 1033.

17. Of course, a few will be entirely innocent victims of such things as misidentification, unjustified police suspicion, or police misconduct.

18. See Lippke, *Rethinking*, 4.

19. Kristina Marlow, "Prisoners' Rights," *Georgetown Law Journal* 86 (1998): 1954.

20. Lippke, *Rethinking*, 129–49.

21. See Duff, "Pre-trial Detention," 125.

22. Improved and less stigmatizing pretrial detention conditions, along with briefer periods of such detention, would make it somewhat easier for those accused of crimes, but who were ultimately acquitted, to resume their lives.

23. Miller and Guggenheim, "Pretrial Detention," 346–54; and Alschuler, "Preventive Pretrial Detention," 512–20.

24. Miller and Guggenheim, "Pretrial Detention"; and Alschuler, "Preventive Pretrial Detention."

25. I say "generally speaking," because it is possible to imagine cases in which, though arrested and charged with relatively nonserious crimes, individuals make

credible and dire threats against those prepared to testify against them. In such cases, pretrial detention might be justified on preventive grounds.

26. There is also the problem with individuals charged with multiple offenses, no one of which might be imprisonable, but the aggregate sentence for which might be a term of imprisonment.

27. See Jenny Roberts, "Why Misdemeanors Matter: Defining Effective Advocacy in the Lower Criminal Courts," *University of California–Davis Law Review* 45 (2011): 281.

28. Miller and Guggenheim, "Pretrial Detention," 407; and Alschuler, "Preventive Pretrial Detention," 566.

29. As Baradaran and McIntyre, "Predicting," demonstrate (535), past violent criminal history and youthfulness are significant predictors of further pretrial crime.

30. Miller and Guggenheim, "Pretrial Detention," 421–22.

31. Miller and Guggenheim, "Pretrial Detention," 412–13.

32. In spite of their general antipathy toward the use of pretrial detention to prevent pretrial crimes, Miller and Guggenheim do seem to embrace the pretrial detention (for preventive purposes) of those who have been charged with "extremely violent crimes." See their "Pretrial Detention," 395. Duff concedes that some persons who appear especially dangerous guilty might be detained pretrial, but he insists that doing so violates the PI and should be recognized as such. See his "Pre-trial Detention," 132.

33. Duff, "Pre-trial Detention"; Baradaran, "Restoring"; Raifeartaigh, "Reconciling"; and Tribe, "Ounce of Prevention."

34. Duff, "Pre-trial Detention," 126; Raifertaigh, "Reconciling," throughout the text; and Baradaran, "Restoring," 731. However, the authors do not squarely face the problem that the majority of criminal defendants, who are poor, will struggle to offer this assurance. In the event that they cannot do so, they might be remanded to custody, whether they are likely to abscond or pose threats to others in the community. Affluent defendants accused of serious crimes might therefore escape pretrial detention, while poor ones charged with less serious ones might not.

35. As Duff admits, "Pre-trial Detention," 125.

36. Though progressively defeasible in the pretrial context, such an account is consistent with holding that it should be fully reinvigorated once a trial is actually under way. Jurors could, at the outset of trials, be instructed to begin with the presumption that accused persons are members in good standing in the community.

37. Andrew Ashworth, "Four Threats to the Presumption of Innocence," *International Journal of Evidence and Proof* 10 (2006): 249; and Hamish Stewart, "The Right to Be Presumed Innocent," *Criminal Law and Philosophy* 8 (2014): 413.

38. Miller and Guggenheim, "Pretrial Detention," 392; Tribe, "Ounce of Prevention," 396–404; Duff, "Pre-trial Detention," 127–28; and Baradaran, "Restoring," 763.

39. Duff, "Pre-trial Detention," 128.

40. Duff, "Pre-trial Detention," 128, concedes that defendants caught (apparently) absconding or interfering with the course of justice might deny that they were doing anything of the sort. If we detain them, it will be for not-yet-proven crimes and so, it seems, in tension with what he claims about the presumption of innocence. Duff suggests that defendants who deny that they were attempting to abscond or interfere with the course

of justice should be given quick hearings on these matters in order to resolve the events in dispute. Setting to one side the difficulties such speeded-up hearings might create for defendants who wish to mount full defenses to the allegations against them, the question remains whether such defendants should be detained until the hearings take place. If so, then it is unclear how such detention is consistent with his claim that the presumption of innocence precludes it.

41. Miller and Guggenheim, "Pretrial Detention," 359–64.

42. Miller and Guggenheim, "Pretrial Detention," 373.

43. Miller and Guggenheim, "Pretrial Detention," 370.

44. Miller and Guggenheim, "Pretrial Detention," 364.

45. Miller and Guggenheim seem uncertain whether to label such detention as "punishment" or not. See "Pretrial Detention," 364.

46. Tribe, "Ounce of Prevention," 404.

47. Such an argument is suggested by Thomas Weigend, "There Is Only One Presumption of Innocence," *Netherlands Journal of Legal Philosophy* 42 (2013): 203.

48. See Duff, "Pre-trial Detention," 118; and Tribe, "Ounce of Prevention," 415.

49. Tribe, "Ounce of Prevention," 415.

50. See Miller and Guggenheim, "Pretrial Detention," 376; and Alschuler, "Preventive Pretrial Detention," 533.

51. See Paul H. Robinson, "Punishing Dangerousness: Cloaking Preventive Detention and Criminal Justice," *Harvard Law Review* 114 (2001): 1429–56; and Stephen J. Morse, "Blame and Danger: An Essay on Preventive Detention," *Boston University Law Review* 76 (1996): 113–55.

52. Tribe, "Ounce of Prevention," 379.

53. For useful discussion of psychopathy, moral responsibility, and the purposes of the criminal law, see Cordelia Fine and Jeanette Kennett, "Mental Impairment, Moral Understanding and Criminal Responsibility: Psychopathy and the Purposes of Punishment," *International Journal of Law and Psychiatry* 27 (2004): 425–43.

54. Miller and Guggenheim, "Pretrial Detention," 377–88; and Tribe, "Ounce of Prevention," 382.

55. Miller and Guggenheim, "Pretrial Detention," 397–405.

56. Alschuler, "Preventive Pretrial Detention," 543.

57. In their recent study, Baradaran and McIntyre attempt to make up for this deficiency in prior studies by contrasting pretrial crime in jurisdictions that rarely impose pretrial detention with ones that do so at much higher rates. They conclude that some categories of defendants (especially those who are young and have histories of violent offending) are a substantially greater threat to the community if released. See their "Predicting," 537–45.

Chapter 8

1. Individuals with lengthy prior criminal records will not have names and reputations to which significantly more damage can be done. This is not a mere idle possibility. Josh Bowers reports that in 2002, in the seventy-five largest counties in the United States, "seventy-six percent of state-court felony defendants had at least one prior arrest, fifty percent had five arrests or more, fifty-nine percent had at least one prior conviction,

and twenty-four percent had five or more convictions." See his "Punishing the Innocent," *University of Pennsylvania Law Review* 156 (2008): 1125.

2. Estimates are the about 60 percent of the individuals housed in local jails are pretrial detainees. See Catherine T. Struve, "The Conditions of Pretrial Detention," *University of Pennsylvania Law Review* 161 (2013): 1055.

3. See the case of Raymond Buckey, described at the outset of the article by Marc Miller and Martin Guggenheim, "Pretrial Detention and Punishment," *Minnesota Law Review* 75 (1990): 335–426.

4. Michael K. Brown, *Working the Street: Police Discretion and the Dilemmas of Reform* (New York: Russell Sage, 1988).

5. Prosecutorial discretion in the United States is substantial. On this see Angela J. Davis, "Prosecution and Race: The Power and Privilege of Discretion," *Fordham Law Review* 67 (1998): 13–67; and Peter Krug, "Prosecutorial Discretion and Its Limits," *American Journal of Comparative Law* 50 (2002): 643–64.

6. The view that legal punishment involves censure and hard treatment is defended by Andrew von Hirsch, *Censure and Sanctions* (Oxford: Clarendon Press, 1993).

7. The vast majority of convictions (about 80 percent in the United States) are for misdemeanors, and thus for crimes concerning which the public is unlikely to be very interested or informed. See Jenny Roberts, "Why Misdemeanors Matter: Defining Effective Advocacy in the Lower Criminal Courts," *University of California–Davis Law Review* 45 (2011): 277–372.

8. On "usual suspects" policing, see Richard O. Lempert, Samuel R. Gross, and James S. Leibman, *A Modern Approach to Evidence*, 3rd ed. (St. Paul, Minn.: West, 2000), 327–28.

9. Kevin R. Reitz, "Sentencing Facts: The Travesties of Real-Offense Sentencing," *Stanford Law Review* 45 (1993): 523–73.

10. Mark A. Franklin and Diane Johnsen, "Expunging Criminal Records: Concealment and Dishonesty in an Open Society," *Hofstra Law Review* 9 (1981): 733–74; and James B. Jacobs, "Mass Incarceration and the Proliferation of Criminal Records," *University of St. Thomas Law Journal* 3 (2006): 387–420. Expungement in some form or other is also available for those with records of convictions in many jurisdictions.

11. Jacobs, "Mass Incarceration," 401.

12. Sadiq Reza, "Privacy and the Criminal Arrestee or Suspect: In Search of a Right, in Need of a Rule," *Maryland Law Review* 64 (2005): 755–874.

13. Juveniles, by contrast, are protected from such disclosure. See Reza, "Privacy," 784.

14. Reza, "Privacy," 795.

15. Of course, some of this risk will be minimized if those charged with crimes are held in pretrial detention.

16. Jessica S. Henry and James B. Jacobs, "Ban the Box to Promote Ex-Offender Employment," *Criminology and Public Policy* 6 (2007): 755–62; Jennifer Leavitt, "Walking A Tightrope: Balancing Competing Public Interests in the Employment of Criminal Offenders," *Connecticut Law Review* 34 (2002): 1281–315; and Ben Geiger, "The Case for Treating Ex-Offenders as a Suspect Class," *California Law Review* 91 (2006): 1191–242.

17. Peter Duff, "The Scottish Criminal Jury: A Very Peculiar Institution," *Law and Contemporary Problems* 62 (1999): 173–201; and Samuel Bray, "Not Proven: Introducing a Third Verdict," *University of Chicago Law Review* 72 (2005): 1299–329.

18. See Andrew D. Leipold, "The Problem of the Innocent, Acquitted Defendant," *Northwestern University Law Review* 94 (2000): 1297–356.

19. See Richard L. Lippke, "The Case for Reasoned Criminal Trial Verdicts," *Canadian Journal of Law and Jurisprudence* 22 (2009): 313–30.

20. Russell E. Lovell II, "The Case for Reimbursing Court Costs and a Reasonable Attorney Fee to the Non-indigent Defendant upon Acquittal," *Nebraska Law Review* 49 (1970): 515–35.

21. Michael Avery, "Obstacles to Litigating Civil Claims for Wrongful Conviction: An Overview," *Boston University Public Interest Law Journal* 18 (2009): 439–51; and Margaret Z. Johns, "Unsupportable and Unjustified: A Critique of Absolute Prosecutorial Immunity," *Fordham Law Review* 80 (2011): 509–35.

22. This formulation of PI_m borrows from Andrew Ashworth, "Four Threats to the Presumption of Innocence," *International Journal of Evidence and Pro*of 10 (2006): 243.

23. I borrow the "responsible citizens" construal of material innocence from Antony Duff, Lindsay Farmer, Sandra Marshall, and Victor Tadros's *The Trial on Trial*, vol. 3: *Towards a Normative Theory of the Criminal Trial* (Oxford: Hart Publishing, 2007), 113.

24. For one account of a defensible plea system, see my *The Ethics of Plea Bargaining* (Oxford: Oxford University Press, 2011).

25. A point made by Antony Duff, "Who Must Presume Whom to Be Innocent of What?" *Netherlands Journal of Legal Philosophy* 42 (2013): 181.

26. Again, the distinction between material (or factual) and probatory innocence is discussed by Larry Laudan, *Truth, Error, and Criminal Law: An Essay in Legal Epistemology* (Cambridge: Cambridge University Press, 2006), 90. See also Herbert L. Packer on the distinction between factual and legal innocence, in *The Limits of the Criminal Sanction* (Stanford, Calif.: Stanford University Press, 1968), 167.

27. See Keith A. Findley and Michael S. Scott, "The Multiple Dimensions of Tunnel Vision in Criminal Cases," *Wisconsin Law Review* 2006 (2006): 291–397.

28. Lempert et al., *Modern Approach*, 327–28.

29. Jacobs, "Mass Incarceration," 411; and Franklin and Johnsen, "Expunging," 742.

30. Though there will be hard cases that put such a policy to the test, such as inquiries by banks or security firms concerning the arrest or charging records of prospective employees.

31. Roberts, "Why Misdemeanors Matter," 281.

32. Reza, "Privacy," 803.

33. Reza, "Privacy," 784.

34. Leavitt, "Walking a Tightrope," discusses the variety of efforts adopted in various states to protect ex-offenders against discrimination. See also Geiger, "Suspect Class," 1201.

35. Leavitt, "Walking a Tightrope," 1294–95.

Chapter 9

1. Jenny Roberts, "Why Misdemeanors Matter: Defining Advocacy in the Lower Criminal Courts," *University of California–Davis Law Review* 45 (2011): 281.

2. Many convicted offenders have one or more prior convictions. See Josh Bowers, "Punishing the Innocent," *University of Pennsylvania Law Review* 156 (2008): 1125.

3. See Marc Mauer and Meda Chesney-Lind (eds.), *Invisible Punishment: The Collateral Consequences of Mass Imprisonment* (New York: New Press, 2002).

4. Jeremy Travis, "Invisible Punishment: An Instrument of Social Exclusion," in Mauer and Chesney-Lind (eds.), *Invisible Punishment*, 15–36.

5. In addition to the authors in the Mauer and Chesney-Lind volume, see Andrew von Hirsch and Martin Wasik, "Civil Disqualifications Attending Conviction: A Suggested Conceptual Framework," *Cambridge Law Journal* 56 (1997): 599–626; Hugh LaFollette, "Collateral Consequences of Punishment: Civil Penalties Accompanying Formal Punishment," *Journal of Applied Philosophy* 22 (2005): 241–61; Gabriel J. Chin, "The New Civil Death: Rethinking Punishment in the Era of Mass Conviction," *University of Pennsylvania Law Review* 160 (2012): 1789–833; and Zachary Hoskins, "Ex-Offender Restrictions," *Journal of Applied Philosophy* 31 (2014): 33–48.

6. Chin, "New Civil Death," 1808.

7. Chin, "New Civil Death," 1791–92.

8. See von Hirsch and Wasik, "Civil Disqualifications," 616–20.

9. Though over two million US citizens are incarcerated, close to seven million are under some form of supervision by the criminal justice system. See "Correctional Populations in the United States, 2013," Bureau of Justice Statistics, at http://www.bjs.gov/index.cfm?ty = pbdetail&iid = 5177 (accessed December 22, 2014). For discussion, see Michael Tonry, "Intermediate Sanctions," in M. Tonry (ed.), *The Handbook of Crime and Punishment* (New York: Oxford University Press, 1998), 683–711.

10. Andrew von Hirsch, *Censure and Sanctions* (Oxford: Clarendon Press, 1993).

11. For a comparative survey of prisons, see D. van Zyl Smit and F. Dünkel, *Imprisonment Today and Tomorrow: International Perspectives on Prisoners' Rights and Prison Conditions*, 2nd ed. (The Hague: Kluwer Law International, 2001).

12. Travis, "Invisible Punishment," 26. Chin quotes a dissenting Supreme Court justice (J. Clark) in *Chaunt v. United States*, 364 U.S. 350, 358 (1960) as capturing the attitude of the law toward individuals with criminal convictions: "The law regards you as having a 'shattered character.' Therefore, in addition to any incarceration or fine, you are subject to legal restrictions on your civil rights, conduct, employment, residence, and relationships. For the rest of your life, the United States and any State or locality where you travel or reside may impose, at any time, additional restrictions and limitations they deem warranted. Their power to do so is limited only by their reasonable discretion. They may also require you to pay the expense of these restrictions and limitations." See Chin's "New Civil Death," 1790.

13. Travis, "Invisible Punishment," 25; and Chin, "New Civil Death," 1815, both suggest that the aggregate effects of collateral consequences amount to a new form of "civil death."

14. See "Invisible Punishment," 34–35; and Chin, "New Civil Death," 1825.

15. The distinction between "overall" (or "cardinal") and comparative (or "ordinal") proportionality in sentencing comes from von Hirsch, *Censure and Sanctions*, 18–19.

16. Again, on this, see Chin, "New Civil Death," 1791–92.

17. Hoskins, "Ex-Offender Restrictions."

18. Hoskins, "Ex-Offender Restrictions," 44.

19. Hoskins, "Ex-Offender Restrictions," 37.

20. Hoskins, "Ex-Offender Restrictions," 42.

21. Von Hirsch and Wasik, "Civil Disqualifications," 605.

22. Von Hirsch and Wasik, "Civil Disqualifications," 621.

23. Antony Duff draws a similar distinction between activities "essential" and "not essential" to a citizen's life in a polity. See his "Who Must Presume Whom to Be Innocent of What?" *Netherlands Journal of Legal Philosophy* 42 (2013): 190.

24. Duff, "Who Must Presume?" argues that if ex-offenders are excluded from public parks or from restaurants, then the civic PI is contravened, but it is not if ex-offenders are denied licenses to drive or practice medicine based on their proven histories of irresponsibility in these endeavors (at 190–92). But is hard to see how exclusion from public parks is "essential" to a citizen's life in a polity, whereas exclusion from her chosen career, for which she has spent years acquiring the education and experience, is "inessential."

25. Von Hirsch and Wasik, "Civil Disqualifications," 616.

26. Von Hirsch and Wasik, "Civil Disqualifications," 606.

27. Von Hirsch and Wasik, "Civil Disqualifications," 612.

28. See Richard L. Lippke, "The Disenfranchisement of Felons," *Law and Philosophy* 20 (2001): 553–80; and Michael J. Cholbi, "A Felon's Right to Vote," *Law and Philosophy* 21 (2002): 543–65.

29. Von Hirsch, *Censure and Sanctions*, 9–14.

30. As von Hirsch and Wasik seem to concede, at least with respect to some common criminal sanctions, "Civil Disqualifications," 617.

31. Von Hirsch and Wasik, "Civil Disqualifications," 617.

32. Nigel Walker, *Why Punish? Theories of Punishment Reassessed* (Oxford: Oxford University Press, 1991), 96–105; and Anthony Duff, *Punishment, Communication, and Community* (Oxford: Oxford University Press, 2001), 134.

33. Von Hirsch and Wasik, "Civil Disqualifications," 618–19.

34. Walker, *Why Punish?* 102. See also Adam J. Kolber, "The Subjective Experience of Punishment," *Columbia Law Review* 109 (2009): 182–236; and Jesper Ryberg, "Punishment and the Measurement of Severity," in J. Ryberg and J. A. Corlett (eds.), *Punishment and Ethics: New Perspectives* (New York: Palgrave-Macmillan, 2010), 72–91.

35. Von Hirsch and Wasik, "Civil Disqualifications," 619.

36. For discussion of efforts to limit discrimination by private employers against ex-offenders, see Jessica S. Henry and James B. Jacobs, "Ban the Box to Promote Ex-Offender Employment," *Criminology and Public Policy* 6 (2007): 755–62; Jennifer Leavitt, "Walking a Tightrope: Balancing Competing Public Interests in the Employment of Criminal Offenders," *Connecticut Law Review* 34 (2002): 1281–315; and Ben Geiger, "The Case for Treating Ex-Offenders as a Suspect Class," *California Law Review* 94 (2006): 1191–242.

37. But see Geiger, "Suspect Class," 1215ff.

38. In fact, even states that have the most stringent provisions regarding discrimination against ex-offenders have various exceptions and qualifications built into them,

ones that take into account such factors as the relationship between an ex-offender's past crimes and the kind of work for which she is being considered. See Leavitt, "Walking a Tightrope," 1287ff.

39. See Bruce Western, *Punishment and Inequality in America* (New York: Russell Sage, 2006), 120–25.

40. As we saw in the previous chapter, there is also the question whether expungement should be partial or complete. In the latter case, legal officials would have no access to records of past offenses once expungement occurs. There could also be staged expungement, with criminal records initially removed from public scrutiny and only after some further time, also removed from official scrutiny.

41. Hock Lai Ho, "The Presumption of Innocence as a Human Right," in P. Roberts and J. Hunter (eds.), *Criminal Evidence and Human Rights* (Oxford: Hart Publishing, 2012), 259–81; and Andrew Ashworth, "Four Threats to the Presumption of Innocence," *International Journal of Evidence and Proof* 10 (2006): 241–79.

42. Stefan Trechsel, "The Human Right to Be Presumed Innocent," in S. Trechsel and S. Summers, *Human Rights in Criminal Proceedings* (Oxford: Oxford University Press, 2006), 153–91; and Hamish Stewart, "The Human Right to Be Presumed Innocent," *Criminal Law and Philosophy* 8 (2014): 407–20.

43. There is only a presumption of guilt at this point, one that is rebuttable if the conviction is overturned on appeal.

44. See Duff, "Who Must Presume?" 187.

45. Duff, "Who Must Presume?" 172.

46. Ho, "Presumption of Innocence," 276.

47. See Richard O. Lempert, Samuel R. Gross, and James S. Leibman, *A Modern Approach to Evidence*, 3rd ed. (St. Paul, Minn.: West, 2000), 327–28.

48. Contrary to Duff, "Who Must Presume?" 180–82.

Epilogue

1. For elaboration of this claim in relation to drug crimes, see William J. Stuntz, "Race, Class, and Drugs," *Columbia Law Review* 98 (1998): 1795–842.

2. Dan Simon, "The Limited Diagnosticity of Criminal Trials," *Vanderbilt Law Review* 64 (2011): 143–223. Simon (at 152) notes that about three-quarters of known false convictions result from witness misidentifications.

3. Simon, "Limited Diagnosticity," 167–70. See also Brandon L. Garrett, "Judging Innocence," *Columbia Law Review* 108 (2008): 75.

4. Kristina Marlow, "Prisoners' Rights," *Georgetown Law Journal* 86 (1998): 1953–2010. See also Richard L. Lippke, *Rethinking Imprisonment* (Oxford: Oxford University Press, 2007), chapter 6.

BIBLIOGRAPHY

Alexander, Michelle. *The New Jim Crow: Mass Incarceration in the Age of Colorblindness*. New York: New Press, 2010.

Allen, Ronald J., and Brian Leiter. "Naturalized Epistemology and the Law of Evidence." *Virginia Law Review* 87 (2001): 1491–550.

Alschuler, Albert W. "The Prosecutor's Role in Plea Bargaining." *University of Chicago Law Review* 36 (1968): 50–112.

———. "The Trial Judge's Role in Plea Bargaining, Part 1." *Columbia Law Review* 76 (1976): 1059–154.

———. "Preventive Pretrial Detention and the Failure of Interest-Balancing Approaches to Due Process." *Michigan Law Review* 85 (1986): 510–69.

———. "A Peculiar Privilege in Historical Perspective." In R. H. Helmholz, Charles M. Gray, John H. Langbein, Eben Moglen, Henry E. Smith, and Albert W. Alschuler (eds.), *The Privilege against Self-Incrimination: Its Origins and Development*. Chicago: University of Chicago Press, 1997, 181–204.

Amar, Akhil Reed. *The Bill of Rights: Creation and Reconstruction*. New Haven, Conn: Yale University Press, 1998.

Ashworth, Andrew. "Four Threats to the Presumption of Innocence." *International Journal of Evidence and Proof* 10 (2006): 241–79.

Ashworth, Andrew, and Mike Redmayne. *The Criminal Process*, 4th ed. Oxford: Oxford University Press, 2010.

Avery, Michael. "Obstacles to Litigating Civil Claims for Wrongful Conviction: An Overview." *Boston University Public Interest Law Journal* 18 (2009): 439–51.

Baradaran, Shima. "Restoring the Presumption of Innocence." *Ohio State Law Journal* 72 (2011): 723–76.

Baradaran, Shima, and Frank L. McIntyre. "Predicting Violence." *Texas Law Review* 90 (2012): 497–570.

Bibas, Stephanos. "Plea Bargaining outside the Shadow of Trial." *Harvard Law Review* 117 (2004): 2463–547.

Blackstone, William. *Commentaries on the Laws of England*. Boston, Mass.: Beacon Press, 1962.

Bowers, Josh. "Punishing the Innocent." *University of Pennsylvania Law Review* 156 (2007): 1117–79.

Braithwaite, John, and Philip Pettit. *Not Just Deserts: Towards a Republican Theory of Criminal Justice.* Oxford: Clarendon Press, 1990.

Bray, Samuel. "Not Proven: Introducing a Third Verdict." *University of Chicago Law Review* 72 (2005): 1299–329.

Bright, Stephen B., and Sia M. Sanneh. "Fifty Years of Defiance and Resistance after *Gideon v. Wainwright*." *Yale Law Journal* 122 (2013): 2150–74.

Brown, Michael K. *Working the Street: Police Discretion and the Dilemmas of Reform.* New York: Russell Sage, 1988.

Campbell, Liz. "Criminal Labels, the European Convention on Human Rights and the Presumption of Innocence." *Modern Law Review* 76 (2013): 681–707.

Cane, Peter. *Responsibility in Law and Morality.* Oxford: Hart Publishing, 2002.

Chin, Gabriel J. "The New Civil Death: Rethinking Punishment in the Era of Mass Conviction." *University of Pennsylvania Law Review* 160 (2012): 1789–833.

Cholbi, Michael J. "A Felon's Right to Vote." *Law and Philosophy* 21 (2002): 543–65.

Davis, Angela J. "Prosecution and Race: The Power and Privilege of Discretion." *Fordham Law Review* 67 (1998): 13–67.

———. *Arbitrary Justice: The Power of the American Prosecutor.* Oxford: Oxford University Press, 2007.

DeKay, Michael L. "The Difference between Blackstone-Like Error Ratios and Probabilistic Standards of Proof." *Law and Social Inquiry* 21 (1996): 95–132.

Dolinko, David. "Is There a Rationale for the Privilege against Self-Incrimination?" *UCLA Law Review* 33 (1986): 1063–148.

Duff, Peter. "The Scottish Criminal Jury: A Very Peculiar Institution." *Law and Contemporary Problems* 62 (1999): 173–201.

Duff, R. A. "Dangerousness and Citizenship." In Andrew Ashworth and Martin Wasik (eds.), *Fundamentals of Sentencing Theory: Essays in Honor of Andrea von Hirsch.* Oxford: Clarendon Press, 1998, 141–63.

———. *Punishment, Communication, and Community.* Oxford: Oxford University Press, 2001.

———. "Strict Liability, Legal Presumptions, and the Presumption of Innocence." In A. Simester (ed.), *Appraising Strict Liability.* Oxford: Oxford University Press, 2010, 125–50.

———. "Presuming Innocence." In L. Zedner and J. V. Roberts (eds.), *Principles and Values in Criminal Law and Criminal Justice: Essays in Honour of Andrew Ashworth.* Oxford: Oxford University Press, 2012, 51–66.

———. "Pre-trial Detention and the Presumption of Innocence." In A. Ashworth, L. Zedner, and P. Tomlin (eds.), *Prevention and the Limits of the Criminal Law.* Oxford: Oxford University Press, 2013, 115–32.

———. "Who Must Presume Whom to Be Innocent of What?" *Netherlands Journal of Legal Philosophy* 42 (2013): 170–92.

Duff, R. A., Lindsay Farmer, Sandra Marshall, and Victor Tadros. *The Trial on Trial*, vol. 3: *Towards a Normative Theory of the Criminal Trial.* Oxford: Hart Publishing, 2007.

Dworkin, Ronald. *Taking Rights Seriously.* Cambridge, Mass.: Harvard University Press, 1977.
Feeley, Malcolm M. *The Process Is the Punishment: Handling Cases in a Lower Criminal Court.* New York: Russell Sage, 1979.
Findley, Keith A., and Michael S. Scott. "The Multiple Dimensions of Tunnel Vision in Criminal Cases." *Wisconsin Law Review* 2006 (2006): 291–397.
Fine, Cordelia, and Jeanette Kennett. "Mental Impairment, Moral Understanding and Criminal Responsibility: Psychopathy and the Purposes of Punishment." *International Journal of Law and Psychiatry* 27 (2004): 425–43.
Fisher, Stanley Z. "In Search of the Virtuous Prosecutor: A Conceptual Framework." *American Journal of Criminal Law* 15 (1988): 197–261.
Franklin, Mark A., and Diane Johnsen. "Expunging Criminal Records: Concealment and Dishonesty in an Open Society." *Hofstra Law Review* 9 (1981): 733–74.
Frase, Richard S. *Just Sentencing: Principles and Procedures for a Workable System.* New York: Oxford University Press, 2013.
Friedman, Richard D. "A Presumption of Innocence, Not of Even Odds." *Stanford Law Review* 52 (2000): 873–87.
Garrett, Brandon L. "Judging Innocence." *Columbia Law Review* 108 (2008): 55–142.
———. *Convicting the Innocent: Where Criminal Prosecutions Go Wrong.* Cambridge, Mass.: Harvard University Press, 2012.
Gazal-Ayal, Oren. "Partial Ban on Plea Bargains." *Cardozo Law Review* 27 (2006): 2295–348.
Geiger, Ben. "The Case for Treating Ex-Offenders as a Suspect Class." *California Law Review* 94 (2006): 1191–242.
Gewirth, Alan. *Reason and Morality.* Chicago: University of Chicago Press, 1978.
Greenawalt, R. Kent. "Silence as a Moral and Constitutional Right." *William & Mary Law Review* 23 (1981): 15–71.
Griffin, James. "Discrepancies between the Best Philosophical Account of Human Rights and the International Law of Human Rights." *Proceedings of the Aristotelian Society* 101 (2001): 1–28.
Hampton, Jean. "A New Theory of Retribution." In R. G. Frey and C. W. Morris (eds.), *Liability and Responsibility: Essays in Law and Morals.* Cambridge: Cambridge University Press, 1991, 377–414.
Haney, Craig. *Reforming Punishment: Psychological Limits to the Pains of Imprisonment.* Washington, D.C.: American Psychological Association, 2006.
Hart, H. L. A. *The Concept of Law.* Oxford: Clarendon Press, 1961.
Helmholz, R. H., C. M. Gray, J. H. Langbein, E. Moglen, H. E. Smith, and A. W. Alschuler. *The Privilege against Self-Incrimination: Its Origins and Development.* Chicago: University of Chicago Press, 1997.
Henry, Jessica S., and James B. Jacobs. "Ban the Box to Promote Ex-Offender Employment." *Criminology and Public Policy* 6 (2007): 755–62.
Heumann, Milton. *Plea Bargaining: The Experiences of Prosecutors, Judges, and Defense Attorneys.* Chicago: University of Chicago Press, 1977.
von Hirsch, Andrew. *Censure and Sanctions.* Oxford: Clarendon Press, 1993.

von Hirsch, Andrew, and Martin Wasik. "Civil Disqualifications Attending Conviction: A Suggested Conceptual Framework." *Cambridge Law Journal* 56 (1997): 599–626.

Ho, Hock Lai. *A Philosophy of Evidence Law: Justice in the Search for Truth*. Oxford: Oxford University Press, 2008.

———. "The Presumption of Innocence as a Human Right." In P. Roberts and J. Hunter (eds.), *Criminal Evidence and Human Rights*. Oxford: Hart Publishing, 2012, 259–81.

Hoskins, Zachary. "Ex-Offender Restrictions." *Journal of Applied Philosophy* 31 (2014): 33–48.

Husak, Douglas. "The Criminal Law as a Last Resort." *Oxford Journal of Legal Studies* 24 (2004): 207–35.

———. *Overcriminalization: The Limits of the Criminal Law*. Oxford: Oxford University Press, 2008.

Jackson, John D., and Sarah J. Summers. *The Internationalisation of Criminal Evidence: Beyond the Common Law and Civil Law Traditions*. Cambridge: Cambridge University Press, 2012.

Jacobs, James B. "Mass Incarceration and the Proliferation of Criminal Records." *University of St. Thomas Law Journal* 3 (2006): 387–420.

Jaconelli, J. "Rights Theories and Public Trial." *Journal of Applied Philosophy* 14 (1997): 168–75.

Johns, Margaret Z. "Unsupportable and Unjustified: A Critique of Absolute Prosecutorial Immunity." *Fordham Law Review* 80 (2011): 509–35.

Kaplan, John. "Decision Theory and the Fact-Finding Process." *Stanford Law Review* 20 (1968): 1065–92.

King, Nancy J. "Judicial Oversight of Negotiated Sentences in a World of Bargained Punishment." *Stanford Law Review* 58 (2005): 293–308.

Kitai, Rinat. "Presuming Innocence." *Oklahoma Law Review* 55 (2002): 257–95.

Klein, Susan R. "Monitoring the Plea Process." *Duquesne Law Review* 51 (2013): 559–93.

Kleinig, John. *The Ethics of Policing*. Cambridge: Cambridge University Press, 1996.

———. "The Hardness of Hard Treatment." In A. Ashworth and M. Wasik (eds.), *Fundamentals in Sentencing Theory*. Oxford: Clarendon Press, 1998, 273–98.

Kolber, Adam J. "The Subjective Experience of Punishment." *Columbia Law Review* 109 (2009): 182–236.

Krug, Peter. "Prosecutorial Discretion and Its Limits." *American Journal of Comparative Law* 50 (2002): 643–64.

LaFollette, Hugh. "Collateral Consequences of Punishment: Civil Penalties Accompanying Formal Punishment." *Journal of Applied Philosophy* 22 (2005): 241–61.

Langer, Máximo. "From Legal Transplants to Legal Translations: The Globalization of Plea Bargaining and the Americanization Thesis in Criminal Procedure." *Harvard International Law Journal* 45 (2004): 1–64.

Laudan, Larry. "The Presumption of Innocence: Material or Probatory?" *Legal Theory* 11 (2005): 333–61.

———. *Truth, Error, and Criminal Law: An Essay In Legal Epistemology*. Cambridge: Cambridge University Press, 2006.

———. "The Rules of Trial, Political Morality, and the Costs of Error: Or, Is Proof beyond a Reasonable Doubt Doing More Harm Than Good?" In L. Green and B. Leiter (eds.), *Oxford Studies in Philosophy of Law*, vol. 1. New York: Oxford University Press, 2011, 195–227.

Laufer, William S. "The Rhetoric of Innocence." *Washington Law Review* 70 (1995): 329–421.

Leavitt, Jennifer. "Walking a Tightrope: Balancing Competing Public Interests in the Employment of Criminal Offenders." *Connecticut Law Review* 34 (2002): 1281–1315.

Lefstein, Norman. "In Search of Gideon's Promise: Lessons from England and the Need for Federal Help." *Hastings Law Review* 55 (2004): 835–929.

Leipold, Andrew D. "The Problem of the Innocent, Acquitted Defendant." *Northwestern University Law Review* 94 (2000): 1297–1356.

Lempert, Richard O., Samuel R. Gross, and James S. Leibman. *A Modern Approach to Evidence*. 3rd ed. St. Paul, Minn.: West, 2000.

Lerner, Craig S. "The Reasonableness of Probable Cause." *Texas Law Review* 81 (2003): 951–1029.

Lillquist, Erik. "Recasting Reasonable Doubt: Decision Theory and the Virtues of Variability." *University of California–Davis Law Review* 36 (2002): 85–197.

Lippke, Richard L. "Criminal Offenders and Right Forfeiture." *Journal of Social Philosophy* 32 (2001): 78–89.

———. "The Disenfranchisement of Felons." *Law and Philosophy* 20 (2001): 553–80.

———. *Rethinking Imprisonment*. Oxford: Oxford University Press, 2007.

———. "No Easy Way Out: Dangerous Offenders and Preventive Detention." *Law and Philosophy* 27 (2008): 383–414.

———. "The Case for Reasoned Criminal Trial Verdicts." *Canadian Journal of Law and Jurisprudence* 22 (2009): 313–30.

———. *The Ethics of Plea Bargaining*. Oxford: Oxford University Press, 2011.

Lovell, Russell E., II. "The Case for Reimbursing Court Costs and a Reasonable Attorney Fee to the Non-indigent Defendant upon Acquittal." *Nebraska Law Review* 49 (1970): 515–35.

Ma, Yue. "Prosecutorial Discretion and Plea Bargaining in the United States, France, Germany, and Italy." *International Criminal Justice Review* 12 (2002): 22–52.

Marlow, Kristina. "Prisoners' Rights." *Georgetown Law Journal* 86 (1998): 1953–2010.

Mauer, Marc, and Meda Chesney-Lind. *Invisible Punishment: The Collateral Consequences of Mass Imprisonment*. New York: New Press, 2002.

Medwed, Daniel S. "The Zeal Deal: Prosecutorial Resistance to Post-conviction Claims of Innocence." *Boston University Law Review* 84 (2004): 125–83.

Mendonca, Daniel. "Presumptions." *Ratio Juris* 11 (1998): 399–412.

Miller, Marc, and Martin Guggenheim. "Pretrial Detention and Punishment." *Minnesota Law Review* 75 (1990): 335–426.

Miller, John. "Compensating Crime Victims within New Zealand's No Fault Compensation Scheme." http://aic.gov.au/media_library/publications/proceedings/27/miller.pdf.

Morano, Anthony A. "A Reexamination of the Development of the Reasonable Doubt Rule." *Boston University Law Review* 55 (1975): 507–28.

Morris, Christopher W. "Punishment and Loss of Moral Standing." *Canadian Journal of Philosophy* 21 (1991): 53–79.

Morse, Stephen J. "Blame and Danger: An Essay on Preventive Detention." *Boston University Law Review* 76 (1996): 113–55.

Nagin, Daniel S. "Deterrence and Incapacitation." In Michael Tonry (ed.), *The Handbook of Crime and Punishment*. New York: Oxford University Press, 1998, 345–68.

Nance, Dale. "Civility and the Burden of Proof." *Harvard Journal of Law and Public Policy* 17 (1994): 647–90.

Natapoff, Alexandra. "Misdemeanors." *Southern California Law Review* 85 (2012): 1313–75.

Nozick, Robert. *Anarchy, State, and Utopia*. New York: Basic Books, 1974.

Nussbaum, Martha. "Capabilities and Human Rights." *Fordham Law Review* 66 (1997): 273–300.

Packer, Herbert L. *The Limits of the Criminal Law*. Stanford, Calif.: Stanford University Press, 1968.

Posner, Richard. "An Economic Approach to the Law of Evidence." *Stanford Law Review* 51 (1999): 1477–546.

Raifeartaigh, Una Ni. "Reconciling Bail Law with the Presumption of Innocence." *Oxford Journal of Legal Studies* 17 (1997): 1–21.

Rawls, John. *A Theory of Justice*. Cambridge, Mass.: Harvard University Press, 1971.

Reitz, Kevin R. "Sentencing Facts: Travesties of Real-Offense Sentencing." *Stanford Law Review* 45 (1993): 523–73.

Rescher, Nicholas. *Presumption and the Practices of Tentative Cognition*. Cambridge: Cambridge University Press, 2006.

Reza, Sadiq. "Privacy and the Criminal Arrestee or Suspect: In Search of a Right, in Need of a Rule." *Maryland Law Review* 64 (2005): 755–874.

Roberts, Jenny. "Why Misdemeanors Matter: Defining Effective Advocacy in the Lower Criminal Courts." *University of California–Davis Law Review* 45 (2011): 277–372.

Roberts, Paul. "Double Jeopardy Reform: A Criminal Justice Commentary." *Modern Law Review* 65 (2002): 393–424.

———. "The Presumption of Innocence Brought Home? *Kebilene* Deconstructed." *Law Quarterly Review* 118 (2002): 41–71.

Robinson, Paul H. "Punishing Dangerousness: Cloaking Preventive Detention and Criminal Justice." *Harvard Law Review* 114 (2001): 1429–56.

Rybert, Jesper. "Punishment and the Measurement of Severity." In J. Ryberg and J. A. Corlett (eds.), *Punishment and Ethics: New Perspectives*. New York: Palgrave-Macmillan, 2010, 72–91.

Saltzberg, Stephen A. "Pleas of Guilty and the Loss of Constitutional Rights: The Current Price of Pleading Guilty." *Michigan Law Review* 76 (1978): 1265–307.

Schulhofer, Stephen J. "Some Kind Words for the Privilege against Self-Incrimination." *Valparaiso University Law Review* 26 (1991): 311–36.

Schwikkard, P. J. "The Presumption of Innocence: What Is It?" *South African Journal of Criminal Justice* 11 (1998): 396–408.

Sen, Amartya. "Rights as Goals." In S. Guest and A. Milne (eds.), *Equality and Discrimination: Essays in Freedom and Justice*. London: Association for Legal and Social Philosophy, 1985, 12–26.

Simester A. P., and Andrew von Hirsch. *Crimes, Harms, and Wrongs: On the Principles of Criminalisation*. Oxford: Hart Publishing, 2011.

Simmons, A. John. *The Lockean Theory of Rights*. Princeton, N.J.: Princeton University Press, 1992.

Simon, Dan. "The Limited Diagnosticity of Criminal Trials." *Vanderbilt Law Review* 54 (2011): 143–223.

Smit, D. van Zyl, and F. Dünkel. *Imprisonment Today and Tomorrow: International Perspectives on Prisoners' Rights and Prison Conditions*. 2nd ed. The Hague: Kluwer Law International, 2001.

Stein, Alex. *Foundations of Evidence Law*. Oxford: Oxford University Press, 2005.

Stewart, Hamish. "The Human Right to Be Presumed Innocent." *Criminal Law and Philosophy* 8 (2014): 407–20.

Strier, Franklin. "Making Trials More Truthful." *University of California–Davis Law Review* 30 (1996): 95–182.

Struve, Catherine T. "The Conditions of Pretrial Detention." *University of Pennsylvania Law Review* 161 (2013): 1009–79.

Stuckenberg, Carl-Friedrich. "Who Is Presumed Innocent of What by Whom?" *Criminal Law and Philosophy* 8 (2014): 301–16.

Stumer, Andrew. *The Presumption of Innocence: Evidential and Human Rights Perspectives*. Oxford: Hart Publishing, 2010.

Stuntz, William J. "Race, Class, and Drugs." *Columbia Law Review* 98 (1998): 1795–842.

———. "The Pathological Politics of Criminal Law." *Michigan Law Review* 100 (2001): 505–600.

———. *The Collapse of American Criminal Justice*. Cambridge, Mass.: Harvard University Press, 2011.

Summers, Sarah J. *Fair Trials: The European Criminal Procedural Tradition and the European Court of Human Rights*. Oxford: Hart Publishing, 2007.

Tadros, Victor. "Rethinking the Presumption of Innocence." *Criminal Law and Philosophy* 1 (2007): 193–213.

———. "The Ideal of the Presumption of Innocence." *Criminal Law and Philosophy* 8 (2014): 449–67.

Tadros, Victor, and Stephen Tierney. "The Presumption of Innocence and the Human Rights Act." *Modern Law Review* 67 (2004): 402–34.

Tomlin, Patrick. "Extending the Golden Thread? Criminalisation and the Presumption of Innocence." *Journal of Political Philosophy* 21 (2013): 44–66.

———. "Could the Presumption of Innocence Protect the Guilty?" *Criminal Law and Philosophy* 8 (2014): 431–47.

Tonry, Michael. "Intermediate Sanctions." In M. Tonry (ed.), *The Handbook of Crime and Punishment*. New York: Oxford University Press, 1998, 683–711.

Trechsel, Stefan, and Sarah Summers. *Human Rights in Criminal Proceedings*. Oxford: Oxford University Press, 2006.

Tribe, Laurence H. "Preventive Justice in the World of John Mitchell." *Virginia Law Review* 56 (1970): 371–407.

———. "Trial by Mathematics: Precision and Ritual in the Legal Process." *Harvard Law Review* 84 (1971): 1329–93.

Turner, Jenia I. "Judicial Participation in Plea Negotiations: A Comparative View." *American Journal Comparative Law* 54 (2006): 199–267.

Volokh, Alexander. "n Guilty Men." *University of Pennsylvania Law Review* 146 (1997): 173–216.

Waldron, Jeremy. *Theories of Rights*. Oxford: Oxford University Press, 1984.

———. "Rights in Conflict." *Ethics* 99 (1989): 503–19.

———. "Rights." In R. E. Goodin and P. Pettit (eds.), *A Companion to Contemporary Political Philosophy*. Oxford: Blackwell, 1993, 575–85.

Walker, Nigel. *Why Punish? Theories of Punishment Reassessed*. Oxford: Oxford University Press, 1991.

Weigend, Thomas. "There Is Only One Presumption of Innocence." *Netherlands Journal of Legal Philosophy* 42 (2013): 193–204.

———. "Assuming That the Defendant Is Not Guilty: The Presumption of Innocence in the German System of Criminal Justice." *Criminal Law and Philosophy* 8 (2014): 285–99.

Western, Bruce. *Punishment and Inequality in America*. New York: Russell Sage, 2006.

Whitman, James Q. *The Origins of Reasonable Doubt: Theological Roots of the Criminal Trial*. New Haven, Conn: Yale University Press, 2008.

Williams, Marian R. "The Effect of Pre-trial Detention on Imprisonment Decisions." *Criminal Justice Review* 28 (2003): 299–316.

Zacharias, Fred C. "Structuring the Ethics of Prosecutorial Trial Practice: Can Prosecutors Do Justice?" *Vanderbilt Law Review* 44 (1991): 45–114.

Zimring, Franklin E., and Gordon Hawkins. *Incapacitation: Penal Confinement and the Restraint of Crime*. New York: Oxford University Press, 1995.

INDEX

Alschuler, Albert 174

burden of proof 48–49
  reverse onus provisions and the 62

Campbell, Liz 34, 42, 46–50
civic trust 74–79
  as unlike trial presumption of innocence 75–79
collateral consequences 8, 213–32
  as adjunct to legal punishment 215, 216
  as conveying censure 217
  as integral to legal punishment 215–26
  ex post facto imposition of 214, 218–19
  human right to be presumed innocent and 227–32
  imposition based on risk 220–21, 222
  proportionality and 217–18
  relation to presumption of innocence 8, 214, 226–32
  and restoration of equal citizenship 219
criminal law
  over-broad provisions 60–65
  presumption of innocence as a constraint on the 1, 5, 18, 58, 62, 63–64
  reverse onus provisions of the 62
  strict liability and the 73–74
criminal record 183, 184–85

due process
  non-presumption of guilt and 51–54
Duff, R. A. 11, 12, 58, 74–79, 169, 228

error
  adjudicative 105
  investigative 144–45, 235
  non-presumption of guilt and avoidance of 144–45
error distribution
  presumption of innocence and 109
  trials as devices for 105, 108–10

fallibility of criminal justice system 49, 52, 55, 57, 111, 124, 142

Guggenheim, Martin 169–70
guilt
  factual (see material guilt)
  material 14, 132
  probative 14, 132

Ho, Hock Lai 34, 50
Hoskins, Zachary 220–21
human rights 35–36, 59, 110
  and justifying infringements of 40–41
human right to be presumed innocent 1, 4, 33, 227–32
  as barrier to police investigation 41
  as procedural 33–35, 36, 51, 52

human right to be presumed innocent (*Cont.*)
- and reputation 43–46
- status characteristics and the 37–38, 55
- Stewart on justifying interferences with the 38–39, 146
- as substantive 33–35, 37, 51, 53, 54

incomplete prosecutions 7, 177–211
- ambiguity of 178
- conceptions of the presumption of innocence and 189
- disambiguating verdicts as a remedy for 187–88
- employment discrimination and 187, 209–11
- expungement and 7, 184–85, 198–202
- factors to be weighed in evaluating 182–83
- malicious prosecutions and 189
- non-presumption of guilt and 179, 193, 195–98, 200–01, 202, 206–07, 210–11
- preserving anonymity of arrested or accused and 7, 185–86, 202–08
- presumption of material innocence and 7, 179, 190–92, 194–95, 198–99, 201–02, 204–06, 209–10, 211
- reasoned verdicts and 7, 188
- required explanations of 7, 184, 194–98
- remedies for 7, 183–89

innocence
- as clean slate 16
- factual (see material innocence)
- material 14, 132
- probabilistic 14–15
- probative 14, 15, 132

Laudan, Larry 25–26, 86, 99–101, 122–27, 130
Laufer, William 25
legal punishment 9
Lillquist, Erik 119

Miller, Marc 169–70

Nance, Dale 58, 74–79
non-presumption of guilt 6, 142
- and due process 51–54
- and error avoidance 6, 142, 235
- distinguished from the presumption of innocence 6
- material 142
- probative 15, 18, 141–42
- the public and the 142
- and a rebuttable presumption of guilt 143–44

plea bargaining 10, 53–54
presumption of innocence
- as attitudinal requirement 24–26
- as based on frequency of alleged crime in population 86
- burden of proof and the 48–49
- as civic virtue 1, 5, 58, 74–79
- clearly defined role during trial of the 102–03
- and collateral consequences 226–32
- as conduct requirement 8, 23–24, 133–34
- as constraint on the criminal law 1, 5, 18, 58, 62, 63–64
- as constraint on the investigation of crimes 38–39, 146–47
- as constraint on the law-making process 1, 65–72
- and crime victims 2–3, 27–28, 132
- distinguished from approaches to trial evidence 87–88
- and due process 51–54
- as equal probability of guilt versus innocence 85
- as framing perspective on the accused 6, 8–9, 23–24, 84, 133–34
- the general public and the 27
- as human right 1, 18, 33
- and incomplete prosecutions 7, 177–212
- as material innocence 84
- as neutrality 85
- as normative construct 83
- as part of the proof structure of criminal trials 6, 51, 81–82, 105

plea bargaining and the 53–54
pre-accusation 1, 18
pre-trial 1, 2, 17, 129–54
and pre-trial detention 7, 149–50
police and the 2, 27, 45–46, 55
probabilistic accounts of 85, 86
as procedural constraint 20
prosecutors and the 2, 27, 45–46, 55
and reputation 21, 43, 47, 50, 147–49
as requiring jurors to focus solely on evidence during trial 86
and right against self-incrimination 30, 95–97, 151–52
standard of proof and the 29, 49
strength of the 21–23
strict liability provisions and the 73–74
as substantive constraint 20–21
trial judges and the 28
presumption of material innocence 84, 132
arguments for trial 89–95
contrasted with alternative framing perspectives on trial defendants 84–87, 88–95
as countering confirmation bias and belief perseverance 93–95
as framing perspective 84, 90–93, 101
Laudan's objections to 99–101
as part of the proof structure of criminal trials 97
as protective attitude 89
and right against self-incrimination 95–97
presumptions
nature of 12, 13
strength of 21–23, 133
pretrial detention 7, 149–50, 155–75
conditions of 7, 158–62
criteria for the imposition of 7, 162–65
negative effects of 155
and the presumption of innocence 7, 155, 157, 165–68
to prevent absconding or interfering with the course of justice 156, 157, 168–72
to reduce the risk of further crime 155, 172–74
pretrial presumption of innocence 2, 129–54
criticisms of a 135–41
police and the 132, 133, 136–40
prosecutors and the 132, 133, 136–40
the public and the 134, 136, 140–41, 145
and reputation 129
principle against punishment of the innocent 5, 59, 72–74
versus presumption of innocence 5, 72–74
proof structure of criminal trials 6, 81, 105
error distribution account of 6, 106, 108–10
moral assurance account of 6, 81, 106–07, 110–13, 120–28
presumption of innocence and 6, 51, 81–82, 105

reasonable doubt standard 119–20
reputation
incomplete prosecutions and 178
role of presumption of innocence in protecting 21, 43, 47, 50, 147–49
Rescher, Nicholas 12
right against self-incrimination 30, 95–97, 151–52
right to trial 113, 114
accused person's to waive 113–15
as second-order right 81, 107

standard of proof 29
relation to presumption of innocence 29, 72
Stewart, Hamish 18, 20, 34, 37–40

Tadros, Victor 59, 60–65
Tomlin, Patrick 58, 65–72
Travis, Jeremy 214
Trechsel, Stefan 21, 33, 34, 42–46
Tribe, Lawrence 170, 173
trials
as error distribution devices 101, 106, 108–10, 110–13
as moral assurance procedures 6, 97–98, 101–02, 110–13

trials (*Cont.*)
process costs of 114
as public events 115–17
role of presumption of innocence in 6, 51, 81–82, 105
waiver of as right of the accused 99, 113–15

unpredictability of criminal justice process 45, 57

von Hirsch, Andrew 217, 221–25

Wasik, Martin 221–25
Weigend, Thomas 151